012843594

29/5/96

LIVERPOOL HOPE UNIVERSITY
THE SHEPPARD - WORLOCK LIBRARY

D1340557

TEACHING RE

IN SECONDARY SCHOOLS

Ideas from the staff room

Edited by

Janet King

with Deborah Helme

MONARCH
ASSOCIATION OF CHRISTIAN TEACHERS

Copyright © Association of Christian Teachers 1994
The right of the Association of Christian Teachers to be
identified as author of this work has been asserted by them in
accordance with the Copyright, Design
and Patents Act 1988.

DISCLAIMER:
Every effort has been made to trace the owners of copyright
material, where this applies, and we hope that no copyright has
been infringed. Apology is made if the contrary is shown to be the
case, and correction will be made at the first opportunity.

First published 1994

ISBN 1 85424 257 1

All rights reserved.
No part of this publication may be reproduced or
transmitted in any form or by any means, electronic
or mechanical, including photocopy, recording, or any
information storage and retrieval system, without
permission in writing from the publisher.

British Library Cataloguing in Publication Data.
A catalogue record for this book is available
from the British Library.

Production and Printing in England for
MONARCH PUBLICATIONS
The Broadway, Crowborough, East Sussex TN6 1HQ
by Nuprint Ltd, Station Road, Harpenden, Herts, AL5 4SE

CONTENTS

SECTION THREE
CLASSROOM PRACTICE

SECTION FOUR
DEPARTMENTAL ISSUES

ACKNOWLEDGEMENT

This book has been produced under the auspices of the Stapleford Project. The Stapleford Project is a curriculum development initiative based at Stapleford House Education Centre. The Project aims to produce materials and offer in-service training to support the teaching of Christianity in schools.

FOREWORD

RE is perhaps one of the hardest subjects to teach in a secondary school. Attitudes which young people imbibe from growing up in an increasingly secularised society, mean that they are often resistant to studying religious issues. The particular burden of RE teachers is to be accused of indoctrination as soon as they suggest that there is knowledge to be learnt in their subject. For many of our students, openness and freedom of choice in religion equates to the idea that any opinion will do. No other subject teachers have to face such resistance, even hostility, and at the same time be expected to run stimulating, discussion-based lessons.

Another important challenge facing RE teachers is isolation. Many work alone in a single person department, with little access to colleagues with whom issues can be discussed and problems shared. Contact with other professionals is a crucial component in professional development. For most teachers this is available in their own staffroom. Not so for many RE teachers. Added to this is the fact that many RE teachers have not had access to specialised training. These problems are being exacerbated by the withering away of local authority advisory services and the likely demise of higher education teacher training institutions. Opportunities for meeting with colleagues from other schools are, therefore, few and far between for many RE teachers.

The Association of Christian Teachers (ACT) recognises that there is no substitute for personal contact. However we also know that having access to the ideas of colleagues in a written form can be an important stimulus, perhaps even a lifesaver, for the hard pressed teacher. During her time as our RE Development Officer, Janet King therefore invited a number of RE specialists to write about their particular area of expertise.

This volume is the result of those invitations. The contributors cover a range of topics from important background issues through to very specific ideas for the classroom. Wherever possible they have sought to deal with practical outcomes. In a number of cases samples of documents like policy statements and units of work have been included as illustrations. Clearly these will not often be directly transferable into other situations, but they are intended to offer guidance as to the sort of documents that can be produced. Our prayer is that reading these ideas from the staffroom will provide much needed information, inspiration and encouragement for colleagues who we know are seeking to do their job against the odds.

Because we have designed this book to be a forum for sharing ideas between colleagues, there is no one overall message, except, of course, that RE matters!

Contributors have simply shared from their own experience and from their own Christian vision. The views expressed do not, therefore, represent the policy of ACT, nor, indeed, do all the contributors agree in the opinions they hold. The coherence for this book comes not, then, from its content, but from its aim, namely to provide access to the stimulation of sharing ideas with colleagues.

Trevor Cooling
Stapleford, Nottingham,
December 1993

SECTION ONE

THE LEGAL FRAMEWORK FOR RELIGIOUS EDUCATION

1 | RELIGIOUS EDUCATION AND THE NATIONAL CURRICULUM IN ENGLAND AND WALES

George Skinner

SUMMARY

Religious Education is compulsory and yet not part of the National Curriculum. Why has this anomaly arisen? What is the relationship between Religious Education and the rest of the curriculum? This article examines these issues.

A CHURCH/STATE PARTNERSHIP

The unique position of Religious Education in British schools cannot be understood without reference to the historical role of the churches in education. Popular education grew out of the Christian Sunday School and church-funded school movements of the eighteenth and nineteenth centuries. Christian instruction was at the heart of the curriculum and an essential aspect of the inductive function of church schools.

The partnership of church and state in education has continued to the present day, despite the ever increasing financial problems faced by the churches in maintaining denominational schools. The church's powerful institutional presence within the education system, together with the long history of Christian involvement in education, has ensured that Britain's education system has never become officially secular. Indeed, until the 1988 Education Reform Act's requirement for a national curriculum, Religious Education was the one compulsory subject in the curriculum. However, confusion continues about the way in which Religious Education should be viewed.

THE BASIC CURRICULUM

The Education Reform Act defines at the outset that the basic curriculum should consist of a National Curriculum of core and other foundation subjects together with Religious Education for all registered pupils. Thus Religious Education is given equal status with other subjects, but is not included in the foundation subjects - it is part of the basic curriculum though not part of the National Curriculum.

The function of the Education Reform Act was essentially to centralise the control of the curriculum. In the case of Religious Education, the reverse was the case. Local control of the Religious Education curriculum via agreed syllabuses was confirmed and strengthened. Unlike other compulsory subjects, Religious Education does not have a national syllabus nor national attainment targets. However since 1992 the English National Curriculum Council has been working on guidelines to help LEAs in drawing up their syllabuses. In August 1993 Baroness Blatch asked the new Schools Curriculum and Assessment Authority to build on this work by drawing up a number of model agreed syllabuses. These will help LEAs to implement the requirement that agreed syllabuses should, 'reflect the fact that the religious traditions in Great Britain are in the main

Christian while taking account of the teaching and practices of the other principle religions present in Great Britain.'[1]

Although the National Curriculum Council was not made responsible for determining the content of Religious Education, the Chairman made it clear from the outset that the Council would establish close links with Standing Advisory Councils and would take a major role in co-ordinating and promoting local responses to Religious Education. The Council published an advisory booklet *Religious Education–a local curriculum framework* and each year produces a survey of Standing Advisory Council Annual Reports. In 1993 it published an analysis of twenty-seven Agreed Syllabuses produced since 1988, pointing out, interestingly, that not one of them matched all the legal requirements of the Education Reform Act.[2] Subsequent to this the Department for Education sent a letter to all LEAs involved requesting that they revise all their syllabuses. This caused some consternation!

In Wales where there is a smaller number of LEAs, the Curriculum Council has played a less interventionalist role. Rather than working on national guidelines or model syllabuses, it has concentrated on providing support materials for teachers. The Welsh National RE Centre has also played a central role in encouraging liaison between the LEAs.

SPIRITUALITY ACROSS THE CURRICULUM

The Education Reform Act requires the basic curriculum to promote the 'spiritual, moral, cultural, mental and physical development of pupils'.[3] What precisely the Act understands by 'spiritual' is open to debate. This is discussed more fully in Chapter 9. However, it can be assumed that RE has a key role to play here.

While Religious Education has a particularly explicit contribution to make in teaching about world faiths; spiritual issues, as understood in the religious traditions, are likely to arise throughout the curriculum. The western philosophical tradition has tended to perpetuate an individualistic and pietistic view which separates religion and spirituality from everyday life. It has failed to recognise that from Biblical times Christians have seen spirituality as permeating all thought and action. This conviction is shared with members of minority faiths in Britain, who often speak of their faith as 'a way of life'. The dualism of religion and science is not found in Islam. Hinduism has no word equivalent to 'religion' in the western sense. Recent research with Hindu children demonstrates a fundamental mismatch between the European word 'religion' and Indian concepts such as 'dharma'.[4] Religion, and therefore Religious Education, cannot be artificially separated from the rest of human knowledge and experience. Fortunately, the National Curriculum recognises this truth in a number of ways.

CROSS-CURRICULAR LINKS

Firstly, the core and foundation subject outlines often refer directly or indirectly to issues of faith or religious practice. For example these issues are important for certain periods covered by the history curriculum, or again can relate to diet in technology.

Secondly, the three cross-curricular elements of 'dimensions', 'skills' and 'themes' identified by the NCC all include religious aspects. The fact that they are by definition cross-curricular implies that they may not be simply left to Religious Education, but must be taken seriously by all curriculum subjects. Thus, cross-curricular *dimensions* seek to cover all aspects of equal opportunities and education for life in a multicultural society. They include extending pupils' knowledge of different cultures and faiths. The personal and social *skills* included among the six cross-curricular skills required to be addressed by all subjects are likely to touch on religious views. The five *themes* include a major section on education for citizenship. As *Starting Out with The National Curriculum* concludes, religion is interwoven with many aspects of life, 'concern for the environment often has a religious rationale, as does the development of personal responsibility and human rights... Religious teachings often lie at the foundation of attitudes to sex education, and aspects of health education'.[5]

ATTAINMENT TARGETS AND ASSESSMENT

There are no national, statutory programmes of study or attainment targets for RE. However, the SCAA has the responsibility to offer advice to SACREs and LEAs who wish to consider drawing up attainment targets and programmes of study for Religious Education and has published a set of guidelines and model syllabuses. The DES recommended that LEAs should determine attainment targets, programmes of study and assessment arrangements to be included in their agreed syllabus.[6] The fact that in 1991 the NCC reported that only about a quarter of LEAs pursued these recommendations suggests some doubt about their value.[7] Indeed, the NAHT commented

> The NAHT has grave doubts as to whether the inclusion of such targets, programmes and arrangements would be beneficial or desirable. An undue emphasis on this approach could limit the contribution of RE to moral and spiritual development, which cannot be measured against attainment targets.[8]

This discussion has been developed further in Chapters 7 & 8.

CONCLUSION

The decision to leave the final control of Religious Education at local level has many advantages. It allows for flexibility, the development of relevant syllabuses and the involvement of the local faith communities. However, the continuing close involvement of the Schools Curriculum and Assessment Authority is the only way forward if Religious Education is to overcome its continuing Cinderella status.

FOOTNOTES

[1] *The Education Reform Act* (HMSO: London, 1988).

[2] *Analysis of Agreed Syllabuses for Religious Education* (NCC: York, 1993).

[3] HMSO op cit.

[4] Eleanor Nesbitt, *My Dad's Hindu, My Mum's Side are Sikhs - Issues in Religious Identity* (The National Foundation For Arts Education & The University of Warwick: Warwick, 1991).

[5] *Starting Out With The National Curriculum* (NCC: York, 1992).

[6] *The Education Reform Act 1988: Religious Education and Collective Worship* (DES Circular No 3/89, January 1989).

[7] *Religious Education - A Local Curriculum Framework* (NCC: York, 1991).

[8] *Guide to the Education Reform Act: 1988* (NAHT: Haywards Heath, 1989).

2 | UNDERSTANDING THE STATUTORY CONFERENCE AND SACRES IN ENGLAND AND WALES

Guy Hordern

SUMMARY

This article traces the development of Agreed Syllabus Conferences and SACREs and examines their nature and purpose. It also considers the part Christians can play in ensuring new Agreed Syllabuses conform with current legal requirements.

UNDERSTANDING THE STATUTORY CONFERENCE

Under schedule five of the 1944 Education Act, Local Education Authorities were required to convene and fund Statutory Conferences whose responsibility it would be to provide a locally agreed syllabus for Religious Education. The conference draws on four groups:

1 The Local Education Authority. This group is often drawn from members of the Education Committee although this is not always the case. The chairman of the statutory conference is often a senior member of the Education Committee.

2 The Church of England. As the established National Church, the Church of England has a group of its own on Statutory Conferences in England. This reflects the Church of England's national responsibility for the teaching of Christianity to the nation and it is both a strategic and a privileged position providing a special opportunity for influencing County Schools not given to other Christian denominations or religions. It is a completely separate

responsibility from the Church of England's own voluntary aided denominational schools.

3 Teachers. This group is normally composed of teachers appointed by the Teacher Unions who have members teaching in schools within the LEA area.

4 The last group is made up of representatives of other Christian denominations, for example Roman Catholic, Baptist, Methodist, Pentecostal, Black Led Churches, House Churches etc and other religions, for example Islam, Hinduism, Sikhism, and Buddhism.

If the Conference cannot reach agreement, the Secretary of State for Education has the power to establish another Conference. Once the Statutory Conference has agreed on a syllabus, the LEA is responsible for its production and distribution.

The 1988 Education Reform Act made explicit that which was understood by the 1944 Act, namely that the content of the Agreed Syllabus should 'reflect the fact that the religious traditions in Great Britain are in the main Christian whilst taking account of the teaching and practice of the other principal religions represented in Great Britain'.[1]

The 1993 Education Act requires all Local Education Authorities who have not produced a new syllabus since 1988 to examine their current Agreed Syllabus in the light of the above Clause 8.3 and, if necessary, create a new syllabus which does comply with this clause. This Act will also result in:

1 Agreed Syllabuses being regularly revised.

2 Conference proceedings being open to the public.

3 A fifth group made up of representatives from the Grant Maintained Sector being added to the Conference once that sector has reached a 75% threshold.

4 Widening the choice of syllabuses available to Grant Maintained Schools to include any syllabus that has been agreed by any Statutory Conference.

5 Committee A of a Statutory Conference (and group A of a

SACRE) being renamed to become, 'Christian denominations and other religions and denominations of such religions'. Legislation also requires that the numbers of people appointed to serve on this group reflect broadly the proportional strength of that denomination or religion in the area.

The 1993 Education Act offers a strategic opportunity to influence Religious Education at a local level by ensuring that legal requirements are met. Religious Education syllabuses and the conferences which produce them should be seen as important resources for creating moral and spiritual values in schools. The National Curriculum Council discussion paper 'Spiritual and Moral Development' (April 1993) says:

> For schools teaching an Agreed Syllabus in line with the Education Reform Act, most attention should be given to Christianity which has contributed so forcibly to the spiritual and moral values of this country whilst also introducing pupils to the other major religions in the community.[2]

In March 1993 the National Curriculum Council published an analysis of the Agreed Syllabuses for Religious Education which have been produced since the 1988 Act and the report concluded (page 7.2) that 'no single syllabus matched all the legal requirements'.[3]

Christians concerned for education within an LEA should prayerfully consider how best to secure decisive membership of their local Statutory Conference. They can make an important contribution to the creation of an imaginative and well understood Religious Education syllabus.

UNDERSTANDING SACRES

The 1944 Education Act made it possible for Local Education Authorities to establish bodies which are called Standing

Advisory Councils for Religious Education or SACREs. The 1988 Education Reform Act made it a requirement that all Local Education Authorities should have a SACRE. The Council is composed of four groups (the 1993 Education Act stipulates that a fifth group representing Grant Maintained Schools be added once a 75% threshold is passed). The groups are drawn from the same sources as those for the Agreed Syllabus Conference described earlier.

The constitution of a SACRE is designed to create a synthesis of interest between four, or probably in the future, five groups representing the educational world and religious groups in society. This is a unique approach to shaping a Basic Curriculum subject area.

THE ROLE OF SACRES

While a SACRE does have some executive functions its role is mostly concerned with offering advice to the LEA which, if accepted, is then passed on to schools. A SACRE advises the LEA on collective worship in county schools and on Religious Education given in accordance with an Agreed Syllabus. This includes advice on methods of teaching, training of teachers, choice of materials and other relevant matters. Local Education Authorities should provide funding for their SACREs and this will enable good advice to be well presented and effectively communicated to schools. The executive duties which belong to SACREs are to publish an annual report, to consider whether or not to require a review of the locally Agreed Syllabus by a Statutory Conference and, since 1988, to consider applications from heads of county schools to be released from having an act of collective worship which is 'wholly or mainly of a broadly Christian nature'.[4] SACREs may also be asked by LEAs to be involved in the statutory complaints procedure and to advise on acts of worship provided for withdrawal groups.

The Education Reform Act re-emphasised the contribution of the curriculum in promoting moral and spiritual development. The National Curriculum Council discussion document *Spiritual and Moral Development*[5] of April 1993 stresses the important contribution which Religious Education and Collective Worship can make in generating this development. SACREs have pivotal roles to play in this work and they offer an opportunity for active Christian ministry in the local community.

FOOTNOTES

[1] *Education Reform Act* (HMSO: London, 1988), clause 8.3.
[2] *Spiritual and Moral Development—A Discussion Paper* (NCC, York, 1993), p6.
[3] *Analysis of Agreed Syllabuses for Religious Education* (NCC: York, 1993).
[4] HMSO op cit.
[5] op cit (2).

3 | RELIGIOUS AND MORAL EDUCATION IN SCOTLAND

Don Hawthorn

SUMMARY

Religious and Moral Education in Scotland has been quietly redefining itself over the last thirty years. This article looks at the progress made thus far and examines the nature and scope of RME in Scotland. Four key historical steps are identified. Finally there is a plea for detractors from the RME 5-14 National Guidelines to join forces to further the development process.

RELIGIOUS AND MORAL EDUCATION 5-14

Religious and Moral Education in Scotland is poised to see some significant development. The final version of National Guidelines on RME 5-14 appeared in November 1992. Regional Education Authorities have had to respond to its recommendations. These specify Attainment Targets and Attainment Outcomes. The Outcomes can be referred to as 'Christianity', 'Other World Religions' and 'Personal Search'. However, strictly speaking, they are not. The Outcomes are the promotion of knowledge, understanding skills and attitudes *in relation to* Christianity, Other World Religions and Personal Search. This is an important distinction. This wording is meant to focus teachers' attention on the educational benefits of studying RE rather than purely on the content of the faiths. It is clearly recognised that there is no intention to cover the whole of Christianity in the school curriculum. Even less so, can Religious Education teachers expect to cover every aspect of five other major world religions, namely Hinduism, Buddhism, Sikhism, Judaism and Islam. Likewise in Personal Search

24

teachers would not expect to exhaust all that might arise. However the promotion of knowledge and understanding, skills and attitudes in relation to Christianity, Other World Religions and Personal Search is targetable and attainable.

Specified attainment levels A to E cover the age range 5-14. A minimum time allocation of 10% of the primary curriculum and 5% over the two years in S1 to S2 (lower secondary) is to be devoted to Religious and Moral Education. All this means there is the potential for real growth and development in the provision of RME from 5-14. In turn, this will mean a significant review of current practice particularly in the early years of secondary schooling and focusing on the question of more effective coordination between primary and secondary teachers.

LOCAL DECISIONS

RME 5-14 leaves many decisions to be taken locally when implementing the general guidelines. The decisions regarding the weighting, balancing and selecting of religions and issues are left to education authorities, colleges, schools and teachers to work out. While the Guidelines make it clear that a programme of RME which fails to draw on all three 'Outcomes' would be inadequate, they leave room for variation to suit local conditions and circumstances. The emphasis should be on process rather than content. All of this represents a major advance in the organisation and provision of Religious and Moral Education in Scotland and should result in significant progress over the next decade. However, this is dependent on the provision of adequate resources, sufficient in-service training and a positive profile for RME in schools. Perhaps the major obstacle will be one of attitude, linked to an inadequate understanding of what is involved in RME.

Recently in Scotland, there have been some interesting reactions to the RME 5-14 reported in the daily and educational newspapers. Many of these reports have persistently presented RME in negative and controversial ways. RME 5-14 has been criticised for being insufficiently Christian in its emphasis because it is too anxious to please everyone. On the other hand, some have accused it of being a biased, even racist, document with its over-emphasis on Christianity at the expense of other world religions. These reactions represent some of the most extreme responses to the document.

In my view, the reality is that RME 5-14, far from sitting on any uncomfortable fences, represents the outcome of a steady process that has been going on over the past thirty years. It is a process in which RME has been quietly redefining itself and its educational role in relation to the wider community. Without suggesting for a moment that there is no room for ongoing healthy debate on a range of issues both within and without RME circles, Religious and Moral Education in Scotland, has matured as a subject. Precisely because it does not try to please everybody, it adopts clear positions that displease some. Although the objections are raised, from time to time, in a way that catches the passing headline, the general trend over the past thirty or so years is one of increasing consensus among those involved in the provision and teaching of RME. More-over, RME 5-14 has been generally well received amongst members of the teaching profession who have expressed appreciation of its clear and helpful guidance.

FOUR KEY STEPS

The nature of the growing consensus in Scotland can be summed up historically in four key steps, with the result that nowadays RME is seen to be:

CHILD-CENTRED

        EDUCATIONAL

                MULTIFAITH

                        NATIONAL.

The First Step

It was in the early 1960s that Ronald Goldman established the need for RME to be child-centred.[1] From this single principle has flowed all the concerns not just to make RME relevant to children's lives but to provide progression in programmes of RME that will relate to their actual stage of development and their ability to cope with ideas and concepts. Nowadays we talk of 'beyond Goldman'[2] recognising that his work which drew on the insights of developmental psychology was a pivotal stage in the development of the subject.

The Second Step

In Scotland, it was the Millar Report in 1972 that established once and for all the educational nature of RE. If RE was to be justified within the state school system, then it had to be on educational rather than purely Christian grounds. The key quotation from the Millar Report is found in paragraph 3.3 dealing with the aims of Religious Education:

> The main body of evidence sees the detailed aims as being governed by an approach which has been summed up by Professor W R Niblett as follows: 'Enlightenment rather than conversion, understanding rather than discipleship are the aims of the school whether in the classroom where religious knowledge is taught or in the periods of worship it conducts.[3]

A desk is not a pulpit. Both represent legitimate means of communication within their own context, but one needs to be clear which is which. In brief, Religious Education was to be educational. From this key principle flowed all the subsequent emphasis upon the nature of RME as one entailing skills of enquiry, investigation, reflection and evaluation. Of course, perhaps unwittingly, the Millar Report also placed its finger on the key issue that is still to be satisfactorily resolved, namely Religious Observance .[4] In Millar's terms, the question might be put as 'Can there be such a thing as "educational worship"?' In terms of the Education (Scotland) Act (1980), the question is simply, 'Are RE and RO compatible?' This is an area where opinions abound without much hard data to go on. I am sure that it deserves the attention of serious research. Equally, I am sure, if we keep the needs and interests of the children foremost in our minds, schools need some form of corporate act of celebration that builds on shared values.

The Third Step

It was the work of Ninian Smart, Donald Horder and others during the 1970s that saw the broadening out of the scope of RE. Faiths other than Christianity were put on the agenda. Publications by the Schools Council and books by such notables as Jean Holm[5] and Michael Grimmitt[6] helped to popularise this process. In those less gender-conscious days, 'Other men's faiths' were now being taken seriously in their own right. This was an important development from Goldman's research, with its focus on Christianity within the state school system, to that of multifaith RE. The pendulum of concern in this area was to swing first one way and then the other, until things settled down into a genuine attempt to find a sustained, balanced approach which focuses on world religions including Christianity.

For me, the growing consensus in this area was beautifully symbolised by the production of the *Multifaith Manchester Agreed Syllabus* in 1985.[7] Some twenty faiths took part in the process leading to its publication and were able to agree unanimously on aims and objectives for RE. These were agreed 'after exhaustive, but very concordant debate'. While much of the initial work in establishing the principle of multifaith RE was carried on in England and Wales, its influence was soon felt north of the border in Scotland. Nowadays, the multifaith dimension is well established and is often allied to further concerns on equal opportunities for race and gender.

The Fourth Step

The last of the four key steps is the fact that with the 5-14 RME we are dealing with a national initiative. The most significant thing for RME is that it is part of a national drive designed to see development in all five curriculum areas of the primary school and their secondary counterparts. These are English Language, Mathematics, Environmental Studies, Expressive Arts and Religious and Moral Education. As such it is much less likely to gather dust on some forgotten shelf. With governmental backing this means there is more chance of effective implementation taking place than on any previous occasion.

RME 5-14 is not the only national initiative that has occurred in Scotland in recent years. National impetus and support can be traced back to the 1970s when a number of developments began. It was following Millar in 1972, that for the first time it became possible to train as a secondary specialist in RE (1974), departments of RE became established, advisers were appointed and the then Consultative Committee on the Curriculum took responsibility for the subject.[8] Certification was to follow much later with the introduction of the 0 Grade, Higher (now revised), and then Standard Grade in Religious Studies, along with Short Courses. This growth spurt in RE which projected the subject rapidly through its adolescence all occurred in the more general educational context of cut-back and contraction. Despite this, steady growth and development took place.

Perhaps one of the most significant developments was in 1983 when RE became for the first time, inspectable. The first report was issued in 1986.[9]

CONCLUSION

In Scotland there has been a growing consensus as to the nature and scope of RME. The role of RME is now well established as a worthwhile, educational area of the school curriculum. There is much to be done to see its further development and many teachers will welcome professional support in a variety of ways if this is to be carried out effectively. The arrival of RME 5-14 augurs well for the future. Perhaps, some of its previous detractors would like now to come on board and help the process.

FOOTNOTES

1 Ronald Goldman, *Readiness For Religion* (Routledge and Kegan Paul: London, 1965).

2 For example: H Peatling, 'On Beyond Goldman: Religious Thinking and the 1970's', *Learning For Living* vol 16 No 3 pp 1-8 (1977).

3 *Moral and Religious Education in Scottish Schools,* Report of a Committee appointed by the Secretary of State for Scotland (HMSO: Edinburgh, 1972). The chairman of the committee was Professor W. Malcolm Millar, CBE, then Professor of Mental Health, University of Aberdeen. Hence the popular name 'the Millar Report'.

4 Religious Observance is often taken by school chaplains. Unlike England and Wales it is not a daily requirement.

5 Jean Holm, *Teaching Religion in School* (Oxford University Press: Oxford, 1975).

6 Michael Grimmitt, *What Can I Do In RE?* (Mayhew-McCrimmon: Great Wakening, Essex, 1973).

7 *Multifaith Manchester: Manchester City Council Agreed Syllabus For Religious Studies* (Manchester City Council Public Relations Office: Manchester, 1985).

8 The Consultative Committee on the Curriculum/Scottish Central Committee on Religious Education (SCCORE) produced two seminal documents namely, Bulletin 1: 'A Curricular Approach to Religious Education' (1978), and, Bulletin 2: 'Curriculum Guidelines for Religious Education' (1981).

9 *Learning and Teaching Religious Education,* Interim Report by HM Inspectors of Schools No 91986 (HMSO: Edinburgh, 1986).
Religious Observance in Primary and Secondary Schools, Interim Report by HM Inspectors of Schools (Scottish Education Department, Edinburgh, June 1989).

4 | RELIGIOUS EDUCATION IN NORTHERN IRELAND

Tom Vance

SUMMARY

This article begins by sketching in the historical background to Religious Education in Northern Ireland. It examines, briefly, both Catholic and Protestant positions before outlining some joint religious developments, recent initiatives and the current situation in Religious Education.

THE CURRENT SITUATION

The present division of Northern Ireland society is obvious. The political and cultural allegiances of loyalists to Britain and nationalists to Ireland closely relate to the associated religious labels Protestant and Roman Catholic, with some exceptions of course. Schools generally reflect this division with the particular exception of the recently formed and growing number of integrated schools which enrol children from both communities. A description of the different types of schools in Northern Ireland can be found in an appendix at the end of this article. Ethnic minority groupings of Muslims, Jews and Hindus total 0.2% of the population.[1]

To understand the present state of Religious Education it is important to understand something of the historical background, the separate Protestant and Roman Catholic systems of Religious Education and the joint ventures of more recent times.[2]

HISTORICAL BACKGROUNDS (1921-1930)

Prior to the establishment of the Northern Ireland State in 1921 nearly all education was provided by the churches. In 1923 the first Education Act was aimed at changing control from the churches to the local civic authorities and to cater for all the children of the community. Lord Londonderry, Minister of Education, regarded denominationalism as divisive. His solution was to avoid denominational religious instruction. Instead he aimed to provide facilities for the clergy to give instruction to those of their own denomination outside the times of compulsory attendance. The education he hoped to provide was described as both 'literary and moral'.[3] All of the churches saw it as a 'purely secular system of education alien to the wishes of the Ulster people, Protestant and Roman Catholic alike'.[4] The Act failed to create a 'universal non-denominational educational system under public control'.[5]

By 1930 schooling was settling into the dual system that we know today. The Roman Catholic Church decided to retain and control its own church school system and to seek on-going public funding. The Protestant churches reluctantly agreed to transfer their schools to the State but with the safeguards that simple Bible instruction would continue to be given by teachers and that there should be provision of Protestant teachers for Protestant children.

PROTESTANT RELIGIOUS EDUCATION

The hybrid state institution resulting from the 1930 Act has been variously interpreted. Roman Catholic writers, perhaps as part of their polemic defence of church based schools, regard the State schools as 'secular' institutions. However, Dr John Greer regards them as 'non-denominational but with a Protestant Christian ethos'.[6]

Subsequently most Protestant schools were transferred to the Local Education Authorities. By the terms of the Northern

Ireland Education Act 1947 undenominational religious instruction based on the Bible was extended to secondary intermediate and grammar schools.

While the same provision for Religious Education was repeated in the Education and Libraries (Northern Ireland) Order of 1972 the oversight of Religious Education has been severely hampered by a legal stipulation which states:

> It shall be no part of the duties of inspectors or other officers...to inspect or examine the Religious Education given in school. Ministers of religion and other suitable persons, including teachers of the schools, to whom the parents do not object shall be granted reasonable access .... to inspect and examine the Religious Instruction given to pupils.

In practice this has often led to unimaginative and uninspiring rote learning of Bible stories and passages in the classroom. An oral examination by the annual mass visitation of the clergy from the three largest Protestant churches (Church of Ireland, Presbyterian and Methodist) led in some areas to unhappy clergy, unhappy teachers and unhappy Religious Education. Elsewhere the system was replaced with regular clergy participation in school assemblies and occasional pastoral visits to the classroom.

Area boards have appointed Religious Education Advisers to support the Religious Education programme in schools and to provide in-service training, but with severely limited powers, for example, no powers of inspection.

Attempts have been made by non-statutory bodies, like the Religious Education Council to provide a programme of primary Religious Education based upon the West Riding Agreed Syllabus. In 1971 'Themes in RE' was published .[7] For various reasons, teachers refused to depart from teaching based on Bible stories and Bible knowledge. In 1981 a curriculum development project of the Religious Education Council produced a replacement biblically-based Religious Education programme for primary school years.[8] Although widely distributed the programme was not widely used, perhaps because of its format or because of growing pressures on teachers and on the timetable.

ROMAN CATHOLIC RELIGIOUS EDUCATION

Today Roman Catholic schools provide education for the vast majority of Roman Catholic pupils. Most church primary and secondary schools are in the maintained school category while church grammar schools are called voluntary schools.

In 1964 the Northern dioceses of the Roman Catholic Church dropped the programme of religious teaching built around the catechism and adapted the 'On Our Way' series developed in the USA by Sister Maria de la Cruz for untrained lay teachers. It was adapted for use in RE in schools throughout Ireland as the 'Children of God' series (1978). Excellent materials are included for pupils, teachers, parents and priests. The teaching covers preparation for the sacrament, penance, first communion in P4 and confirmation in P7. Then in 1980 the 'Christian Way' was designed for use with 12-15 year olds and especially less able pupils.

Diocesan RE Advisers are appointed by the Catholic Commission for Maintained Schools (CCMS) and are responsible for the inspection of schools and the supervision of the RE programme and the in-service training of Roman Catholic teachers of Religious Education.

GENERAL CONSIDERATIONS

Teachers are trained for the Roman Catholic schools in St Mary's College, Belfast, and for controlled schools in Stranmillis College, Belfast. The latter is a non-denominational college and has a number of Roman Catholic students. However, such students graduating must complete a special Roman Catholic diploma in Religious Education before they are permitted to teach RE in maintained schools.

A conscience clause operates in controlled schools which permits teachers to contract out of teaching RE and parents to withdraw their children from RE classes. Some parents who are Jehovah's Witnesses and Exclusive Brethren do withdraw their children from RE classes. Roman Catholic teachers in church schools are required to teach religion if requested.

JOINT RELIGIOUS EDUCATION DEVELOPMENTS:

a) Peace Education: The Irish Council of Churches[9] and the Irish Commission for Justice and Peace[10] have produced peace education material for primary and secondary schools.

b) Religion in Ireland: A curriculum development project based at the University of Ulster at Coleraine has produced teaching materials for secondary schools to develop pupils' sensitivity to religious traditions other than their own .[11]

c) Public Examination: From 1973 pupils from both sectors followed common examination courses provided by the Northern Ireland Schools Examination Council for the Certificate of Secondary Education (CSE) and the General Certificate of Education (GCE) Ordinary level ('O') and Advanced level ('A'). Many pupils were entered for these examinations. In 1982 for CSE Mode 1 3,475 students sat the exam, for CSE Mode 3 a further 1,790 students were entered, 4,257 students took the 'O' level exam and 4,081 the 'A' level. The implementation of GCSE with its emphasis on world religion has been less popular and a substantial number of maintained schools have opted for the Northern Examining Board syllabus which is particularly suited to Roman Catholic teaching.

d) Core Syllabus in RE: The Northern Ireland Education Reform Order 1989 introduced the possibility of inspection of RE. This would be done by the Department of Education for Northern Ireland (DENI) at the request of a school governing body. It also gave DENI power to specify a core syllabus for the teaching of RE in grant aided schools, that is both maintained and controlled schools.

Under the sponsorship of the Roman Catholic, Presbyterian, Church of Ireland and Methodist churches and with the approval of DENI a drafting group was established in October 1990 to draw up proposals for a core syllabus in RE .[12] These were published in 1991 and were due to be implemented in both primary and secondary schools in September 1993. However, just before the term began, the Minister for Education for Northern Ireland, Michael Ancram, who had recently been appointed, decided that the Core Syllabus would not be implemented in primary schools that year. Yet the plans for implementing it into secondary schools went ahead as intended. At the time of writing it is still not clear when the Syllabus will be introduced in primary schools. The Syllabus focuses on the study of Christianity, the three attainment targets being:

1 The Revelation of God (Old Testament and New Testament)
2 The Christian Church (origins, history, prayer, worship)
3 Morality (respect for self, other, God, environment)

Jeremy Hanley MP, the Minister for Education at the time, decided not to approve some important recommendations of the drafting groups. These included assessment for controlled schools, a statutory development body for RE, proposals for a new GCSE syllabus and change regarding in-service training. Contrary to the vast majority of teaching opinion, the minister encouraged schools to include the study of other world religions within their total RE programme.

CONCLUSION

An informal observer of RE in Northern Ireland will soon be aware that the subject is in a healthy condition in maintained schools largely due to a closely monitored and controlled structure. In the controlled sector there is a great variation. The weaknesses of the controlled system are more than compensated for by the very large percentage of committed Christian teachers. The growing demands and pressures on teachers and school timetables from the educational reforms are seriously impairing Religious Education. Where there is a lack of teacher commitment Religious Education is often totally neglected.

The legal implications of the new Core Syllabus, implemented in September 1993, have resulted in a flurry of activity in the controlled schools, as primary RE coordinators have been appointed, and as a significant number of secondary schools have advertised for RE specialists.

FOOTNOTES

[1] *The Northern Ireland Census 1991* (HMSO: Belfast, 1991).

[2] John Greer, 'RE in Northern Ireland Up To 1970', *A Dictionary of RE*, J M Sutcliffe (Ed) (SCM Press: London, 1984).

[3] Norman Atkinson, 'The 1923 Education Act', *Irish Education* (Allen Figgis: Dublin, 1969).

[4] ibid.

[5] ibid.

[6] John Greer, 'The 1930 Education Act', *The Northern Teacher* vol 14:1 (Autumn 1982).

[7] Anon, *Themes in Religious Education for Primary School Children* (Religious Education Council Century Services Ltd: Belfast, 1971).

[8] A Programme for Religious Education in the Primary School, Learning Resource Unit, Stranmillis College, Belfast, 1981.

[9] Irish Council of Churches, 48 Elmswood Avenue, Belfast 9. Catalogue available on request.

[10] Irish Commission for Justice and Peace, 169 Bootertown Avenue, Blackrock, Co. Dublin. Catalogue available on request.

11 Religion in Ireland Project, University of Ulster, Coleraine, Northern Ireland.
12 Curriculum Council of Northern Ireland, Stranmillis College, Belfast.

FURTHER READING

'RE in Northern Ireland up to 1970' *The Fourth R – The Durham Report* SPCK 1970.

APPENDIX A

Controlled Schools

These consist of largely Protestant pupils. They are provided by Education and Library Boards and managed through Boards of Governors. This category includes secondary and grammar schools.

Maintained Schools

Pupils attending these schools are mainly Roman Catholic. They are provided by voluntary school authorities and managed by Boards of Governors.

Voluntary Grammar Schools

This category includes schools that can be mainly Protestant or mainly Roman Catholic. They are provided by voluntary bodies, including the main churches, and managed by Boards of Governors. Their running costs are largely met from block grant payable by the Department of Education.

Integrated Schools

These schools enrol Protestant and Roman Catholic pupils in equal numbers. They began as independent schools and qualified for public funding when their longer term viability had been adequately demonstrated. New integrated schools can now receive public funding right from the start.

IMPORTANT ISSUES FOR RELIGIOUS EDUCATION TEACHERS

5 | MULTIFAITH MATTERS?
Jean Mead

SUMMARY

This chapter deals with issues raised by multifaith RE and suggests some practical strategies to help teachers handle it honestly, effectively and professionally. The specific questions that concern Christian teachers, in particular, are addressed.

TO TEACH OR NOT TO TEACH

Multifaith RE can pose particular problems for people who have a strong commitment to one faith; yet these are the very people who are often asked to teach RE without specialist training. If you are a non-RE specialist who has been asked to 'help out' with RE, the chances are pretty high that the request might have been prefaced by 'You go to church don't you?' or 'I know you used to teach Sunday School...' I know someone who became an RE teacher on the strength of once having sung in a church choir! There may also be Christians, some with degrees in theology, who are happy to teach Bible-based RE, but have reservations when faced with the requirement to teach multifaith RE.

It would be a loss if fears about multifaith RE precluded Christians from being able to contribute to the subject, but it might also be a danger professionally, if they taught it without being aware of the issues involved. It could also be a source of personal and spiritual conflict especially if teachers felt they were being pressed into teaching other faiths against their consciences. These are the six key questions which concern many Christians.

SHOULD WE TEACH ABOUT OTHER RELIGIONS?

Multifaith RE features in most RE syllabuses. Since 1988, the law in England and Wales requires that agreed syllabuses 'take account of the teaching and practices of the other principle religions represented in Great Britain',[1] although the emphasis on the teaching of Christianity is increased. The 1993 Education Act requires all LEAs to align RE syllabuses with the requirements laid down in 1988.[2] In Scotland the national guidelines include teaching other religions as one of the three Attainment Outcomes.

Christian teachers have a responsibility to display a positive attitude to their work. It is important to be sensitive to the feelings of pupils from a variety of world faiths. From personal experience, I know this is not always the case. I once heard an advisory teacher, supporting bilingual children, say, 'It's a dreadful school, the staff are all Christians!' I was ashamed to have to admit that there was an element of real truth in the comment.

Some Christians perceive multifaith RE as being in conflict with their own faith, but this is not necessarily so. Others are happy to get involved provided they can do so without being compromised. For a wider discussion in such issues see the booklet 'Calling or Compromise'.[3]

HOW SHOULD CHRISTIANS HANDLE MULTIFAITH RE?

Those with a strong commitment to one religion need to be able to find strategies that enable them to teach about the commitment of others without compromising their own. For Christians teaching 'Christianly' does not necessarily mean teaching about Christianity only. How should Christians handle multifaith RE in relation to their own faith? Here are some suggestions from my own experience:

Fairly

We should take scrupulous care to present all faiths authentically, not in biased terms. We should also examine our selection of material, and ensure that we do not compare the best of one religion with the worst of another. We should not 'load the dice' in favour of Christianity!

Honestly

We should not be expected to teach as truth, what we do not believe to be true, or pretend neutrality. If we make belief statements we should openly identify them as such, and acknowledge that not everyone believes the same.

Humbly

We should not make derogatory statements or implications about any faith, or use judgmental terminology that is offensive. I find it helpful to have an 'imaginary friend' from the faith I am presenting sitting at the back of the classroom. We should also be humble enough to admit that we do not know everything.

HOW CAN WE TEACH SOMEONE ELSE'S FAITH WITHOUT HYPOCRISY?

We should be clear that our teaching aim is educational. Our objective is to promote understanding rather than religious belief or commitment. This is a professional responsibility, which should not offend our consciences.

We should always 'ground' belief statements in the faith to which they belong. For example, a Christian or even an atheist could teach without hypocrisy that 'Muslims believe that the Angel Gabriel revealed the Qur'an to Muhammed' for this statement is true whether or not we ourselves believe that it actually happened that way.

HOW CAN WE TEACH OUR OWN FAITH WITHOUT INDOCTRINATION?

An added bonus is that the same strategies which help teaching about other faiths can also be used when teaching about our own faith to protect us from indoctrinating pupils. If we use our own faith as a resource, ('As a Christian I believe . . .') we must keep the professional and 'believer' roles clearly distinct. We should not talk as if we assume the pupils share our beliefs.

HOW DO WE DECIDE WHICH FAITHS TO TEACH ABOUT?

The syllabus may well dictate this for us, but if it is vague (or non-existent) we may need to make our own decisions. These can be based on a variety of criteria.

If we have children in our classes from a range of faiths this gives a clear criterion for selection. It is good for the pupils to have their religious background acknowledged and valued, and an excellent opportunity for their classmates to learn what is important to them. We should, however, be sensitive about using pupils as an example, as it could have a high 'cringe factor'! Faiths represented in the school or the local community are those which children are likely to encounter and need to know about.

In England, the DFE requires pupils to study all the principal religions of Great Britain in the course of their compulsory education. This reflects the belief that pupils need an awareness of diversity of religion and a suitable range can be covered over time. It is not wise, however, to attempt five major faiths in every term!

Some faiths link particularly well to aspects of cross-curricular themes. If RE is linked, for example, with other humanities subjects, this may provide a more co-ordinated syllabus.

A teacher's personal interest, expertise or the availability of interesting resources could be practical reasons for a specific focus. If you are new to teaching world religions, you may have limited knowledge of the subject. If so, David Day's advice to 'start small' and his discussion of how a little knowledge can go a long way, is encouraging.[4]

The choice should not be an arbitrary hotch-potch of assorted faiths. It should fit into a coherent progression of RE objectives appropriate to the age of the pupils. Ask yourself how your chosen material can be used to help further the pupils religious understanding or spiritual development.

HOW DO I ANSWER 'BUT IS IT TRUE MISS/SIR?'

Pupils are entitled to help and support as they think through questions of truth and meaning. We should not abandon them at their point of need in the interests of objectivity. Teachers are also entitled to their honest opinion. However, ethical integrity and professional responsibility should prevent teachers of whatever religious or non-religious persuasion, from abusing their position by manipulating children into accepting their belief. Christian teachers must be above reproach in this respect, although no one can prevent teachers praying for their pupils!

With these principles in mind how then can we respond honestly and professionally to such questions? Whilst we can clearly state our own opinion, we should balance it by referring to other views. A special use of this strategy is available if teachers agree to use each other's stance as a point of reference, enabling comments like, 'I don't actually believe it myself, but Miss Ahmed does.'

Discussion is a useful approach in exploring what is going on in the pupils' minds, rather than terminating their questions prematurely with a pat answer. Teachers' normal skills in questioning and leading discussion should still operate. Answering a question with another question, a noted delight in Jewish dialogue, is effective at opening rather than closing minds. A particularly fruitful line of discussion can be 'What do you mean by true?' A debate on different types of truth might then follow. Pupils are often grappling with such questions and need to develop into mature thinkers. It is worthwhile RE to help pupils cope intelligently with different literary genres in the Bible and elsewhere.

When a pupil asks a personal question in the midst of a class debate, it may give them more freedom for an honest discussion if their teacher arranges an opportunity to talk to them later in a quieter, more private environment. This provides the pupil with a chance to be honest about the issues that multifaith RE raises for them, without the pressure of their peers' opinions.

FOOTNOTES

[1] *The Education Reform Act* (HMSO: London, 1988).
[2] *The Education (Schools) Act 1993* (HMSO: London, 1993).
[3] *Calling or Compromise* (Association of Christian Teachers, St Albans, 1990).
[4] David Day, *'Teaching World Religions–Can I? Should I? How Do I?'* in Alan Brown, *SHAP Handbook on World Religions in Education* (The Commission for Racial Equality, London, 1987) p11.

6 DEALING WITH CONFLICTING TRUTH CLAIMS IN RELIGIOUS EDUCATION

George Skinner

SUMMARY

Religious Education raises questions of ultimate truth. Such questions need careful handling in the classroom. This article challenges teachers to consider their own position and the appropriate ways to approach these issues.

Religions are often studied in school in largely descriptive ways with the result that central theological questions such as the nature of God and the means of salvation are dodged or shelved. Similarities, real or apparent, between religions are often emphasised in order to avoid divisiveness and to give the impression that we are basically all the same; religion is mankind making meaning. The problem with concentrating on the externals of a religious faith, is that Religious Education may become little more than lessons in history, geography or social anthropology. However, anything other than a superficial study of world faiths soon raises questions about ultimate truth. The answers given by different world faiths to such questions as, 'What is God like?', 'What is the meaning of suffering?' are patently not the same. The different religions may well give conflicting answers. Should such issues be tackled in the classroom?

CULTURE CONTACT THEORIES

The answer to that question depends very much on what you think Religious Education is for. The Swann Report on the education of ethnic minority pupils argued strongly that RE has a vital role to play in promoting inter-cultural understanding and harmony.[1] Such a motive is indeed to be applauded. Yet often current RE Agreed Syllabuses appeal for RE to fulfil social or even anti-racist functions, making the assumption that familiarity with other faiths will breed tolerance. This may well reflect a naive optimism in the potency of simply learning about those who are different from us. The irrational nature of prejudice means, however, that such 'culture contact' theories are inevitably flawed. As one Year 10 Asian Muslim girl observed about a white classmate during a research interview with the author, 'She went on the RE trip to the mosque and said it was great—but she still calls us names!' Accurate knowledge about religious and cultural practices can certainly help undermine the myths on which intolerance is built. However, on its own, it is not enough to combat prejudice.

There is a further problem with this approach to promoting harmony. Religions, at heart, deal with underlying beliefs about human beings and the nature of God. When RE steps beyond the bounds of a descriptive social anthropology and begins to explore the philosophies and theologies of faith, conflicting truth claims are inescapable.

PHENOMENOLOGICAL APPROACH

Phenomenology has given much to the study of religion. It has challenged approaches which seek to explain religious beliefs and practices in terms of the observer's assumptions. Its emphasis is on understanding a religion from the point of view of the adherent and suspending one's own judgment in order to be objective in one's study. However, phenomenology in its highly simplified form adopted in a lot of Religious Education lessons, has often been concerned with only external, describable 'public phenomena'. It has failed to grapple with the inner subjective experience and truth claims of individuals. To hold back one's own judgment while studying another's faith is one thing. To assume that judgment, interpretation and subjectivity are not at the heart of religious faith is another.

In the seventies, RE teachers who had doubts about the trend towards phenomenology were sometimes heard to say that the trouble with comparative religion is that it makes pupils comparatively religious. More seriously, John Taylor in 1976 warned against the danger that it was initiating children into agnosticism.[2] Eight years later, Edwin Cox expressed concern about the way in which preoccupation with the outward expressions of religion may miss the truth claims which lie at the heart of all faiths.[3] Since then, some movements in RE have tried to take more seriously the experiential dimension in religion.[4]

PHILOSOPHICAL APPROACH

Can Religious Education transcend the informative? If it attempts to, will it not threaten the security of those who have a faith or confuse those who have none? Might it not lead to conflict and polarisation rather than harmony, as the conflicting nature of truth claims becomes apparent? No teacher will embark on a course of Religious Education which so emphasises theological differences that it undervalues the many shared values and experiences of people from different faith backgrounds. However, as Edward Hulmes observed, to subtly disguise truth claims in the name of social cohesion or classroom unity is to do a disservice to both religious faiths and pupils.[5] How this can be handled in the classroom is still open to debate.[6] Yet, the point is that, rather than avoiding controversy, RE should perhaps recognise it as part of the price of the quest for truth. RE should be more 'philosophical' in its orientation, helping pupils to recognise truth claims and to develop the skills which enable them to discuss and evaluate them.

HONESTY AND OPENNESS

Such matters also raise the question of the position of the RE teacher. If the teacher's role is essentially one of conveying information, then accurate knowledge and teaching skills are the primary requisites. If the RE teacher is in the business of helping pupils to explore issues of truth and reality, qualities of another kind may be required.

How does the teacher handle his or her own commitments? Of course, every teacher brings commitments to the classroom and all curriculum areas make huge assumptions about truth and reality. The quest for the objective and neutral RE teacher was always doomed to failure. What is needed is not neutrality, but honesty; not objectivity, but openness. The teacher's commitment, rightly handled, is not an obstruction to good Religious Education but a valuable teaching resource.[7]

FOOTNOTES

[1] *The Swann Report: Education For All* (HMSO: London, 1985).

[2] John Taylor, 'Initiation into Agnosticism', *Learning For Living* vol 15.4 (1979).

[3] Edwin Cox, 'Religion in Schools Today and Tomorrow', *RE News & Views* (ILEA: London, 1984).

[4] Hammond et al, *New Methods in RE Teaching: An Experiential Approach* (Oliver & Boyd, Harlow, 1990).

[5] Edward Hulmes, *Commitment and Neutrality in Religious Education* (Geoffrey Chapman: London, 1979).

[6] For example, Werner Haussmann, 'Walking in Other People's Moccasins', *British Journal Of Education* vol 15/2.

[7] ibid 5.

Also see Chapter 7: *What Makes a Good RE Teacher?* by George Oliver.

7 | WHAT MAKES A GOOD RELIGIOUS EDUCATION TEACHER?

George Oliver

SUMMARY

This article is devoted to examining some aspects of what good practice entails. The ideas emerge from my experience of nearly thirty years as teacher, adviser and inspector of Religious Education. I have learnt many of these things in the most direct and painful way of all, by making the mistakes and having to pick myself up afterwards. Other comments are the product of long term reflection and observation. All are deeply rooted in the realities of the classroom.

THE RIGHT ATTITUDE

All too often, I have observed colleagues fall into one or other of two traps in their role as a teacher. One is to suppose that it really does not matter at all what we do in the classroom. It has absolutely no impact. The other extreme is to reckon that what we do is all-important, so that our least word can lead to untold consequences. We end up believing that every detail of the content and tone of our lessons is likely to affect our pupils' attitudes about religion for life.

Either of these positions is apt to lead to teacher paralysis. Why, after all, should we bother to put ourselves out in planning or delivering lessons if we do not believe they have any effect? On the other hand, if everything we do may have powerful, lifelong effects on our pupils, we shall be fearful of doing anything lest we, however unintentionally, brainwash or indoctrinate them.

Both of these positions are gross exaggerations, of course. In

53

reality good, honest RE teachers *can* have a lasting effect in imparting information and changing attitudes. Modern young people, however, are open to a wide range of influences on their beliefs, values and attitudes, and the content of school RE lessons will very rarely be swallowed uncritically. The personalities and observed lifestyles of admired teachers, however, can be influential. It matters what kind of impression we leave on our pupils, but we as teachers are unlikely to be the central, determining factor in their finding their own religious identity.

BE YOURSELF

My second and related point is that we are much more likely to make a positive, healthy contribution to the education and development of young people, especially in the fields of religion and morality, if we are 'ourselves' in school. The attempt to be neutral and detached when teaching about religion is a misconceived and unhelpful way to deal with a highly controversial area. None of us, in the end, is neutral about the ultimate questions of religion. We all have our own, working, day-to-day pragmatic answers, however provisional, to the questions about God, life, human destiny, purpose and meaning which are the stuff of religion. Attempts to conceal these from our pupils will often be in vain. Even if we succeed in seeming detached, our very success will convey all too often its own message: 'It doesn't matter what you believe', or 'Intelligent, modern people don't believe in any of these religious ideas'. Unfortunately this message will then be transmitted in a way which will not easily permit it to be challenged–it will come across insidiously as an unspoken assumption: 'Right thinking people are detached from such matters'.

It is more honest and, therefore more educational, to aim not at detachment, but at fairness. Much of the best and most open RE I have seen has taken place where the teacher's own personal convictions were clearly on the table, sometimes even the starting point of the lesson. 'This is what I believe' presented in an atmosphere of trust and discussion enables beliefs to be challenged. This kind of approach effectively says: 'Religious differences matter; they can be discussed rationally; your point of view is entitled to a proper hearing'. This is a positive, educational way of handling the fact of differing religious commitment.[1]

PRESENT ALL RELIGIONS FAIRLY

Related closely to the last point is the issue of how we actually present different religions. They should be presented so that their adherents will recognise them. Often there is a good deal of pressure to play down controversial parts of a faith to avoid offending anyone. However, religions must be given the fundamental, basic right of fair presentation. We may earnestly and usefully discuss in class whether the claim that Jesus is God's Son is valid; but we may not conceal or even play down the fact that this is a central claim in historic Christianity. Equally, we may discuss the validity of the Muslim claim that the Quran is uniquely, word for word inspired by God; but we may not conceal its importance for Muslims.

There is an influential approach that says that all religions are different routes up the same mountain, leading to the same ultimate goal. Certainly there are Christians, Hindus, Jews and others who believe this and their views should be represented in Religious Education. However, it should not be presented as the ultimate educational orthodoxy, overriding all exclusive claims. To do that would be to misrepresent the position of Muslims, most Christians and many others. I would go further. When Muhammad proclaimed the words of Allah, he did so to challenge men and women to conversion and commitment. The Ten Commandments and the Sermon on the Mount are equally strong, intended to challenge with a view to commitment. Any presentation of religion which plays down this element, which makes it all bland, which removes the controversial element, is a bad presentation. Moses, Jesus and Muhammad alike were commanding, controversial figures. They sought radical changes in peoples' beliefs and consequent lifestyle. RE which does not make this plain is bad RE. There is a built-in challenge to the claims of the great world religions. Something of the excitement of the subversive quality that caused people to accuse Paul and his companions of 'turning the world upside down' must be communicated in RE. Religious commitment affects peoples' lives deeply. Young people need at the very least to get an idea of why people are prepared to die for their faith.

Furthermore a good RE syllabus should not be written in a way which suggests that RE is about studying religion as something which is alien, outside ordinary experience; something which 'other people' do. Good classroom RE takes account of the religion some young people themselves hold dear. In a relationship of trust between teacher and class it becomes possible to use the children's own experience of being part of a faith community, and, with due care, their own personal religious questions and commitment. It is important that teachers should recognise, acknowledge and value the religious commitments and affirmations which young people bring with them into the classroom. I have encountered young people whose religious faith has, they claim, been attacked, even ridiculed in RE lessons. Teachers should be especially careful not to be insensitive and dogmatic in ways which could lead to this accusation. Courteous, careful listening and, when necessary polite and reasoned disagreement should be our trademark. Among its advantages it teaches, by example, how to listen and how to disagree.

Beyond this, most of us, in a society with such wide varieties of religious belief, can learn a good deal from pupils, especially older ones, with a religious commitment which is different from our own. We should, of course, not expect young people to be experts in the traditions of their religious community. Still, in the right classroom atmosphere, the simple personal statement of faith from a young person can bring to life, for more secular friends, the whole area of religion in a way that no amount of effort by the teacher can match.

BUILD UP COMMUNITY LINKS

A surprisingly large proportion of young people have at least occasional links with a faith community, and it is worth taking the trouble to find out what contacts exist in your classes. Through such young people it may be possible to establish fruitful contacts with the leaders and pastors of different religious groups. This can provide local links with men and women of deep religious conviction. These are an essential contribution to the curriculum if the many secular young people in our classes are ever to develop any realistic understanding of why people are religious and of how this affects their lives. I recall taking a lively, normally sceptical class to a synagogue to meet the local rabbi. They were politely interested up to the point they learned that the rabbi's whole family had perished in the holocaust. 'But you still believe in God?' someone asked. From then on they were involved. But what really impressed them was the rabbi's comment, 'I knew Hitler could never win when he declared war on God by burning the synagogues.' That remark somehow confronted them with real faith, and they talked about it for weeks.

DEAL WITH THEIR QUESTIONS

We should take seriously young people's questions and questioning. How many RE schemes of work leave space for the pupils to write their own agenda items? What do they want to know about, to question, to argue about? Too many of our syllabuses are exclusively concerned with the material and issues adults think young people need to tackle. If a child has a problem about suffering, perhaps based on personal experience in the family, then he or she needs to be able to raise this matter.

We must take trouble to find out what our pupils are concerned about and give time to discuss their theological and moral questions. For several years I wrote into my teaching programme lessons simply devoted to grappling with the questions pupils wrote down, anonymously if they wished, and put into the question box. It was invariably worthwhile in itself, and the questions often gave helpful clues for further modules of work.

KEEP SCHEMES FLEXIBLE

We rightly spend a lot of time constructing syllabuses and schemes of work. These are important guides for our classroom teaching. They are, we think, logical: they progress and they cover all the important issues in an appropriate order. Often we are very proud of them. Our pupils, however, do not normally view them or experience them as we do. We produce a five year scheme of work. How many of our pupils will actually work right through such a scheme? Some of them will move in or out of the school part way through. Contingencies arise, causing us to change things. Other teachers will interpret our scheme very differently. We ourselves will, in any case, need or want to revise the whole thing. Even the minority of the students who actually work through the whole of our carefully articulated sequence will rarely, if ever, see it whole, even in retrospect.

While we need schemes of work, we need also to avoid treating them with too much respect. Part of the art of good RE teaching is to know when to depart from them, perhaps to deal properly with students' questions as suggested earlier.

CONCLUSION

I conclude with three succinctly expressed warnings.

First, it is worth listening respectfully to outside opinion; parents, religious leaders, clergy and even politicians often have useful comments to make. However, remember that in the end you are the one who confronts 11C on a wet Thursday afternoon. The authority of experience is yours. You know the limits of what can and can not be done in your particular situation in a way that well-meaning advisers from the sidelines rarely do.

Secondly, for heads of departments especially, avoid strait-jacketing teachers. I have seen many good RE teachers, and some who were quite outstanding. The one thing the good teachers have in common is that they are individuals, each with his/her own unique way of tackling the general task. Teachers will find their own methods, their own ways in, and, within limits, often their own subject material in detail. Despite the risk of their making mistakes, teachers, and inexperienced teachers in particular, need to be given the scope to develop their own styles, and the encouragement to produce their own, unique brand of excellence.

Finally, in RE teaching sensitivity is all. Over the years, your classes will contain 'orthodox' believers from many faith traditions, followers of sects and cults, atheists, humanists and agnostics. Your pupils will come from every kind of background and among them will be those with all kinds of problems and questions. Teaching RE well is treading among peoples' dreams and nightmares. Humour is an essential tool, but the only safe person to laugh at is yourself. Readiness to listen and a respect for your pupils will be a safeguard against most dangers.

Above all, the Christian teacher, seeking to have the mind of Christ, will care for and pray for those entrusted to him/her. This is Christian love, and will compensate for most of the mistakes we all make in tackling this uniquely difficult work.

FOOTNOTES

1 See George Oliver, *Ten Tips For Tightrope Walkers* (CiE, London, 1987). Obtainable from Christians in Education, 53 Romney Street, London SW1P 3RF.

Alternatively, see *Calling or Compromise* (ACT: St Albans, 1990). Available from Association of Christian Teachers, 94A London Road, St Albans, Herts AL1 1NX.

8 | SPIRITUAL DEVELOPMENT
Joan Furlong

SUMMARY

This article seeks to provide answers to such questions as: What is spirituality? How do people develop spiritually? How can we evaluate this area of experience? It also offers a practical framework for teachers to use in the classroom and gives guidance on strategies to promote spiritual development, especially within the RE context.

The spiritual realm is referred to in many educational documents. The 1944 Education Act says the Local Education Authority is responsible for contributing to the 'spiritual, moral and physical development of the community'.[1]

The 1988 Education Act describes a balanced and broadly based curriculum as one which 'promotes the spiritual, moral, cultural, mental and physical development of pupils'.[2] The DES document, Curriculum 11-16 (1985), lists eight areas of experience, the first of which is the spiritual.[3]

Many recent agreed syllabuses of Religious Education refer to the spiritual dimension. A typical attainment target category for RE is 'Personal Understanding and Response'–interpreted as pupils being enabled to understand their own spirituality and uniqueness. Pupils are encouraged to respond to ultimate questions and values which, for some, may lead to a faith commitment or belief in God.

WHAT IS SPIRITUALITY?

Spirituality has to do with us as people, mind, body and spirit. It is not bound by any agreed definition and yet, paradoxically, in order to communicate we must attempt definitions. Here are some starters:

Spirituality

-is a universal or innate feature of human nature which values the inner self and self-knowledge.
-is associated with a search for the meaning of life and the development of personal beliefs.
-can be examined by reason, but cannot be contained by it.
-explores, reflects and responds to mystical, numinous (holy) and transcendent experiences.
-enables wholeness both in our inner being and in relationship to others.
-enables an awareness of the presence of God, the divine, the Sacred.

It is 'the development of that awareness that there is something more to life than meets the eye, something more than the material, something more than the obvious, something to wonder at, something to respond to'.[4]

HANDLING SPIRITUAL DEVELOPMENT IN THE CLASSROOM

Spirituality is not simply about prayer and worship. It also includes knowing and being ourselves, knowing the world around us, and being aware of and caring for others. At this level it is possible to recognise the potential for spirituality in each individual pupil.

As in any other area of the curriculum, pupils need to acquire skills, attitudes and explore and assimilate knowledge within the spiritual area. The difficulty is to contain the spiritual experience within the cognitive stages of learning, since the spiritual often defies verbal description, calling for pupils to respond creatively or intuitively. The teacher must be aware of potential spiritual experience without always insisting that such experience is written down.

To gain access and respond to spiritual experiences the pupils need to acquire the following developmental skills: reflection, stilling, questioning, interpretation, searching for meaning, the ability to communicate feelings and sensitivities, and empathy with others. These skills take time to acquire and need to be practised. This can occur across all areas of the curriculum, but in Religious Education lessons, time and space must consciously be given to ensuring that their development can occur. As these skills are explored and developed, the spiritual rights of every child should be recognised. These include:

Initiation into the spiritual heritage of the culture into which one is born.

Expression of one's own spiritual belief without discrimination.

Choice to deepen, doubt or alter one's own spiritual commitment.

Support complementary to one's own spiritual development.

Protection from spiritual damage and handicap.

Teachers will need to foster the growth and development of spiritual sensitivities and capacities. This could be done through encouraging thoughtful and imaginative contemplation of a wide range of issues, for example awe and wonder at the mysteries of life. It is also important that they promote awareness that life involves moral choices which could have a dark side containing suffering, pain, decay and loss. The teacher must encourage empathy towards the way others respond to their faith, provide pupils with guidance on how to be aware of their own uniqueness and worth, and encourage them to communicate with increasing confidence and self-esteem.

SPIRITUALITY ACROSS THE CURRICULUM

All sorts of areas foster spiritual growth. The DES recognised this, identifying spirituality as a cross-curricular dimension. RE has often been linked to humanities and viewed as the study of another dimension of human experience alongside history, geography, moral education and life skills. RE also has a close link with art, music, drama and English–all these subjects having a definite 'spiritual dimension'. However, it could be argued that in science we should also seek to engage pupils imaginatively and evoke from them their personal response, rather than simply requiring from them a scientific report of what is observed. Similar links could be observed with history, geography, technology and maths. Other languages enable us to perceive the variety and complexity of world-wide communications and cultures. Even in PE we can celebrate the wonder of our human bodies and sense achievement when a new skill is developed.

SPIRITUAL DEVELOPMENT AND RELIGIOUS EDUCATION

The special relationship between Religious Education and spiritual development has long been assumed. For some people the terms 'religious' and 'spiritual' are synonymous. This leads to the assumption that RE alone is responsible for the spiritual. In one way this is true, for the spiritual search is at the heart of all religious experience and activity. The experiential approach to teaching [5] reflects this in its three basic principles:
- –to take seriously the inner experience of the religious believer
- –to enable pupils to have a practical and humane understanding of the religious impulse
- –to encourage increased respect for personal inwardness and awareness.[6]

All areas of the religious curriculum should be characterised by a search for personal understanding and response, so that pupils are enabled to understand their own spirituality. However, the spiritual is not only expressed in religious terms—it has much wider boundaries permeating all human experience and understanding. So, response to the spiritual can be seen in a heightened awareness of a sunset, a feeling of loss or sadness, or in the motivation of a life spent in caring for others.

HOW DO WE PROMOTE SPIRITUAL DEVELOPMENT IN OUR SCHOOLS?

The RE curriculum should be familiar to everyone in school. It should be highlighted and given time in INSET planning alongside the provision of appropriate resources. Such training offered to teachers should heighten their awareness that recognising and developing spirituality across the curriculum is fundamental to the development of the whole child.

Acts of collective worship and religious observance should encourage spiritual growth through the fostering of sensitivities, capacities and skills relating to the spiritual area of the curriculum. Spiritual development should not, however, be limited to collective worship and Religious Education. The spiritual dimension should be mapped out across the whole curriculum and through the ethos of the school. These should support and give legitimacy to the exploration of feelings, the development of positive attitudes and ideas, and the inspiration of the imagination.

In the learning process pupils must be encouraged to think about the process of good or bad habit formation. They too must be asked to question assumptions about what a person is and what gives that person value. Stillness and silence should be given value as well as activity. Finally pupils' inner experiences, that is their feelings, intuitions and responses, should be dealt with in a way that gives them value and legitimacy.

If these principles are born in mind and made real in practice, pupils will experience religion in its proper context of care and love and in so doing grow spiritually in a positive and supportive environment.

INSPECTING PUPILS' SPIRITUAL DEVELOPMENT

The consultation paper for the Inspection of Schools,[7] suggests that each pupil's spiritual development can be gauged through their response to collective worship, aesthetic opportunities and reflection about philosophical and religious questions. Evidence about these responses can be drawn from discussion with the pupils about their beliefs, understanding, feelings and values.

HOW CAN WE PROVIDE INDICATORS FOR SPIRITUAL DEVELOPMENT?

The very nature of the RE curriculum provides an educational process from knowledge to understanding. It is hoped that the pupil will be able to internalise this understanding in relationship to their own spiritual quest.

Within the ethos of the school, pupils should be developing personal values, having explored those presented to them via the many relationships that make up school life. It would be all too easy to set up benchmarks of development which assume every child travels the same pathway and emphasise the cognitive aspects of this spiritual trail. This could be done without ensuring space was left for the non-verbalised aspects and responses to the transcendent. In other words if we contain the spiritual, we may end up losing it. So let us rejoice that this area of experience is a different way of knowing and a different way of becoming, and enable pupils to grow in their awareness of 'something more'.[8]

FOOTNOTES

[1] *Education Act* (HMSO: London, 1944).

[2] *Education Reform Act* (HMSO: London, 1988).

[3] *The Curriculum From 5-16* (DES: London, 1988).

[4] Terence Copley speaking on the video *Educating For Spiritual Growth* New Era Series. (Marjon: Plymouth, 1989).

[5] See: John Hammond et al, *New Methods in RE Teaching: An Experiential Approach* (Oliver & Boyd: Essex, 1990).

[6] Ed. Alison Jones. *Making RE More Affective* Religious Education Research Project, Paper 1 (University of Nottingham: Nottingham, 1986).

[7] *Framework For The Inspection Of Schools; OFSTED Paper For Consultants* (HMSO, London, 1992).

[8] *Spiritual and Moral Development: A Discussion Paper* (National Curriculum Council: York, April 1993).

9 | PERSONAL, SOCIAL AND MORAL EDUCATION AND RELIGIOUS EDUCATION

Brian Wakeman

SUMMARY

What is the current scene and legal position concerning PSE? What is Personal, Social and Moral Education? What can RE contribute to PSME? This article discusses these three important questions.

It is widely agreed that the responsibilities of teachers in state education include pastoral care, and personal, social and moral education (PSME). These are intended to promote the general progress and well being of the pupils and protect their health and safety. Schools are expected to have clear policies, and effective systems and practices for pastoral care and PSME. This emphasis is highlighted by the new Office For Standards in Education (OFSTED) in England which include these issues in their focus.[1]

We are all familiar with the responsibility of schools to provide a broad and balanced curriculum. This should promote the spiritual, moral, cultural, mental and physical development of pupils at the school and prepare them for the opportunities, responsibilities and experience of adult life. Schools have been responding to the challenge of providing this by reviewing their work and formulating policies and development plans.

Many schools have had tutorial arrangements, a pastoral curriculum, or a personal social and health education programme for years. These are organised in various ways, for example in tutorial periods, special timetabled courses, or whole school cross-curricular approaches. Many have been very successful, but there have been problems, for example co-ordination; appropriate staffing; need for in-service training;

pressures for extra time from other statutory subjects; quality of curriculum design and resourcing; depth of commitment by staff. More recently schools may have been reviewing the curriculum to map the cross-curricular dimensions, themes and skills specified at national level. Many schools have been prompted to look again at their approaches to PSME because of its cross-curricular implications with themes like Economic and Industrial Understanding, Guidance, Health Education, and Education for Citizenship. Others, however, have abandoned tutorial periods and a 'pastoral curriculum', yielding to pressures for more time for academic subjects. Some are delivering PSME themes across the curriculum, and others are devising special courses to deliver particular themes with staff who have volunteered for the task.

With so much stressful change associated with the curriculum, the commitment to PSME in schools has often waned. However, the government's renewed interest in these areas has put Personal, Social and Moral Education higher on schools' agendas.

WHAT IS PERSONAL, SOCIAL AND MORAL EDUCATION?

In a very helpful review of thinking about PSME, Her Majesty's Inspectorate of Schools said that PSME is not just a timetabled subject but 'those aspects of a school's thinking, planning, teaching and organisation explicitly designed to promote the personal and social development of the pupils'.[2]

The work of the National Curriculum Council in England has been helpful to teachers in unpacking what those aspects are, both in terms of the aims quoted earlier and in their analysis of the cross-curricular elements.

In one sense PSME is one of the most important responsibilities laid upon teachers. They must be concerned with the education of the 'person' as a physical, rational, sentient, moral, social, economic and spiritual being.[3]

We can take each part of PSME, or PSHE (Personal, Social and Health Education) and ask further probing questions. Is *personal* education about privacy or about the development of self-awareness, esteem or autonomy? Is the *social* to do with other people in life, training pupils in acceptable codes of sociable behaviour, or in helping them to fit into helpful roles prescribed by societies, employers or politicians? Is the *moral* about codes of conduct suitable for good classroom behaviour or principles such as 'telling the truth', 'keeping promises', 'acting considerately towards others', 'respecting the rights and property of others' and 'helping the less fortunate'?[4]

In one early definition of PSME this author wrote:

The *personal* refers to the growing self-awareness of pupils, their self-esteem, understanding of the process of growing up and awareness of their attitudes, emotions, values and beliefs. It will also include personal health.

The *social* refers more to the place of others in the pupil's life, their relationships, feelings about those close to them, and the way they might fit into groups of people. It includes wider issues—not only self-consciousness in relation to others—but awareness and understanding of other people, the institutions of society, and the problems of both the local and wider communities. The relation of the individual to the state, concepts of a more political nature, such as use of power, government, beliefs about how society should be organised, the place of law, police, crime and punishment—all these are what I loosely term 'social'. The world of work, the production of wealth, the preparation of children for adult roles which has been denoted 'Careers Education' also come under this umbrella.

The *moral* has more to do with the way an individual behaves towards others. It is concerned with questions of 'ought' and 'should', of 'duty' and about principles which regulate the private and public lives of individuals. It is about the principles by which I arrive at my behaviour. Judgments about right and wrong, about the nature or development of virtue or the good life, and how best to practise it – these are ethical or moral concerns. Moral Education is that part of PSME which helps the young person to understand what moral questions are about, how to recognise moral issues, how to arrive at a moral decision. Moral Education is the consideration of principles and codes of moral life. It includes reading accounts of people exemplifying the 'good life'. Moral Education consists not simply of teaching moral reasoning, but also of encouraging young people to practise their principles. PSME cannot be limited to one subject. We are talking about realms of experience here, dimensions of the whole curriculum and what has been called the hidden curriculum. All that the school plans, organises and implements contributes to the PSME of the pupils. The unintended as well as the intended contributes to the PSME of the pupil.[5]

This attempt at filling out what is meant by PSME still begs questions which I believe thoughtful teachers need to ask. Underlying PSME programmes in schools are presuppositions about the nature of persons, a vision for society, what constitutes the 'moral' dimension, and how people ought to behave. We all bring our values and presuppositions to our work in PSME.

Christians will wish to bring a Christian mind to PSME. If they think Christianly, that is bringing the Biblical insights of Creation, Fall and Redemption to their thinking and action, what differences does it make?[6]

Is there a Christian view of persons, of a vision for society, and of morality, virtue and nature of the good life? The answer is that Christian beliefs and practice have an enormous contribution to make. What then does a Christian world-view mean for PSME?

You might find it helpful to try sketching out your understanding and ideas on the 'value of PERSONS'; 'a vision of SOCIETY'; and 'MORALITY, virtue and the nature of the good life'. Then compare your ideas with the values of your school, or the PSME programme. How can you introduce your commitments in your teaching of PSME in a legitimate way? Ought you to? Can you avoid it?

While acknowledging the worth that other perspectives bring, I have suggested elsewhere[7] some distinctive and unique contributions Christians can make to PSME, but these ideas need developing by individual Christian teachers .[8]

What does God require of Christians in their service to children in schools? How can they work out the Creation Mandate and Great Commission of the Bible (Genesis 1:26-28 and Mark 16:15) in a secular setting? For those readers who are theists, surely we believe that God is still interested in his World, in education, in what we teach in PSME and how we teach? The other articles in this section will help in providing guidelines for answering these questions.

WHAT CAN RE TEACHERS CONTRIBUTE TO PSME?

Many RE teachers will be responding to the stimulus of the National Curriculum, and defending their curriculum time and resources from the eroding forces of 'hard' subjects, such as Maths, English and Science. We need to work out how we contribute to the aims discussed earlier. What do we have to contribute to the cross curricular dimensions and themes? RE plays a major role in education for a multi-cultural society, and in Citizenship Education. Your RE department should generate policy statements on the topics, concepts, skills and abilities, and attitudes and values you contribute to cross-curricular aspects of school learning, and to your PSME programme in particular. RE teachers need to be 'in' on the planning and review of PSME and cross-curricular courses or arrangements.

We cannot claim any exclusive rights in pupils' personal, social and moral development, but we do have legitimate claims to make. We contribute a lot in common with other curriculum areas to PSME, but we also bring distinctive knowledge and understanding, qualities and skills to PSME. The enquiry, discourse and traditional territory of Religious Studies includes reflections about meaning and purpose, the questions that the life experiences of pupils raise and the relation between belief and behaviour. There are further religious perspectives on PSME topics which may be missed without the RE teacher.

We can claim that RE deepens and structures pupils' thinking of some PSME themes, questions, socio/moral issues, mysteries, and exploration of beliefs. The disciplined enquiry of RE promotes tolerance, investigative skills, powers of thinking about controversial issues, understanding of people and culture, critical openness and a quest for truth rather than just the formulation of opinion. There is a sense in which RE makes the 'wisdom of the ages' available to pupils rather than the sum of pupils' limited experience through discussion, as in some PSME lessons. Neither should the skills and qualities that the RE teacher models be underestimated. These may include experience of the spiritual dimension of life; quest for meaning and purpose; search for truth; tolerance of mystery and partial understanding; longing to know God and understand revelation; commitment to religious and moral discourse, practice of agape love; and insight into pastoral care.

In conclusion, Religious Education can make a rich and powerful contribution to the wider curriculum in knowledge of topics, understanding and skills. We need to know what we are doing to promote the various aspects of pupils' development and prepare them for their life in society. It is essential that RE teachers contribute to PSME planning and development. An RE element or involvement in your school's PSME and cross-curricular learning will enrich and deepen your pupils' experience.

FOOTNOTES

1 *The Handbook for the Inspection of Schools,* (OFSTED: London, 1992).
2 *Curriculum Matters No 14 – Personal and Social Education from 5-16* (HMSO: London, 1986).
3 Richard Pring, *Personal and Social Education in the Curriculum* (Hodder & Stoughton: Sevenoaks, 1984).
4 Nicholas Pyke, 'Pascal's Weighty Moral Legacy', *Times Educational Supplement* (April 9th 1993).
5 Brian Wakeman, 'Religious Education and Personal and Social Development', Bill Greenwood, *Perspectives on Religious Education and Personal and Social Education* (CEM: Isleworth, 1986).
6 See Albert Wolters, *Creation Regained* (IVP: Leicester, 1985) and David Cook, *Moral Maze* (SPCK: London, 1983).
7 Wakeman op cit.
8 See Brian Wakeman, *Personal, Social and Moral Education* (Lion: Tring, 1984).

10 CROSS-CURRICULAR LINKS
Chris Wright

SUMMARY

This chapter looks at various approaches to cross-curricular links and asks where RE fits in. Arguments for and against forging cross-curricular links between RE and other subjects are also examined.

Two trends have been noticeable in the recent position of RE in the curriculum. Firstly, in some cases despite its statutory status the subject has become marginalised. The school timetable has been naturally concerned with delivering the 'core subjects' such as English, Maths and Science. RE has consequently been relegated, in some schools, to the position of a minor luxury subject. The second trend has been towards more subject specialism.

In the past, three approaches have been adopted by those forging links between RE and other subjects in the curriculum:

1 Integrated studies: Subject specialities contribute to a general theme–which can be made up of a number of contributory units (religious, historical, geographical etc). Within this context individual teachers do not divide up by their subject specialism but contribute to the general theme.
2 Interdisciplinary studies: Here subject specialists teach their own subject with the aim of contributing towards some common themes. They all contribute their own subject-specific perspective upon the theme.
3 Liaison: Here the individual subjects maintain their own identity. However, teachers from a number of disciplines liaise to identify cross-curricular issues. This can work in

one of two ways. Firstly, by being aware of common skills, attitudes and knowledge which the subjects within a faculty/curriculum area are attempting to develop. Secondly, by liaising with subjects outside individual curriculum areas. For example, the RE teacher may well make links with the home economics department when doing work on kosher food.

WHERE DOES RE FIT IN?

In the past RE has been organised under a number of different umbrellas. Some schools have placed it with Personal, Social and Moral Education and therefore aligned it with the tutorial programme. This approach has stressed the natural links with the personal and moral development of the pupil. The inherent danger of this approach is that RE will lose its individual identity and become subsumed within the tutorial programme. Furthermore, RE has sometimes become squashed into a mish-mash of PSE–sometimes only receiving thirty minutes of study a week. One teacher commented that 'my department is subsumed into PSE–I have to compete with Health Education, PE and Social Education'.[1]

A more mutually beneficial relationship would appear to credit the potential cross-curricular liaisons with PSE rather than teach both together within an integrated course. Such courses as, for example, 'Christian Perspectives on Moral and Social Issues', are very popular at GCSE level. However, even within this setting it is important not to lose sight of the religious dimension of the course. Many examiners' reports have cautioned against the tendency to turn the course into social studies.

Other schools have included RE within the Humanities faculty along with History, Geography and Sociology. This has drawn on the trend to study religious phenomena in the objective way that has characterised Religious Studies over the past decade. The general unifying theme has been a study of humanity–its geography, history, beliefs and values. 'If Humanities is about people and the world in which we live then "Belief" is an integral part of understanding, along with Geography and History.'[2] Religious Studies, according to this model, has been taught largely from a sociological perspective. The danger here is that it can be criticised as a rather 'dry bones' approach to RE, 'often overlooking the experience and spirituality of believers'.[3]

The National Curriculum offers explicit opportunities for forging links between History and RE. For example, the History General Requirements for England state that History should be taught from a variety of perspectives including the religious. The National Curriculum History document draws attention to the need to look at religion in the Roman Empire (KS3), the Church in mediaeval society and the beliefs of the Aztecs, Greeks (KS2), Anglo-Saxons and Vikings (KS2). Islam features as a supplementary study unit on the Crusades and Islamic Civilisations (KS3). The Holocaust (KS4) is another area where cooperation between History and RE is essential. The explicit attention which the teaching of History now gives to beliefs and values is something which ought to please the RE teacher and it provides opportunities for the two curriculum areas to enrich one another. From the RE angle it offers a useful reminder that beliefs arose within an historical context. Whilst it is important that students understand the beliefs, values and practices of believers today, it is also important that they understand the historical context for the rise of the religions.

Course planners should also be aware of the potential pitfalls inherent in making such cross-curricular links. For example, as W Owen Cole has asked, how does one deal with Roman religion? (KS3), 'Are its adherents to be called "pagans"?; is Christianity to be presented as superior to the "superstitions" which it replaced? In RE we have stopped using value-laden terms such as "pagan" and "superstition".' He goes on to ask, 'Will children learn them from less careful colleagues?'[4] If care is not taken religious material could be used in a way with which many religious educators would be unhappy. A vital question for the RE teacher must be, 'Is it history or RE?' However, it would be naive to presume that since religious belief is being taught in history there is no need to have separate RE lessons.

Other schools have seen natural links with the creative and expressive arts (literature, music, art and drama). All these have been employed by religious believers down the centuries to express their most deeply held convictions. Such a rationale draws attention to the fact that the arts are 'witnesses to experience, experience which cannot be adequately expressed by simple statements. Religious experience is also experience which goes beyond words'.[5] A brief glance over some attainment targets for RE draws attention to the possible links with the arts: For example at Key Stage 3 pupils should, according to the FARE project, be given the opportunity to develop creative responses to experience and to explore the use and effectiveness of different language forms.[6] Similarly in the Westhill Project under attainment 9 it is said that pupils should 'be able to interpret meanings from examples of rituals, artifacts, art and music'.[7]

Placing RE within the realm of the arts offers access into the affective element of the subject since 'spirituality is most likely (to be) manifest in the practical process of creative action', because 'in the day to day struggle with paint, ink and glue (not to mention dance and music) the act of making became a form of dedication, and it was by these means that the metaphysical and spiritual dimension became manifest'.[8]

'For RE to affect the personal, moral and spiritual aspects of pupils, it must engage in that which is creative and artistic, for not to do so will de-personalise religion and so we shall once again end up with dry bones, collections of facts and figures which only have significance in terms of curiosity value'.[9]

Other RE departments have forged natural links with the science department. Topics, in the primary school, on water and air lend themselves to both science and RE as pupils are encouraged to express their wonder at the natural world. Similarly, in secondary schools, when exploring subjects such as birth, it is important that this is approached from both the biological and spiritual side as pupils are, for example, encouraged to reflect on what it is to be human. In PSME courses such as 'Religious Perspectives on Moral Issues' there are natural links with the science department (eg issues related to alcohol, drugs, contraception etc). At sixth form level it is usual for many departments to put on courses exploring the relation between science and religion.

Though this paper has concentrated on outlining four areas for curriculum links, this is not to say that RE does not have links with all subjects within the curriculum. For example, English literature is often used as a basic resource for the RE classroom.

WHAT ARE THE ARGUMENTS FOR AND AGAINST CROSS-CURRICULAR LINKS BETWEEN RE AND OTHER SUBJECTS?

Arguments in Favour

Pupils should be aware that religion is a part of life and is not to be compartmentalised into its own specialist arena. It helps pupils to make links between belief/faith and lifestyle. Religion does not exist within a vacuum – it affects other areas of life and in turn is affected by them. What people believe affects how they respond to issues, for example war and pacifism (history) or how they treat the environment (geography).

Bringing RE into a larger collective of subjects can give the subject a greater status and more time on an equal footing with other subjects within the same curriculum area. One teacher writes:

> Pupils feel that RE is irrelevant, so it is good for them to see it's not just about learning slabs of information, but it's a living experience for people. It is also good for me because as a one-man department I can feel a bit isolated.[10]

Some argue that links are more appropriate at some times than others. For example, at an early age linkage can aid an holistic approach and avoid giving the impression that RE is about weird and wonderful things not relevant to ordinary people. The same case for an integrated approach can be made at sixth form level where students should be encouraged to explore the synthesis of distinctive and individually valid subject strands.

Arguments Against

There is a practical issue to face when considering the integrated approach. Many secondary schools employ more history and geography specialists than RE specialists. Since it is natural for teachers to teach out of their own specialist interests, the RE element of the theme can have a raw deal. RE is a recognised shortage subject for teachers. There are not enough RE specialists to go around.

It is important from the outset to see RE as a full partner in a Humanities programme. If this is not the case it is easy for it to become subsumed into other subjects. Thus, one teacher voices a concern held by many more when she writes that it 'easily gets lost'. Another teacher stated that she had 'deliberately avoided being lost in a Humanities mishmash'.[11]

The identity of RE can be watered down into something other; for example, one teacher argued that 'RE when taught with Humanities seems to evaporate into social studies...it has the lowest common denominator effect and tends to diminish the specifically religious content to become a mild phenomenology'.[12]

There is also the concern that when RE is taught in integrated studies, not only will the content be subsumed into other subject bases, but the nature of the subject will be changed. John Hull makes this point in his discussion of multi-faith RE which he accuses of encouraging 'moral relativism and secularism by concentrating on social and political issues'.[13] This is even more of a danger when RE is taught within a larger integrated course.

There is the fear that when non-specialist teachers from other disciplines are called to teach RE within an integrated course, they do not always have the skills with which to carry out the task, prompting one teacher to complain that, 'this places a huge INSET burden on RS staff–often only one person'.[14] Furthermore, when RE is taught within an integrated course it is important that it is preserved as a distinctive discipline, teaching specific skills and concepts. This is reflected in the views of another teacher, 'too many compromises have to be made regarding both content and skills–the whole programme becomes too vague'.[15]

The Culham report on 'RE and the Humanities' concludes that the 'risks outweigh the advantages' of teaching RE through integrated courses. The responses from their questionnaire indicate that teachers 'wish RE to exist in its own right inside and outside of any collaborative arrangements, whilst taking and making opportunities to co-operate with other disciplines in the service of pupils' general education'.[16]

ISSUES TO BE TAKEN INTO CONSIDERATION WHEN CONTEMPLATING CROSS-CURRICULAR LINKS

There should be a careful identification of the right propriety in the relationship. The RE component within any course, whether it be integrated studies, interdisciplinary studies or cross-curricular liaison, needs to be planned coherently and separately from the other components. This is to ensure that RE is not lost within the whole. In other words, RE needs to be firmly focused. The RE syllabus applicable to the school must be delivered.

The RE contribution needs to arise out of the inner logic of the subject. This will ensure that superficial links are not made which pay only token homage to RE.

FOOTNOTES

1 *RE & Humanities* (Culham College Institute: Abingdon, Oxon, May 1990).
2 ibid p 2.
3 Christine Bedford, 'Religious Education and The Arts', *Resource,* vol 14 no 3 (Summer 1992): p 3.
4 W Owen Cole, 'History and RE: the Need for Cooperation', *RE Today* vol 9 no 3 (Summer 1992): p 9.
5 Bedford op cit.
6 *Forms of Assessment in Religious Education: The Main Report of the FARE Project* (University of Exeter: Exeter, 1991).
7 Attainment in RE: A Handbook for Teachers (Westhill: Birmingham, 1989) p78.
8 Richard Yeomans, 'Islamic Art in The Primary Classroom', *Resource* vol 15 No. 2 (Spring 1993): pp 4- 5.
9 Bedford op cit. p 4.
10 Culham op cit.
11 Culham op cit.
12 Culham op cit.
13 John Hull, *Mishmash–RE in Multicultural Britain: A Study in Metaphor* (CEM, Birmingham, 1991), p 12.
14 Culham op cit.
15 Culham op cit.
16 Culham op cit.

SECTION THREE

CLASSROOM PRACTICE

11 THE BIBLE IN THE SECONDARY SCHOOL

Trevor & Margaret Cooling

SUMMARY

This article examines important issues relevant to teaching the Bible in schools and looks at three dimensions which need to be part of one's approach. Following the article, there are two sample lessons which show how Biblical concepts and material may be handled in the secondary school.

For the RE teacher there are two facts which are important when thinking about teaching the Bible.

FACT 1: The Bible is the foundational text both for Christianity and for understanding the culture of modern Britain.

This means that every RE teacher will have to teach the Bible. The amount of time devoted to the topic will vary. In some schools, for example in Northern Ireland, in some church and independent schools in England and in certain examination syllabuses, the Bible will constitute the majority of the work. In others it will form one aspect of a study of Christianity, as for example in the Scottish schools using the national RE guidelines. However, in every school it will figure somewhere in the syllabus.

FACT 2: Large numbers of school children and adults know very little about the Bible.

Two national newspapers published surveys on Easter Sunday 1993, reporting that about one-third of people did not know why Easter was celebrated. A 1991 MORI poll showed that 62% of 18 to 24 year olds did not know who Pontius Pilate was. There can be little doubt that most of these people were taught the Easter and Christmas stories at some stage in their school careers. What this adds up to is a third important fact:

FACT 3: *The teaching of the Bible in British schools has been patently unsuccessful.*

From my experience, I suggest that this is because our approach to teaching the Bible has been unappealing to young people.

Two of the answers that have been given to the question 'Why teach the Bible?' have not helped.

These are:

ANSWER A: WE TEACH THE BIBLE BECAUSE IT IS THERE.

When I first started work as an RE teacher I planned my syllabus on the basis of a chronological study of the Old and New Testaments. It soon became obvious that, although I could make the pupils learn about Abraham, Moses, Elijah, Paul and so on, they did not like it. I then began to ask myself why teaching the chronology of the Bible was important anyway and the only answer I could give was because that was the way I had been taught. The chronology was simply there. My students needed a better reason than that, because they couldn't see any relevance in, for example, learning about Elijah on Mount Carmel. Bible knowledge for its own sake was not helping them.

ANSWER B: WE TEACH THE BIBLE BECAUSE IT WILL MAKE CHILDREN MORAL.

Following riots in Newcastle a clergyman is quoted as saying; 'You may be happy with children who know nothing of the Bible. You wouldn't be if you were a headteacher on Tyneside, with police having to protect your school.'[1] The implication was that Bible knowledge would make children more moral. It is this feeling that lies behind calls to teach children the Ten Commandments, as though being able to recite these would immediately ensure they followed them. A brief study of the history of Christianity is enough to show that such knowledge is no guarantee of moral behaviour.

The problem with these two approaches is that they ignore the pupil's perspective. The first assumes an intrinsic interest in learning the Bible passages. The truth is very few pupils, even those who come from a Christian home, are interested in this. The second makes the pupils feel the Bible is being forced on them as a form of social control and therefore they resent it.

In order to overcome this resistance and apathy, I suggest that there are three dimensions which have to be part of our approach to teaching the Bible.

DIMENSION ONE: THE MESSAGE, NOT JUST THE CONTENT, IS IMPORTANT.

There can be no doubt that knowledge and understanding of the Bible are essential in Religious Education. That, however, is very different from passing on mounds of Biblical content for pupils to remember. That is to do little more than to train up potential 'Blockbusters' contestants or prepare students for a life of crosswords. The Bible authors did not write databanks for memorisation, rather they were seeking to communicate ideas. For them it was the message they had to share that motivated them and governed their choice of the information they chose to record. For example, the gospel writers each had a distinctive understanding of Jesus which they wanted to communicate.

To grow in knowledge and understanding of the Bible is to grasp these messages, not to memorise information. An approach which emphasises ideas is intrinsically more interesting than one which harps on information. It is ideas which capture people's imagination and changes their thinking. Information becomes important in the context of ideas, because it is the ideas which give that information importance and significance. To know the details of a Roman crucifixion may perhaps appeal to our more morbid instincts. To set that in the context of the idea that this was God dying to redeem the human race is an altogether more revolutionary encounter with the story of Easter.

A very important way of communicating these messages is to emphasise their significance for Christians in the modern world. All too often we leave pupils thinking that the Bible is a relic from the first century. My wife recounts the story of a fifteen year old student who suddenly blurted out, 'You mean people today believe in this?' whilst studying the resurrection accounts in the gospels. It had taken eleven years of formal education for this to dawn and it was quite a stunning revelation.

DIMENSION TWO: TEACHING ABOUT THE BIBLE SHOULD CONTRIBUTE TO THE PUPILS' OWN PERSONAL DEVELOPMENT.

Put simply, this means that pupils learn about the Bible in order to learn from it. The RE department at the University of Birmingham have coined the phrase 'Gift to the Child' to describe this. By this, they mean that the study of the Bible can help pupils in their understanding of themselves and of the world even if they themselves are not Christians. So the Bible makes a non-religious gift to the pupil. For example studying the episode of Peter's betrayal of Jesus after his arrest and his subsequent reconciliation with him by the Sea of Tiberias, can help students deal with their own sense of guilt when they fail badly according to the standards set by their own ideals.

An important way of linking dimensions one and two is to structure pupils' exposure to the Bible around key concepts. These are the big ideas which form the skeleton of the Bible and a grasp of which is essential to developing an understanding of the messages the authors were communicating. An example would be the concept of the resurrection. However, not only do these key concepts give us a way of understanding the significance of the information recorded in the Bible, they also offer a bridge which enables pupils to use the Bible in forwarding their own personal development. So an idea like 'resurrection' raises fundamental questions about the destiny of human beings and the purpose of suffering which are part of our shared human experience. Reflecting on the Biblical response offered through the concept of resurrection can stimulate the pupils in their own search for personal response to these issues which life throws up for us all.

Perhaps I can give an example which I heard given by Jack Priestley, the principal of Westhill College, Birmingham. He cited a class doing work from Genesis on the story of the Fall of Adam and Eve. They had produced a display which included Eve being persuaded by the serpent to eat the forbidden apple. The class went out to play at break during the course of which one pupil started a fight. Another child came running in to inform the teacher of the incident. In the course of trying to explain what had happened, she said that James (the assailant) had 'eaten the apple'. What this showed was that learning about the concept of the Fall and the imagery of the biblical story had given her a powerful tool for grappling with the rights and wrongs of the playground situation.

DIMENSION THREE: THE WAY IN WHICH CHRISTIANS READ THE BIBLICAL TEXT SHOULD BE TAKEN SERIOUSLY.

Here we move into a more sensitive area, which entails recognising that the Bible means different things to different Christians. Certainly by the time the students reach the end of their school career, they ought to be aware of some of the challenges involved in reading the Bible. The technical terms for these areas of study are hermeneutics and contextualisation. The first is the study of interpreting the Bible, the second is the application of the Bible to situations in the modern day world. There are three things of particular significance for school Religious Education which arise from these areas of study:

1 Pupils should become aware that the message that people find in the text is not always the same. What is read in the Bible depends not only on the words, but also on the interests and priorities of the people reading it.

   To give a simple example, there are some Christians who believe that the Bible teaches what is called 'prosperity theology'. This is the belief that followers of Jesus Christ can expect to benefit materially as a reward for their faith. Other Christians find what they call 'liberation theology' in its pages. By this they mean that God has a bias to the poor, and that the Christian calling is to identify with and work for those whom society does not favour. It should not be surprising to know that it is the particular circumstances of the individuals involved that often leads them to hold their interpretation. So, prosperity theology is mainly a North American phenomenon, although an influential advocate is the pastor of the largest church in the world in South Korea, whereas liberation theology has arisen in the slums of South America. Being aware that the questions we ask the text can predetermine the answers we get, should make us wary of assuming that our reading of the Bible is the only legitimate one. We can all be guilty of distorting the meaning of the text.

2 Pupils should know that there are different traditions of doing theology. Probably the key distinction for them to understand is between conservative traditions and liberal or radical traditions. The former work on the assumption that there is a body of authorative teaching which is to be found in the Bible and can be applied in the modern world. The latter sees the Bible as literature which invokes and inspires a way of life, but is not a source of doctrines that are literally true.

   An example from a school textbook I once found may

help. Discussing the resurrection, the author compared it to the story of the Good Samaritan. As the point of the story of the parable did not depend on the real existence of any Good Samaritan, so too, he said, the story of the resurrection did not depend on Jesus rising physically from the dead. That is an example of a radical interpretation. As an evangelical I would disagree with this because I would distinguish between these two stories. In the parable it clearly does not matter if the Good Samaritan existed or not. In writing the story the gospel writers did not intend us to worry about that. However, in my opinion in the case of the resurrection, Paul and the gospel writers did intend that we accept it as a physical event. My position is an example of a conservative interpretation. In that case what matters is the intention of the original author. There are, therefore limits to my freedom to re-interpret the text. In liberal/radical traditions it is quite legitimate to re-interpret the text in the light of the modern world.

3 This leads to the third point that students should become aware that there are different types of literature in the Bible. The Good Samaritan is clearly story, while the description of the stoning of Stephen is history. Being aware of the genre is an important element in reading a biblical passage correctly. There are, of course, disputes between the theological traditions as to which genre particular passages belong—for example the miracles performed by Jesus.

4 Finally in an age of increasing anti-Semitism, it is important for pupils to be aware that the New Testament was written in the context of some conflict between the Jewish and emerging Christian communities. There is a danger that pupils can assume that this may legitimise certain attitudes to Jews which are quite anti-Christian if they are not made aware of this specific background to the New Testament.

Hopefully these four brief discussions are enough to establish my point. Students will have a very unhelpful and naive view of the Bible if they emerge at sixteen still viewing it as a source book of proof-texts or pre-packaged answers. Instead it should be seen as a book which requires thoughtful and careful interpretation and application.

A survey of syllabuses will reveal four things which secondary school pupils are expected to cover in their study of the Bible:

1 Its origins, including original languages, formation of the canon, translation etc.
2 Its content.
3 Its use within the Christian community.
4 The different attitudes to its interpretation.

If we are to avoid producing further generations who have no interest in or knowledge of this book, then our teaching of these areas will have to take more seriously the three dimensions I have discussed.

FOOTNOTE

[1] David Holloway, 'Multifaith Confusion–Challenging False Assumptions', *From Acts to Action* (Christian Institute: Newcastle, 1991).

These two examples illustrate an approach to teaching the Bible which seeks to take dimensions One and Two seriously.

CREATION

AIM

To explore some of the Christian concepts of creation and encourage pupils to appreciate the beauty of the world.

UNPACKING THE CONCEPT

First the teacher needs to unpack the Christian concept of
creation for it has many facets. This helps in the planning
process. For example:
–making
–designing with a purpose
–being pleased with what you have made
–not blind chance

PUPIL EXPERIENCE

Find parallel or similar experiences within the pupils' world to
help them understand the ideas inherent in the creation story.
–When or why do they make things?
–Pupils can bring in the things they have made.
–Ask the pupils to think of one thing that they've made with
  which they were really pleased.
–Bring in a number of unusual items and ask the pupils to guess
  their purpose.
–Use the lego activity below to explore chance.

ACTIVITY

Give the pupils (in groups) a pile of lego and give them five
minutes to design something. Using the same lego give the
pupils a coin and a dice. Each pupil in the group rolls the dice
and flips the coin in turn. If it is 'heads' the pupil adds lego
bricks to the right. If it is 'tails' the pupils adds lego bricks to the
left. The dice tells them how many to add.

After five minutes ask the pupils to compare their changed
design with their thought-out creation.

BIBLICAL MATERIAL

Look at the account of creation in Genesis 1-2. God takes delight in making. It is not blind chance, the Bible describes creation as purposeful action, but God's purpose is not made explicit. Why make a world?

Look at the poem below.

What does this poet say is God's reason for creating? Do you think he is right?

REFLECTION

Ask the pupils to think quietly about creation and write down five things which are really good about creation, five things that the world would be worse without.

THE CREATION by James Weldon Johnson

And God stepped out on space
And He looked around and said:
'I'm lonely—
I'll make me a world.'
And as far as the eye of God could see
Darkness covered everything,
Blacker than a hundred midnights
Down a cypress swamp.
Then God smiled,
And the light broke,
And the darkness rolled up on one side,
And the light stood shining on the other,
And God said: 'That's good!'...
...Then God walked around
And God looked around
On all that He had made.

He looked at His sun,
And He looked at His moon,
And He looked at His little stars;
And He looked on His world,
And all its living things,
And God said: 'I'm lonely still.'
Then God sat down—
On the side of a hill where He could think,
By a deep wide river He sat down;
With His head in His hands,
God thought and thought,
Till He thought: 'I'll make me a man!'
Up from the bed of the river
God scooped the clay;
And by the bank of the river
He kneeled him down;
And there the great God Almighty
Who flung the stars to the most far corner of the night
Who rounded the earth in the middle of His hand;
This great God,
Like a mammy bending over her baby,
Kneeled down in the dust
Toiling over a lump of clay
Till He shaped it in His own image;
Then into it He blew the breath of life,
And man became a living soul.
Amen. Amen.

(From *Presenting Poetry 2,* by P McCall and S Palmer, Oliver & Boyd, 1986.)

SIN

AIM

To explore some Biblical images of sin and forgiveness, to use those images to help pupils consider their own response to wrong and failure to live up to standards.

UNPACKING THE CONCEPTS

There are many words used in the Bible for sin. It proposes the idea that all have sinned, no one is perfect, but it also recognises various types of wrong.

In Biblical terms, sin is not just breaking a list of rules. It is breaking a relationship, but a relationship which can be healed through forgiveness and change.

Some Biblical ideas about sin:
- Some sin is falling short of God's standard. It is missing the mark.
- Some sin is wandering off the straight path of God's standard.
- Some sin is chosen, deliberate rebellion.
- God forgives sin, but forgiveness also demands change.

PUPIL EXPERIENCE

These ideas can be parallelled in the pupils' experience. For example:
- Use a sport video or safe (velcro) dartboard to illustrate missing the mark or falling short.
- Talk about the ideal images we have of ourselves and how we fail ourselves as well as others. Pupils can think about the sort of comment they would like to have on a report. If we are

honest, we all know that we do not live up to those sort of comments all the time.

–No one is perfect. This can be illustrated by a piece of fabric with a fault or talking about a car with a steering fault. The design is still good, but it is not as the designer intended.

–Sometimes we deliberately say or do something to wreck our friendships. Pupils can write a list of 'Four Easy Ways To Lose A Friend'. Link each of these ideas to the Biblical images.

ACTIVITY

Pupils can illustrate an image of sin or of forgiveness. This can be done in cartoon or poster form.

BIBLICAL MATERIAL

All have sinned–no one is perfect: Romans 3:23 and John 7:19. Forgiveness: Psalm 103:12, Micah 7:19, Isaiah 38:17, Isaiah 1:18.

These pictures show God is willing to forgive. Guilt is a burden people do not have to bear.

Read the poem, 'Forgive My Guilt'. Forgiveness is the lifting of the burden that sin causes. What sort of sin would you say the writer of this poem committed?

REFLECTION

How easy do you find it to say sorry and ask forgiveness? Is admitting you were wrong a sign of weakness or strength?

FORGIVE MY GUILT by Robert P Tristram Coffin

Not always sure what things called sins may be,
I am sure of one sin I have done.
It was years ago when I was a boy,
I lay in the frost flowers, with a gun,
The air ran blue as the flowers, I held my breath,
Two birds on golden legs slim dream things
Ran like quicksilver on the golden sand,
My gun went off, they ran with broken wings into the sea,
They cried like two sorrowful high flutes,
With jagged ivory bones where wings should be.
For days I heard them when I walked that headland
Crying out to their kind in the blue,
The other plovers were going over south
On silver wings leaving these broken two.
The cries went out one day, but I still hear them
Over all the sounds of sorrow in war and peace
I ever have heard them, time cannot drown them,
Those slender flutes of sorrow never cease.
Two airy things forever denied the air!
I never knew how their lives at last were spilt,
But I have hoped for years all that is wild,
Airy, and beautiful will forgive my guilt.

(From *Presenting Poetry 4,* P McCall and S Palmer, Oliver &
Boyd, 1986.)

12 | EXPLORING VALUES
Stephen and Wendy Kenyon

SUMMARY

In considering teaching a module on Christian Values various themes may be explored. This article offers two examples. The approach adopted is ideally suited for thirteen to fifteen year old pupils.

VALUES–AN INTRODUCTION

Before the course can tackle specifics, pupils need to consider what values are.

Exercise One:

a) Put questions to the class to define the word 'values'. For example, 'What do people mean when they say, "Members of my family have very different values" '; or "We are similar in the values we hold"?' Alternatively, use a brainstorming approach with 'values' in the centre of a board. Look for answers such as 'morals', 'ideals', 'accepted standards' and 'things we believe are important'.

Pupils need to personalise this if it is to be meaningful. Consequently they should be able to think about their own values and the values promoted in our society or sub-sets of society. For example, there may be differences between the general media message and that of certain ethnic minority groups.

Exercise Two:

a) One of the most effective ways to help pupils personalise this is to construct a questionnaire (possibly devised by the class) to discover what priorities people have in life. Questions could be along the lines of 'What possession do you most value and why?', 'What is the most important thing you can have in life?', 'What is your most important ambition and why?' and so forth. Answers could be categorised into sections entitled 'Wealth', 'Sentimental Value', 'Relationships', 'Health' and 'Faith'. The questionnaire becomes particularly interesting when carried out with different groups in society. You might set a homework for each pupil to ask one teenage girl, one teenage boy and one adult the same questions. Class time would then be needed to categorise the answers. Interesting patterns can emerge, leading to illuminating discussions about the different values held by teenagers as opposed to adults, or differences between boys and girls.

b) Alternatively set the task of making a collage of advertisements which tell us what we are supposed to be like, have or do if we are to be successful and fulfilled. This too yields immediate results which can be discussed in class in small groups or as a whole, considering 'Are these things really necessary?', 'Do they lead to fulfilment?', 'Do adverts convince people that they should buy the product?', 'What is not covered by these adverts which is important in life?' etc. The following two lessons will examine some values commonly held in society.

MONEY

It is appropriate to anticipate that one of the most commonly held values in our society, (as confirmed in the class investigations) is that of materialism. The desire to accumulate wealth and possessions and secure a financial future is very strong in our society.

Exercise One:

Use a piece of drama as a different and stimulating thought-prompter. The sketch on page 105 requires two people for speaking parts and a few others for mime. It is open to adaptation but could work well if a group of volunteers prepared it (with guidance!) prior to the lesson.

Alternatively, if there is less time available, the 'Materialist Creed' on page 104 could be used. Either of these could be followed by immediate feedback in a discussion time but it may be more effective to turn to the Bible straight away for a stark contrast in Jesus' teaching. Suggested passages are: the rich fool or foolish farmer (Luke 12:13-21), our inability to serve two masters (Matthew 6:24) and the rich young ruler (Luke 18:18-27).

Exercise Two:

Response to the Biblical passages: In the case of 'You cannot serve two masters' it can be helpful to encourage consideration of what it might have been like to be a slave or servant. This analogy can be carried through to being a slave or servant to money as opposed to letting money serve. Topical examples of the farmer could be gamblers, drug addicts and misers which illustrate this point.

The rich young ruler is often taken out of context to suggest that Christians should give away all that they own. The key idea here is that this man had made no investment in life other than his wealth (as seen in the parable of the rich fool).

Questions to consider might be:-

'To what extent can a Christian serve God and be rich?' (Cliff Richard, Whitney Houston etc.)

'What does it mean to invest in eternity?'

'What kinds of investment do we make in life which do not involve money?' (eg relationships, faith, etc)

'Can we differentiate between the cost of everything and the value of nothing?'

'Can your life be 'rich' if you have little or no money?'

'Does money make you happy?'etc.

SELF-WORTH

It should become evident, if it is not already, that lack of self-worth is rife amongst our young people and arguably in our society as a whole. This is rarely questioned and making the issue explicit can be a starting point in redressing the balance.

Exercise One

At the beginning of the lesson, ask pupils to divide a sheet of paper in half, making two columns. One column should be headed 'weaknesses', the other 'strengths'. Assure them that anything that they write will remain confidential, and can if they wish, be destroyed later. Give them one minute to write in the first column everything that they can think of that they do not like about themselves or are unable to do well. Give them a further minute to write all the things that they do like about themselves and are good at in the 'strengths' column. It is usual for less to be written in this column and for there to be awkwardness at this stage.

To follow this up all that might be necessary is to ask which list was easier to compile and why that might be. Ask why people/they find it hard to admit to themselves or others what they like about themselves. Remind them of Jesus' teaching, 'Love your neighbour AS YOURSELF' (see Luke 10:27). Why do we rarely speak of loving ourselves? (Answers may include concerns about arrogance, rejection or other negative responses etc).

Exercise Two

Read the parable of the Talents, or pounds (Matthew 25:14-30). If the talents/pounds are seen as 'gifts' (things we are good at) what is its main message? Using our gifts and investing them will cause them to grow and develop. Whilst hiding or neglecting them will cause us to lose them. You can emphasise the practical nature of this message by inviting examples of how this is true of our talents–learning to play an instrument, listening to others etc. Ask the group as individuals if they really know what their talents are. Generally they will not.

Exercise Three

For these follow up activities, you must know the class you are teaching well and feel secure in instilling a sense of care and responsibility in the group.

a) Each pupil writes their name on a sheet of paper and then draws around one of their hands. Class members choose one hand to write one positive comment about that person along one finger. A hand will be completed when there are five comments written on it. Every member of the class is responsible for ensuring all the comments are true and positive and for checking that no one's 'hand' is left blank or unfinished. It can be helpful to compile a list of varied gifts on the board before embarking on this.

ALISON SUTHERLAND

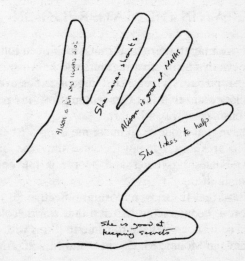

b) Allow for a confidential self-appraisal through the following exercise. Give everyone a sheet of paper, and if possible, an envelope. Ask the class, rhetorically, what they hope to have gained, learnt or avoided by the time they are thirty years old. They are given the task to write a letter to themselves to be read when they are thirty years old, telling them what they think of themselves now and what they hope they will be like when they read this in the future. The letter can be sealed and taken home, entitled, 'To be opened on my thirtieth birthday'.

Exercise Four

Questions for discussion or further development might be:
    How can talents be used for evil? (eg holocaust, atomic bombs).
    If there is no God can we be of value? (Our self-worth depends ultimately on God valuing us).

MATERIALIST CREED

I BELIEVE IN THE STATE RELIGION

–I believe that all there is, is that which I can touch and see.
–I believe in *adverts,* that perfume will improve my sex appeal, that happiness is a cigar, that chocolate has everything to do with love, and that fast cars will improve my performance in life, business, love and sport.
–I believe that money will make me happy. I believe that rich people are always happy because they can buy what they want. Possessing things and people is the only aim worth having in life.
–I believe that the most important objective for my country to achieve is economic growth and that world ecology and third world countries will have to come to terms with that.
–I believe in Money, Materialism and Myself. AMEN.

TOPSY-TURVY SKETCH

Narrator (N) is Mr Topsy—fatherly but not patronising.
Turvy (T) is simple, childlike, enthusiastic and naive.
This sketch can be kept up-to-date by selecting the most recent
television advertisements.

T: Mr Topsy...Mr Topsy...Mr...

N: Yes, yes Turvy, I'm here. I heard you the first time.

T: Mr Topsy..I've decided on something very important.

N: Oh yes...what's that then?

T: Don't say it like that Mr Topsy...like you all don't believe
me.

N: No, I didn't mean that, Turvy. Tell me.

T: Well, I've decided, you know, about what we were talking
about yesterday.

N: Yes.

T: Well, I've decided that I want to be happy in my life.

N: Well, that is an important decision, Turvy.

T: I mean I want to make it my aim in life to be happy.

N: And you're sure you've thought about this?

T: Oh yes a lot! Well, aren't you pleased for me, Mr Topsy?

N: Um, yes.

T: Mr Topsy—there's something you want to tell me, isn't
there?

N: Well, Turvy, how are you going to be happy?

T: Ah well, I've thought about that and I thought I'd ask you.
You can tell me how to be happy, can't you?

N: So that will be today's lesson? How to be happy?

T: Oh yes please, Mr Topsy.

N: Right. Well come and stand over here and I'll show you how
to be happy.

ADVERT 1 (4 characters)

A: People nowadays are getting more out of life–more out of music–more out of shopping. And now there's even more to Mars–more chocolate, more caramel and it's more chewy.

B: Mmm, more chocolate

C: Mmm, more caramel

D: Mmm, more chewy too

A: Now there's more to Mars!

ADVERT 2 (2 characters)

Enter A, sits down, tries to get tomato ketchup out of a bottle. Can't. Music.

B: Happiness is a cigar called Hamlet.

ADVERT 3 (2 characters)

Enter A. Irons a shirt and looks perplexed.

B: Do you want to be really fulfilled in your life? Do you want everything to be 'just so'? Do you want even your husband's shirts to smell fresh? Then you need Radion! Radion washes whiter and removes the smells that ordinary powders leave behind.

SCENE RETURNS TO TOPSY & TURVY

N: Well, Turvy, there you have it. That's how to be happy.

T: A cigar, a Mars bar and some washing powder?

N: Yes, and all the other things you can buy. For instance, if you got rid of all those spots, showered yourself with perfume, shaved with the best razor a man can get, use one bottle not two to shampoo and condition your hair and had the fastest car around, then you'd be happy.

T: I don't believe you, Mr Topsy, no one is stupid enough to believe that buying things could make them happy!

N: Lots of people do, Turvy.

T: So what did Jesus say?

N: Good question, he said something like this:

ADVERT 4 (1 character)

A: People nowadays are finding there's more to life. More than simple adverts, more than the consumer dream. And there's more to following Jesus. More challenge, more excitement, more fulfilment. Jesus said, 'Follow me and I will give you fullness of life'.

N: Turvy...Turvy

T: Mmmm?

N: Alright Turvy?

T: Just thinking.

N: Help me read this, Turvy.

T: Alright, Mr Topsy:

A BLOXHAM PROJECT PRAYER

I asked God for strength, that I might achieve;
I was made weak, that I might learn to humbly obey.
I asked for health, that I might do greater things;
I was given infirmity, that I might do better things.
I asked for riches that I might be happy;
I was given poverty that I might be wise.
I asked for power that I might have the praise of men;
I was given weakness that I might feel the need of God.
I asked for all things that I might enjoy life;
I was given life that I might enjoy all things.
I got nothing that I asked for,
but everything that I had hoped for.
Almost despite myself, my unspoken prayers were answered
I am among all people most richly blessed.

13 | RESOURCE BASED LEARNING
Alison Wilkinson

SUMMARY

This article examines resource based learning as a teaching method and learning strategy. It attempts to show how it works and how it can be managed. It includes an example of a worksheet and sets out some of the benefits to be gained from this approach.

Have you ever wondered, after hours of preparation and a meticulous execution of a lesson, why there are students who seem no more enlightened when they leave a lesson than when they arrived fifty minutes earlier? I wish I could say this was not a frequent occurrence! Yet every teacher wrestles daily with the question of why some students find a particular lesson exciting, challenging and thought-provoking, while others remain bored and uninterested. If we are to be effective in our teaching we ignore this challenge at our peril.

The fact is that individuals learn in very different ways. We all respond differently to the range of influences that affect learning, from our physical surroundings to our relationship with the teacher. Balancing the needs of our students may seem more like spinning a roulette wheel than a carefully planned process!

Resource based learning is a student centred approach to educating which attempts to solve this problem. Whether we teach upper or lower secondary students, we will be faced with a variety of interests, concerns and abilities. Resource based learning offers a range of experiences in which the students take some responsibility for their learning. It also improves pupil motivation and is an effective way of achieving differentiation.

WHAT IS RESOURCE BASED LEARNING?

Resourced based learning is exactly what its name implies *learning which is focused upon resources*. Instead of having one major resource in the class, that is the teacher, resource based learning demands a number of resources. Pupils may focus on a variety of areas within a topic so that their learning opportunities are as wide as the resources that can be made available. Before you throw your hands up in horror and see your tiny capitation disappearing on one lesson, there are ways that it can be practically managed.

At Beauchamp College in Oadby where I worked, a particular way of planning resource based learning was developed. The strategy was that for each module in the course, each student's task was to produce an in-depth assignment which focussed on a question that the student decided was important and interesting. My Head of Department described this as being a mini PhD! The stages in the teaching process we used were as follows:

1 *Lead Lessons:* Every student experienced these. They were an introduction to the subject matter. A variety of input methods were used; teacher explanation, video, visitors, visits etc.

2 *Devising The Question:* Each student was required to define a question that they wished to investigate on the basis of the lead lessons. A bank of questions was available for those students who found it hard to think of their own. The question was negotiated with the teacher. This was a key stage in the differentiation process with students, negotiating a question appropriate to their own learning needs.

3 *Refining The Question:* Each student then devised other questions which arose from the main question. These formed the basis of the main 'chapter headings' in the final assignment.

4 *Designing The Work Plan:* Each student then devised a simple plan as to how they were going to answer their question. This was then broken down into a more detailed plan. For example, 'questioning the visitor' was analysed further so the

student was clear as to exactly what information they wished to elicit from the visitor.

5 *Research and Write Up:* The student carried through the investigation and prepared their assignment.

An example of the guide that was given to help students through this process is included here (p117–121).

HOW DOES IT WORK?

The key is a variety of resources. If you are studying one topic then clearly differentiated resources are helpful, but often students resent being identified as 'less able' which, in their frame of reference, just means they are stupid. If a variety of sources are used, students of different abilities can be guided without it being immediately obvious that they are using simpler forms of the same work. This is very important when students worry about the views of their peers. In addition, the more able will naturally seek out and deal with more demanding sources and therefore be stretched without seeming to be punished by having to do more work than others.

However, this can be broadened even further if pupils were able to study different aspects of the same topic. This element of choice in work begins to develop students' responsibility and 'ownership'. If a student has, for example chosen 'Hindu worship' as a topic and the work is dull or difficult, then the student must accept at least some responsibility for this. That is the negative side. The positive side is, of course, having chosen the topic themselves, they are usually more motivated in their work. If students are motivated, they are far more likely to produce their best work.

Perhaps I can outline a specific example to illustrate the basic concept. One area covered in our GCSE Religious Studies course was 'Conflict, War and Peace'. All students would have around eight to ten lessons of material designed to stimulate them and introduce the different areas of work that would be covered. These included work on conflict management styles and areas where teenagers experienced conflict at school and home such as bullying and in families. We would examine questions of how to apply religious principles to everyday situations. For example, what does Sikhism have to say concerning bullying, or conflict between parents and children at home? We also looked at figures like Ghandi and Martin Luther King and concepts such as Just War, Pacifism and Jihad. All students would not only have a taste of studying these issues but would examine in detail one or two religious approaches to them.

The aim was to make the study of the religion life-centred and to encourage the student to transfer dogma to practice, so that they developed living concepts of faith and belief. This means that books are only one of many possible resources available. General text books on major religions are useful, but articles from newspapers, religious tracts and literature, videos and people themselves all become an immensely valuable means of resourcing classroom work.

During the Gulf War we happened to reach the 'Conflict, War and Peace' section of our course. Students were being bombarded by the media and could not fail to pick up opinions on Islam and of course 'Jihad', the Muslim belief on Holy War. I will never forget the impact of a white, middle-class, western Muslim woman talking about Jihad and relating it to the Gulf War. Students came face to face with someone from their own culture who represented the very different culture which they had seen portrayed negatively by the media. In dialogue with her, they were able to learn about Muslim belief in a way that a textbook could not have communicated.

Resource based learning also encourages good scholarship from an early age. Students need to deal with a great variety of material and perhaps a diversity of opinions within a belief system. Although this can be very challenging, students need to learn that life is never quite as simple as saying things such as– 'all Muslims think this about the Gulf War'–even if they want to say it.

In some topics, the relevant information sources will not be available for giving directly to the students. In these cases it is the teacher's responsibility to produce a 'user friendly' worksheet. See, for an example, the worksheet on 'Christianity, Violence and Sport' on page 114.

I am not suggesting that resource based learning is a cure for all classroom ills, but perhaps it begins to offer some solutions in the difficult situations we face daily with pupils who are not easy to motivate.

GETTING STARTED IN RESOURCE BASED LEARNING

Clearly, you do not change to resource based learning overnight! It is probably best to begin with one topic or module from your syllabus on an experimental basis. Even developing two or three different resources begins a movement towards a situation where a whole number of options can be offered. Resource-based learning can continue to grow and develop by continually adding new materials. It is also cheaper to use smaller numbers of each resource rather than attempting to continue to buy class sets of books which may mean only one book per student and years before other class sets could be purchased.

'Live' resources are an excellent addition to the range, but they bring their own difficulties. Suitable visitors may be hard to find and maintain contact with. Not all religious leaders can communicate well with students! Obviously, it will mean trial and error until you develop a group of people whom you can readily rely upon to deal helpfully with young inquiring minds. Listen to what your students tell you—they may know people in the community who would otherwise escape your attention. People who frequently do assemblies and have contact with particular age groups may be better than just picking a source at random.

A number of Mosques, Temples and Gurdwaras have specially trained people who show school groups round and can speak into youth culture in an understandable way. They may be able to suggest people to you. You may meet parents who would be willing and available to answer questionnaires or write to students, even if they are not able to attend during a lesson. Speak to other RE teachers in your area about sharing resources and contacts.

CONCLUSION

Ultimately resource based learning should be seen as a process for developing innovative and varied learning strategies, not a teaching style which you either adopt or reject. It can be introduced gradually and evolve over a number of years to a multiresourced facility for learning. It may appear a lot of hard work. This cannot be denied, but the benefits to you as a teacher and to your students will be well worth the time and trouble that it takes.

This is an example of a worksheet which Alison used with some of her classes to encourage resource based learning.

SPORT, VIOLENCE AND CHRISTIANITY

THE TEACHING OF THE NEW TESTAMENT ABOUT VIOLENCE

a) Jesus:

> You have heard that it was said, 'an eye for an eye and a tooth for a tooth.' But I say to you, Do not resist one who is evil. But if any one strikes you on the right cheek, turn to him the other also; ...
>
> You have heard that it was said, 'You shall love your neighbour and hate your enemy.' But I say to you, Love your enemies and pray for those who persecute you ... ' (Matthew 5:38-39 & 43-44).

At the arrest of Jesus, the night before his crucifixion, the gospel of Matthew states;

> Then they came up and laid hands on Jesus and seized him. And behold, one of those who were there with Jesus stretched out his hand and drew his sword, and struck the slave of the high priest, and cut off his ear. Then Jesus said to him, 'Put your sword back into its place; for all who take the sword will perish by the sword. Do you think that I cannot appeal to my Father, and he will at once send me more than twelve legions of angels?' (Matthew 26:50-54).

b) Paul:

Repay no one evil for evil, but take thought for what is noble in the sight of all. If possible, so far as it depends upon you, live peaceably with all. Beloved, never avenge yourselves... Do not be overcome by evil, but overcome evil with good (Romans 12:17–19, 21).

c) Peter:

For what credit is it, if when you do wrong and are beaten for it you take it patiently? But if when you do right and suffer for it you take it patiently, you have God's approval. For to this you have been called, because Christ also suffered for you, leaving you an example, that you should follow in his steps. He committed no sin; no guile was found on his lips. When he was reviled, he did not revile in return; when he suffered he did not threaten; but he trusted to him who judges justly. He himself bore our sins in his body on the tree, that we might die to sin and live to righteousness. (1 Peter 2:20-24).

Question: How can this teaching be applied to sport?

SOME OF THE TEACHING OF EARLY CHRISTIANS AFTER THE NEW TESTAMENT

The Romans were the superpower 2,000 years ago when the Christian Church was established. Some of the 'sports' then included gladiator contests, fighting wild animals etc. They were very violent sports that often involved the death of humans. How did the early Christians respond to these sports? The following two quotations from early Christian writings give some ideas: 'A charioteer, an athlete, a gladiator, a trainer of gladiators, or one who fights wild beasts or hunts them or holds public office at the circus games shall give it up or be rejected.' Hippolytus, *Church Order in the Apostolic Tradition 16,* about 218 AD.

'We are forbidden so much as to look at gladiator fights lest we (see) and (become) participants in murder! We also consider it immoral to watch other shows, because our eyes and ears will not be defiled with sympathy for acts of murder as they are celebrated there in song' (Theophillus of Antioch, *To Autolycus* Book III.15).

Question: How can these quotes be applied to:

a) boxing and wrestling?
b) contact sports like football and rugby?
c) fox hunting?
d) motor racing?
e) athletics?

Question: Would early Christians who tried to live peacefully in love and unity have been against any competitive sport?

Question: What do modern Christians think? See if you can interview a minister or priest.

BIBLIOGRAPHY

Eberhard Arnold, *The Early Christians After The Death Of The Apostles* (Plough Publishing House: Rifton, New York, 1970), pp 108, 121.

GUIDE TO R.E. ASSIGNMENTS
– Modular GCSE

....

Introduction

For your assignment you should choose a Question and work on it through 4 stages:

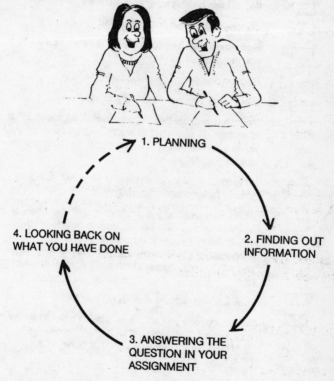

1. PLANNING

2. FINDING OUT INFORMATION

3. ANSWERING THE QUESTION IN YOUR ASSIGNMENT

4. LOOKING BACK ON WHAT YOU HAVE DONE

You will need to show by written work what you have done at each stage. More details about each step are as follows:

1 PLANNING:
Choosing a Question and planning to answer it.

You need to choose a Question that interests you. You have to do a written plan of how you are going to go about answering your Question. Here are some suggestions for a simple plan worth 6 marks:

Tick here when done   **Planning Steps**

☐ Write down heading: *Assignment Plan*

☐ Choose a Question. Write it down.

☐ Brainstorm the Question by writing down all the ideas you can think of.

☐ Choose one or two religious viewpoints.

☐ What other viewpoints could you use?

☐ You need chapter headings in your assignment. What questions do you need to ask to help you answer your assignment Question? Write these down as possible chapter headings.

☐ What kind of information do you need to find out to answer these chapter headings?

☐ Where can you find this information? Write down possible books, Holy books, leaflets or videos you could use. Think of people you could survey or interview. Which libraries and places of worship could you visit? What organisations and people you could write to.

☐ How will you present your assignment?

☐ List all the jobs you will have to do in order to complete your assignment. Now put all these jobs down on a TIME PLAN so you get your assignment done by the DEADLINE.

If you want to go on and try and get a full 8 marks for planning then do the following tasks:

☐ Produce another complete plan for another Question.

☐ Say with reasons which plan would be the best one to use.

2 FINDING OUT INFORMATION

This is a very important stage. You have already begun to find out information for the planning stage above. Keep a careful note of where you have got your information from. For 4 marks you will need a detailed *Bibliography* at the end of your assignment. This should contain ALL your sources of information including books, leaflets, interviews, surveys, videos etc. Set it out as follows:

Books: A. Author; Title: (Publisher, year) pages.
Leaflets: A. Author: 'Title'; (Publisher, date).
Interviews: Who, Where, When.
Surveys: Topic, When, Where, What kind of people, how many.
Letters: From whom, date, topic.
Film/Video/Tape: Title: Company, date.
Bible: e.g. Isaiah 2:2–4.

Start a rough bibliography NOW!

Do NOT copy word for word unless you put it in 'Quotation Marks' and say where the quote is from.

For another 4 marks you need to do a chapter on *Reviewing Sources of Information.* This chapter goes just before the last chapter in your assignment.

3 ANSWERING THE QUESTION IN YOUR ASSIGNMENT

In this stage you produce an assignment. You should give evidence and an answer to your Title Question.

YOU SHOULD PRODUCE AN ASSIGNMENT CONTAINING THE FOLLOWING:

☐ Title 'Page' with the title Question, your full name and RE class, teacher, and school.

☐ Contents Page (done last!)

☐ Introduction: (done next to last!) In your introduction give your full title Question. Say briefly why you are interested in it and how you have gone about tackling it.

☐ 'Chapters'. One of these at least must be a religious viewpoint. Each chapter should have a heading — in a question form if you can manage it. Say what you have found out. At the end of each chapter have a summary paragraph summarising what you have found out and saying how it connects with the title Question.

☐ Next-to-last Chapter: *Reviewing Information.* This is worth 4 marks. See sheets on how to do this if you want to go for the 4 marks here.

☐ Final Chapter with your title Question as your heading. This is the most important chapter of your assignment. It's here you bring everything together and really answer your assignment title Question.

Read through your assignment and summarise arguments and evidence *for* the title Question.
Summarise arguments and evidence *against* the title Question.

(It is *very important* to include religious arguments and evidence). Then weigh up the strength of the arguments on both sides and write a careful conclusion in answer to the title Question.

Do this in rough first. Then think about it. Then do it again in neat. You need to do at least two sides for this final chapter to get 16 marks.

4 LOOKING BACK ON
WHAT YOU HAVE DONE

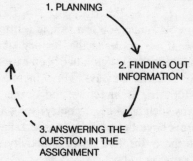

1. Briefly describe how you did the assignment. (2 marks)

2. (a) What have you learnt from doing this assignment? Give examples.
(b) Is there anything you have learnt that you can apply to your own life? Write down anything you can think of. (2 marks)

3. What did you do *well* in the assignment in each of these steps, 1 — 3: (1 mark)

1. PLANNING

2. FINDING OUT INFORMATION

3. ANSWERING THE QUESTION IN THE ASSIGNMENT

4. If you were going to start all over again, how would you improve what you did the second time in each of the steps 1 — 3? Give examples. (1 mark)

5. If you were going to do more work on this question, where would you go from here?
i.e. What new areas have opened up?
What questions still need to be answered? (1 mark)

6. Was your plan on how to tackle this title Question the best one? Could you think of an improved way of planning? Which way would be the best way? Give your reasons.
(1 mark)

(Fourth Edition Sept. 1991).

14 | ACTIVE RELIGIOUS EDUCATION: WITH SPECIAL REFERENCE TO DRAMA AND MOVEMENT

Petra Owen & Joanne Pimlott

SUMMARY

Using drama and movement in Religious Education can be an exciting and meaningful method of exploring religious concepts and ideas. This article looks at a variety of ways in which this can be done.

ACTIVE RELIGIOUS EDUCATION

Active Religious Education is a simple term with wide ranging implications. If we look at the history of religion, it soon becomes apparent that religion has been expressed and communicated in many different ways. These include art forms such as painting, sculpture, architecture and drama, as well as more obvious forms such as stories, poetry, song and dance. Indeed most art forms have their beginnings in religious devotion. So why not use these different types of activity to help our pupils understand religion today?

These activities can provide pupils with the opportunity to learn from their own experience as well as through the experience of others.

The approaches used in Religious Education are often concerned with the feelings, emotions, impact on the senses and a child's natural capacity for awe and wonder. One way religion can be described is as, 'the outward expression of the inner feeling'. Active Religious Education in its various forms encourages the pupil to explore this dimension.

DRAMA

Drama is a relevant way of teaching Religious Education. It is a valuable, experiential learning tool. As religion is concerned about meaning in life and the world, drama can be used to explore that meaning–through movement, mime, representation, character analysis, watching others, story and creativity. Drama is a useful way of adding a new dimension to Religious Education. It allows for self-expression in a safe 'other person' mode. Through drama concepts can be introduced before making them 'religion specific'. Drama can be flexible and motivating. It offers the opportunity to raise and prompt discussion on important elements in Religious Education lessons. It can also break through ethnic and social barriers. Drama encourages active rather than passive involvement by communicating visually to contributors and observers. Active participation also helps young people to develop confidence and self-esteem. It encourages them to take an interest in, and respect, the views and lifestyles of others.

Representational Drama

Directly acting out a particular situation or story is probably the most widely used drama technique. This can be a very effective means of communication and can be adapted easily to many different aspects of RE syllabuses. Teachers can use a wide variety of resources as a basis for this sort of work. Scripts, parables, simple biographies and stories of various kinds may all prove invaluable to those wishing to take the first steps in using drama in an RE class.

Using Drama To Investigate

Rather than simply acting out parts of a story or incident, this type of drama aims to look at issues in more detail. Through investigative drama pupils can be encouraged to carefully examine historical questions. For example, in a series of lessons on the death and resurrection of Christ, the teacher could set up a courtroom investigation called, 'The Case Of The Missing Body' (see pp 128 ff). This can be done by giving each pupil a different character in order to explore the different points of view and opinions involved. A lesson plan developing this idea can be found at the end of this chapter. A similar approach could be used with many historic or modern day situations.

Exploring Issues Through Drama

Improvisation is another great way of stimulating discussion and insight, giving a lively context in which to explore issues. A good starting point is to use some form of stimulus to interest the pupils and provoke thought and discussion. For example, a controversial letter from a problem page or a newspaper article containing conflicting views could be used here. The class can then be allowed to explore the issue or situation concerned through role play or producing short plays in groups.

Improvisation is a particularly useful way of looking at moral dilemmas and personal conflict. Concepts such as forgiveness, justice, responsibility, good, evil and love can be explored, whilst still providing the students with the chance to be one step removed from such emotive themes. It is also a way to focus on relationships–with the family, with others, and with God.

Experiential Drama

This form of active Religious Education is designed to expose pupils to something which is beyond their normal day to day experience, perhaps as a starting point to questions such as 'Who am I?' This could involve changing their environment through darkness, light, smell or sound. Alternatively, the pupils could be brought into a situation where they are confronted with a particular emotion, for example, alienation could be explored with pupils standing in a circle with their backs turned in, excluding one person. Although this kind of work can be very effective and powerful, there are obvious dangers of which the teacher needs to be beware. This approach often demands a high level of vulnerability from the pupils, and may bring to the surface quite personal or disturbing emotions. The teacher concerned needs to make sure that effective provision is made for discussion, feedback and follow up which is not always possible in the confines of the average school day.

MOVEMENT

This is valuable and successful if you have the space and confidence to do it! Stimulus material is the key to success. Here the teacher must act as a guide and just 'let them go'. They should not interrupt on the basis of their judgment of 'good' or 'bad' effort. If the child is still, allow the stillness as this in itself is expressing a feeling or thought. Several different types of stimuli could be used. Music, for example, can be chosen to evoke a response, such as fear, or left open-ended. Objects can also act to provoke movement, for example the amnesty symbol of a candle surrounded by barbed wire. Guided thought journeys, if explained carefully and ended in an appropriate manner, can result in movement of the mind. There are many more!

A VARIETY OF RESOURCES

Many different resources can be of use to the RE teacher who wishes to use drama in the ways described above. Stimuli can take various forms and can be used as part of the initial activity to provoke thought, discussion or action and/or follow up work to enhance the pupil's expression of the experience. Some ideas are listed below. These could be used individually or mixed together for different occasions.

Visual Creativity—mobiles, painting, pictures, slides, videos, cartoons, flick books, food, classroom layout, puppets, masks, costumes

Creativity with sound–dance, narrated mime, raps, speaker, voice, radio play, interviews

Written Creativity–scripts, newspaper accounts, diary form, story, monologue, poem, problem pages, newspaper headlines.

POINTS TO CONSIDER IN MULTI-CULTURAL SCHOOLS

Muslims believe that it is a sin (Shiric) to liken God to any created thing. He must not be represented in any way. It is also undesirable to represent any of the prophets or Kaliphale. Another cause of offence is the use of improvisation and role play about life/moral issues, especially those which explore opposite-sex relationships. Use of some types of music and costume would also be deemed undesirable.

Sikhs use wonderful stories to illustrate life stances and good practice. However many Sikhs participate in such activities, you will rarely find them at dances or watching a play.

Jewish law stresses that Jews are forbidden to watch or take part in anything immodest or obscene. There are different interpretations of what this includes: for example, parents may consider participating in a role play about abortion to be immodest.

Some Christian parents object to their children engaging in any methods of drama in respect to any faith other than Christianity.

Hindus rarely object as their festival celebrations include dramatic performances and dance.

OVERCOMING PROBLEMS

There are exceptions to the above, but in situations of doubt the following solutions may help:

1 Send a letter home explaining what you are going to do

and the reason for doing it, asking for the parent's permission.

2 Seek guidance from the particular faith leader.

FURTHER HINTS

When using drama, be confident and take a risk! However, there are things that will have an influence on the activity before it has even begun. For example, the mood of the day – the class may be too excitable or too sombre. External circumstances, such as the weather, the lesson before, and the next lesson will also be relevant to the class dynamics. Practical limitations such as the size and layout of the classroom need to be considered.

During the activity, pupils may respond surprisingly slowly if they are not used to 'active Religious Education' or they may be able to take the activity on further than you planned, so be prepared for the unexpected! The same exercise may work well with one group but not another, so it can be worth persevering with an idea. The visual usually creates visual – it has a knock on effect: this means plenty of stimuli and resources are needed, which can be a lot of work initially, but the results make it worthwhile.

The atmosphere created through active Religious Education can easily be lost through unexpected disruptions. Some of these can be prevented by putting a sign on the door asking visitors to come back later. It is also very important that the pupils are warmed up properly and able to discuss and learn from their experiences.

Active Religious Education and its many forms is an exciting way to discover new insight. Let the pupils explore this as much as they can!

FOOTNOTES

[1] John Hammond et al, *New Methods In Religious Education* (Oliver & Boyd, Harlow, 1990).

THE CASE OF THE MISSING BODY–LESSON PLAN

This lesson plan assumes that the pupils already know the story of the death and resurrection of Jesus in some detail. It would probably be most useful as a summing up or drawing together a lesson after initial work has been done. It could also be used for revision purposes and with minor adjustments, would probably work with most secondary age groups.

OBJECTIVES

- To explore / revise / discuss the story of the resurrection.
- To look at and express both sides of an argument.
- To help pupils develop their own opinions on the story.
- To encourage pupils to express opinions 'in character', which they don't necessarily agree with.

PREPARATION

This activity demands quite a high degree of preparation, particularly with a younger class. The teacher needs to ensure adequate knowledge of the story. Cue cards, examples of which are shown below are a very useful way of preparing and prompting the central characters. The layout of the classroom can provide atmosphere and create a sense of excitement. Depending on the group this may or may not be desirable!

The lesson will work most effectively if the group is aware beforehand what is going to happen and who is going to take which role. Perhaps part of the previous lesson could be spent in preparing small groups.

MATERIALS

Cue Cards
   Small hammer or ruler (for the judge to 'keep order')
   Any other items the teacher feels will add to the atmosphere.

LESSON PLAN

The teacher introduces the theme and seats the characters in groups:
eg Defence lawyers
     Witnesses for the defence: Disciples
                                   Mary and the other women
     Prosecution lawyers
     Witnesses for the prosecution:
                                High Priests
                                Roman Soldiers
    Jury—the rest of the class

Ideally the teacher or a very mature pupil should play the judge, who keeps order, introduces the witnesses and allows the witnesses to be questioned by the lawyers and if necessary members of the jury. The judge needs to be sensitive to the abilities and confidence of the group and to intervene if a witness is questioned too violently.

The judge can begin the proceedings with the following statement:

'This court has been brought together to examine the case of the missing body. Members of the jury, you will hear how the body of Jesus of Nazareth, who was recently crucified, has disappeared. Some of his followers claim that he has risen from the dead. Several very respected members of the community claim that the body has been stolen by these followers. It is for you to decide.

'I call the first witness for the prosecution.'
The witnesses are then called by the judge who allows them

to be questioned by the lawyers. If time is a problem, then perhaps the questions can be limited to two or three per witness.

When the witnesses have all been questioned the whole group can take part in the vote 'out of character' if this is appropriate, or the lawyers and the judge could announce the verdict.

IDEAS FOR FOLLOW UP WORK

Newspaper article describing their view of the death and resurrection of Jesus.

Newspaper articles about the trial itself.

Summaries of the cases for and against the resurrection.

EXAMPLES OF CUE CARDS

Mary Magdalene

You were the first person to discover that the body had disappeared. You went to the tomb with your friends Joanna and Mary (mother of James) to put spices on the body. When you arrived at the tomb the stone at the door had been rolled away. An angel told you that Jesus had risen from the dead as he said he would. On your way back to tell the disciples, you saw Jesus and touched him. He told you to go back and tell the disciples what had happened (Matthew 28:1–10).

Chief Priest

You hear that the body had disappeared and were very concerned. You are convinced that the body has been stolen by the disciples as you do not believe that Jesus was the Son of God, as he claimed to be. Because you have no proof, you gave the guards of the tomb money to say that the disciples came and stole the body in the night. You will not admit this in court of course, and you will have to think of some 'evidence' that will convince the jury that you are right (Matthew 28:11–15).

Other useful passages from the Bible are:

The guard of the tomb (Matthew 27:62-66).
The resurrection (Matthew 28, Mark 16, Luke 24, John 20 and 21).
The burial of Jesus (Mark 15:42-47, Luke 23:50-56, John 19:38-42).
Jesus predicts his death and resurrection (Matthew 16:21, Mark 10:32-34, Luke 18:31-33).

15 USING MIND MAPS IN RELIGIOUS EDUCATION

Adrian Brown

SUMMARY

This article examines the technique known as mind mapping and looks at its potential for use in Religious Education. It also shows how to mind map and when this approach can be used.

Mind mapping is a note making technique developed by Tony Buzan.[1] Whether your approach is phenomenological or conceptual it offers a powerful tool for handling material. It concentrates on key words and the way they are linked together. Students themselves are encouraged to focus on the essentials of each topic. The method is visual and non-linear, so it can appeal to both the artistic and the less literate, as well as students for whom more traditional note making is no problem. Each mind map is unique and therefore offers scope for creativity, originality and variety. It is likely that youngsters will meet mind mapping in their RE lessons before anywhere else (inspired by teachers who have read this chapter!) giving the subject another shot in the arm and another mark on the scale of curriculum kudos.

WHY MIND MAP?

Some of us were introduced to the ideas of Tony Buzan via the BBC television series and accompanying book he produced in the early 1970s entitled *Use Your Head*. Since then he has written many books on learning methods,[2] and produced a recent video with Lana Israel which works particularly well with secondary school aged children.[3]

Dr Gordon Howe of Exeter University, among others, did some research into different kinds of note making to discover which were the most effective. Results indicated that the best techniques were those that involved a key word approach. Within reason, the fewer key words used the better the results. Key words were defined as 'those which incorporated the most relevant sense in the shortest way possible, and which gave the most immediate recall when the notemaker was tested.'[4]

When you consider that most people can recall only a very small number of complete sentences they have read or heard during their whole lifetime, it is clear that our brains do not store information in this way. On the contrary, it appears that key words act as triggers and when we have these key words in our consciousness they spark off a myriad of associated ideas. They are like the labels on a file in a filing cabinet or the key search words on a CD-ROM for the more modern reader! Provided the other relevant knowledge has been met and associated with these key notions, we can access it very easily.

Thus the notion of key words is central to the technique of mind mapping. In addition, because the method eliminates padding–unnecessary words in sentence form–it is faster to make a mind map and to use it afterwards. As it is non-linear, the creative potential is increased. You can employ colour, arrows, diagrams and special codes to immediately show where the relationships lie between key concepts. It lends itself to emphasising material by using three dimensional images, variations in size, outlining and underlining as well as colour. It makes note-making fun!

HOW TO MIND MAP

I introduced the technique in a number of ways with my students. Sometimes they just picked it up, with a few hints thrown in from watching me use it on the board. At other times I have used the video mentioned earlier and/or an A3 worksheet on how to use mind mapping. This is outlined below. On the reverse of the worksheet pupils were asked to do their own revision mind map of an entire topic. In this instance, Hinduism was the subject by Year 9 pupils.

The technique of mind mapping is easy to learn. By using non-linear methods, the idea is that you can use more of the right hand side of your brain. Ideas are reduced to KEY WORDS. Maximum use is made of INTERCONNECTIONS, PICTURES, COLOURS and your IMAGINATION.

There are very few rules to follow, but they are important ones:

- use the plain page long side across ie landscape
- put the main headings in the centre of the page
- sub-headings branch off from this
- even smaller heading grow out from the sub-headings
- use capital letters
- group ideas together using colour
- use pictures, diagrams, graphs etc. wherever possible
- be imaginative
- have fun!

The idea can be seen in the following example, which will summarise what we know about Hinduism.

First start with the major heading in the centre of the page, using an image that represents Hinduism to you:

Secondly, write down as branches off the main topic heading some of the major areas of Hinduism that you have studied. Here three different ways of doing this are shown:

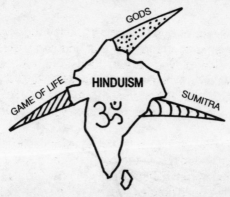

Thirdly, concentrate on the special section of work we did together on Hindu Karma, through the Game of Life.

-Have a sub-heading MAIN IDEAS, and use this as the centre of the main ideas we covered in the game:

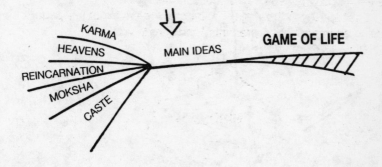

Fourthly, expand on the ideas of caste. Write down the different castes in order. Show this using an arrow. Note the sub-human lives:

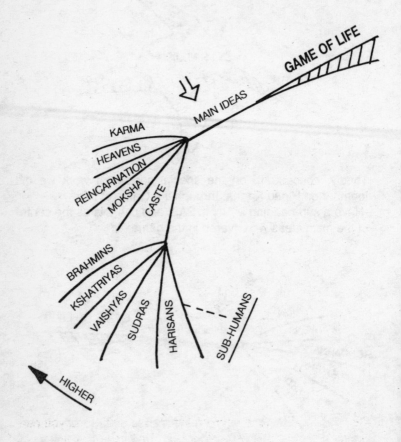

Fifthly, add some relevant pictures that summarise the key points. Put a bubble around them to separate them from other sections you might draw. This is often left until the end, in case you discover connections as you produce the whole mind map:

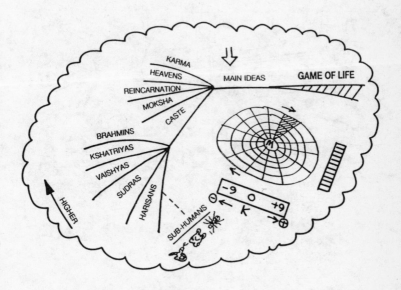

After this, or when the whole mind map is done (and you can always add things later), colour it in. Underline in colours, or shade in similar sections. Be bold and imaginative, but focus on the content of the mind map and its subject matter.

Now it's your turn. Using a blank sheet of paper, have a go at a mind map of Hinduism as a topic. Remember to follow the guidelines above. Good luck!

Below is a black and white copy of the mind map that was done by Katie Higgs as a homework in response to the above worksheet. You should note that this is her first attempt at this technique. All the other pupils produced excellent summaries, including those with learning difficulties who relished the opportunity to get away from writing lots of sentences.

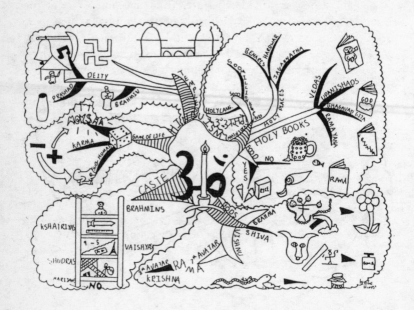

WHEN TO USE MIND MAPS

Mind maps can be used whenever you want to. The method is especially potent in summarising material, whether in an overview given by the teacher or in revision of a section of work. Experienced users make notes in lectures or lessons using mind maps. Essay plans are ideally suited to the method. Once all the material is mind mapped, the order of paragraphs can be superimposed upon it, and the essay written. Books and articles can be prepared in this way too. There are few limits to what can be done. The spirit needs to be willing, but experience shows that with a little encouragement most students take to it very quickly. Do start lower down in the school though; older clients are notoriously resistant to new ways of working. Enjoy your mind mapping!

FOOTNOTES

[1] A registered name.
[2] A complete list can be obtained from Buzan Centres Ltd, Suites 2/3, Cardigan House, 37 Waterloo Road, Winton, Bournemouth, Dorset, BH9 1BD.
[3] Tony Buzan, *Get Ahead* (Island World Communications Ltd: UK, 1992).
[4] Tony Buzan, *How to Make the Most of Your Mind* (Colt Books: London, 1977), p 105.

16 | MOTIVATING FOURTEEN TO SIXTEEN YEAR OLDS
Paul Bee

SUMMARY

No one would pretend that motivating fourteen to sixteen year old pupils is easy. Topics need to be chosen with great care and a variety of strategies employed. This article looks at these issues and offers some ideas for successful lessons.

'Graveyard RE' is not an uncommon description of Religious Education in the last two years of compulsory schooling. For the pupils it is 'dead boring' and 'irrelevant' and for the teacher it is liable to be the last resting place of their career ideals and ambitions. Fifteen year olds are probably the most difficult age to teach, their adolescent hormones wreaking the maximum havoc with their temperaments and concentration. Keeping them gainfully occupied in their mandatory Religious Education lessons would tax even the patience of St Francis of Assisi. Every other class may be wonderful, but if this one is going badly it can have an impact out of all proportion to its relative importance.

A DIFFICULT TASK

The hardest task faces those who have to teach a sixty minute period to a non-exam class every week of the academic year. Sustaining even a modicum of interest over such a long period can be extremely difficult. More usually, Religious Education is provided for as part of a modular Personal and Social Education class. Each group spends about five or six weeks doing Religious Education before moving on to something else such as economic awareness, sex education or careers. In my own situation, Religious Education contributes two six week modules to the lifeskills programme, making the total amount twelve double seventy-minute lessons. If you face the prospect of lessons this long, beg or bribe the deputy head or whoever is responsible for timetabling into scheduling these lessons in the morning. A few years ago I taught Year 11 Religious Education last thing on a Friday afternoon! Telling Duane and Dominic that their lives have cosmic significance is difficult at the best of times...but Friday afternoon when their minds are planning the weekend's social events?

Motivation is a serious problem. You may believe (I hope you do!) that what you are doing is important but the system is sending out a very different message. It is saying, 'this is non-exam so don't try too hard', 'it's an add on, an afterthought', 'no grades are awarded, no certificate bestowed, no prizes given so there is no need to take it seriously'.

The Religious Education teacher has to provide his or her own motivation. This may be in the form of an end of unit review or test, or it may just involve extra praise, smiles and encouragement for tasks done well and work properly completed. You may not want to make a rod for your own back by insisting that reports are given and grades allotted as per exam subjects but some kind of formal assessment could repay the time spent preparing and marking the pupils' work. If you are motivated the pupils will be infected by your enthusiasm. If you convey an air of defeatism when you walk in, then the smouldering embers of teenage interest are unlikely to be fanned into a forest fire of commitment to investigation and learning.

CHOOSING THE TOPICS

Motivation is also dependent on the subject matter chosen for study. At this age, more than any other, using the pupils' experience as a starting point is imperative. Find out what interests them and within the bounds of the Agreed Syllabus begin from there. The following study units taken from the Gloucestershire Syllabus suggest topics for Years 10 and 11 that I would recommend:

Religion and Science
Religion and Ethics
Marriage and the Family
Death
Modern Religious Movements
Education
Sexuality
Work and Leisure
Wealth and Poverty
Religion and Race
Law and Order
Mass Communication
War and Peace
Conservation
Health Matters.[1]

Many of these are very topical and teenagers will readily relate to them. Keep an eye out for newspaper cuttings which will keep the subject matter pertinent and up to date. One of my favourite opening gambits is to select a controversial article, read it to the class and then ask them to write down their ideas on slips of paper which I collect and read out. This ensures that even the shyest pupils have a chance to air their views and it heightens interest by encouraging them to take sides. The best comments, and some can be excellent, provide an invaluable prompt for further discussion.

Motivation can also be assisted by holding out the carrot of a visit or a visiting speaker in return for good work and behaviour. Care should be exercised here though. Check the person you invite or the place you plan to visit will capture pupil interest. An Arabic speaking Ayatollah discoursing for an hour on how Muslims work out their calendar and the dates of

Ramadan for the next twenty five years is unlikely to hold the attention of such a demanding audience for very long!

VARY YOUR STRATEGIES

Ironically fourteen to sixteen year olds seem to have a shorter attention span than their juniors so keep the lesson tasks short and accurately targeted. Have some good video clips ready; Amnesty's Human Rights pack or some of the social issues covered by BBC 'Scene' documentaries/plays go down well. ITV's 'Starting Out' seldom misses either but be selective—it is supposed to be Religious Education. (Don't let the religious aspect get squeezed out because you are too busy finding out whether Zoe is pregnant or whether Wayne is going to get off after stealing the motor bike!) Ten minutes on any one task is ample. Halt it and move on. Sustaining the pace of the lesson with this age group is crucial.

It is a temptation to resort to drama and discussion when all else fails, but be wary—they are not easy strategies to handle with this age range particularly if you are inexperienced. Drama needs to be very carefully structured and planned and runs the risk of total disaster if Dean and Darren become overheated about the issue of a 'Just War'. However, a properly structured, planned and apposite role play can be a great success. For example put one of the pupils on trial for an offence like sabotaging a nuclear weapons installation. Develop the role by telling the class that the man/woman before them is a Quaker pacifist but that as a result of his/her sabotage activity a security guard was killed. Then ask the class to devise some questions to ask him/her to ascertain guilt or innocence. If you choose a sharp-witted pupil with plenty of confidence for the main role this has plenty of potential as an ethical/religious investigation into the morality of war and weapons of mass destruction. Further ideas for using drama and role play in Religious Education are developed in the *Active RE* article.

Whole class discussion is undoubtedly the hardest teaching

strategy to supervise in this context because young adults are moving beyond the hands up stage and are inclined to discuss with their neighbour rather than listen to the class. Everything can disintegrate very rapidly in this situation. Try these strategies instead:

1 Agree/Disagree–choose a statement that is likely to divide the class eg 'Christians, Muslims and Jews should all be educated in separate schools' and then ask pupils to express their agreement or disagreement by standing at one end of the room or the other (by the Agree or the Disagree sign). Quiz one or two at each end to discover why they agree or disagree. Three or four statements are quite sufficient for this activity and between five and ten minutes should be adequate.

2 Partner Discussion–read a question to the class eg 'Do you think a Christian should work for a company which produces cigarettes or weapons?' and then ask them to discuss it with a partner for one minute with one person in the pair writing down the views expressed. Allow brief class feedback before moving on to another question and another partner. With a seating plan in operation order can be quickly restored by sending everyone back to their seats if things get out of hand.

3 Questions in a Jar–select the questions you want the class to discuss, a minimum of ten will be needed, and after reproducing them cut them up and place them in separate jam jars. There should be enough jars for your intended number of groups. In a class of thirty, six groups of five would be about right. The person with the jar takes out the first question, reads it to the rest of the group and gives their own opinion. When he/she has finished anyone else can chip in. The jar is then passed to another person who follows the same procedure. This continues until the jar is empty. Pupils could then be encouraged to take one of the questions and write about it more fully in their exercise books.

4 Picture Response–this operates in a similar fashion to the 'statement response' described earlier except a picture replaces the statement. Distribute slips of paper and then show a picture (perhaps photocopies are handed round or a slide is shown) of something enigmatic or unusual eg Muslim women in traditional dress wearing the veil. The pupils write down their responses. These are collected by the teacher and read to the class.

5 Circle Response–divide the class into groups and sit them in circles of about five or six (arranging the furniture before the class arrives is a good idea). Have some discussion questions ready on slips of paper and hand them to one member of each group who reads the question to the group before voicing their own opinion on the matter. The slip of paper is then passed on to the person sitting next to them. Only the person holding the question can speak. When discussion is completed groups can exchange questions. This encourages everyone to contribute instead of just the ones who like expressing their opinions.

When it comes to discipline, try to anticipate the problems a particular group is likely to throw up. Who are the problem children? Can they be separated *before* and not *after* they cause mayhem? A seating plan is often a good idea. Ignore the moans and groans which will be plentiful. These will soon subside and when settled, the class is more likely to give their full attention to you than to one another. Be ready armed with your answer for that hot chestnut, 'Why are we doing this Miss?' It is not because the law says so, although technically that is true, it is because they have reached an age when they are more capable of handling abstract concepts and should not neglect their moral and spiritual development.

Here are some examples of topics that could be used.

THE ROLE OF WOMEN

Aim: To contrast and compare the role of women in Islam and Christianity.

Approach: Statement response. Read article 'Ayatollahs unleash new reign of terror' which describes how, in a crackdown on permissive attitudes, women caught wearing make-up or showing too much leg were dragged off the streets.

Two young women working at a trade stand at the Tehran Business Fair were grabbed, punched and lipstick and mascara wiped from their faces. Explain and discuss some of the beliefs that led to these actions.

Exposition: Divide the class into small groups. After providing them with the necessary resources ask half of the groups to discover as much as they can about Christian attitudes to women and the other half to investigate Muslim attitudes. Compare the results, writing the discoveries up on the board or a chart which all pupils can then copy into their exercise books or folders.

eg Some Muslims believe women should cover all of their bodies.

Some Christians believe man was created first so they have authority over women.

Prepare a brief Fax to send to The Tablet or The Tehran Chronicle explaining why you think women have an important role in society and why their rights should be respected.

Conclusion: Banners and badges. Imagine you are taking part in a demonstration which is campaigning for the rights of women. Design some badges and banners that the demonstrators could wear and hold. Think up a meaningful slogan.

WORK AND LEISURE

Aim: To assess the relevance of Christian teaching on work.

Approach: Wire sculpture. Distribute three or four pipe cleaners to each child and ask them to design a sculpture to illustrate what the work means to them personally. Show sculptures and briefly explain what attitudes they represent.

Exposition: Consider Christian teaching on 'work'. In groups pupils can draw a four frame frieze to illustrate the main purpose of work according to a Christian understanding. Groups then take it in turns to show their friezes using them to explain what they have learned about Christian teaching. Apply these beliefs to jobs. Study a variety of occupations and say which ones Christians would not do.

Conclusion: Scrambled message. Write out and reproduce the fourth commandment referring to the sabbath day as a day of rest. Cut it up and place the pieces in an envelope. Give one to each group to see if they can discover what it says. Use it as a starter for discussion of the Christian view of leisure.

ANIMAL RIGHTS

Aim: To consider the treatment of animals in the light of Hindu and Muslim beliefs.

Approach: Graffiti wall. On a piece of paper, either in groups or individually, pupils spend five minutes expressing their ideas about animals in the form of a graffiti wall. Eg ANIMALS ARE–Cuddly, Pests, Vital in the cycle of life etc.

Exposition: Discover what Islam and Hinduism teach about animals perhaps in the form of a treasure hunt. Have the necessary resources spread around the room and give each group ten things to find out as quickly as possible. For example the animal sacred to Hindus or rules for ritual Muslim slaughter. Show a filmstrip or video about animal rights. A BBC 'Scene' programme dealt with the subject and Animal Aid have an education pack. Consider vegetarianism in Hinduism and highlight Hindu beliefs about reincarnation and the cycle of life.

Conclusion: Devise a charter of rights for animals along the lines of the United Nations Declaration on Human Rights.

BIBLIOGRAPHY

Cole, W Owen. *Moral Issues in Six Religions*. (Heinemann: Oxford, 1991).
Jenkins, Joe. *Contemporary Moral Issues*. (Heinemann: Oxford, 1992).
Thompson, Mel. *Guidelines for Life*. (Hodder: London, 1990).
Bailey, John. *Religious Beliefs and Moral Codes*. Schofield & Sims: Huddersfield, 1988).
Hunt, Dilwyn. *Muslims 4*. (Stanley Thornes: London, 1989)
BBC Scene programmes.

17 | USING GAMES IN RELIGIOUS EDUCATION
Adrian Brown

SUMMARY

Why should we use games in the teaching of Religious Studies? What do we understand games to include? When can they be employed? Where do games fit into a balanced programme of Religious Studies? This article grapples with some of these issues.

WHY USE GAMES?

Game playing is a widely recognised form of active learning. Its virtues are many, including the ability to:
- enhance and complement other forms of classroom learning
- help develop group-work skills, especially in cooperative rather than competitive game play
- revise material originally taught in some other way
- provide a means of assessing pupils in a context different from that imposed by traditional learning structures
- last, but emphatically not least, provide fun and raise the profile of pupil expectation in RE![1]

WHAT ARE GAMES?

The term 'game' is something of a catch-all for many activities. These can range from simple card or board games to role play simulations through to more sophisticated multi-layered activities where the participants are involved in 'getting inside' a situation in order to 'feel' the part, exploring the world of the game in an open-ended fashion.

The common feature of most games, and certainly those in use in the world of Religious Education, is their non-passive nature. The players have to become actively involved with the material in the game and with the other players. Inasmuch as life is a game, this is a miniature simulation of some aspect of the real world. Much education offers pupils opportunities to explore aspects of the real world, in a safe manner, but to do so vicariously. Games are an ideal vehicle for this.

An important distinction in gaming is between the form of the game and its content.[2] FORM refers to the design of the game in terms of appearance, strategy, rules and so forth. CONTENT is the specific subject matter being used in it. In other words, form is largely about the medium, and content the message. The initial interest of the pupils is likely to be captured by the form of the game, and certainly when devising their own this is their dominant focus. It is incumbent upon teachers to ensure that in the event, the content is not lost in the enthusiasm for play. However, experience strongly suggests that pupils learn a tremendous amount of content simply by playing with it.

WHO USES GAMES?

It is in the nature of Religious Education that pupils are required to investigate the life-stances and beliefs of others. The use of games offers a way into what are often alien situations. Published games can certainly be successfully employed in the service of this goal. Perhaps, however, more interesting is the involvement of students in the creation of their own games as a way of looking at a topic. Teachers should not be excluded from the category of students either! When pupils and teachers are partners in learning there are exciting possibilities.

For starters it is perhaps best to use an already tried and tested RE game. Some of these are content specific, others can be adapted to fit a variety of requirements.[3] Experience with this way of learning can be built upon, and the adventure (and risk) increased!

Inevitably, it seems, it is the pupils who have the best ideas. They, after all, tend to be culturally more attuned to games than most adults. When devising games an element of plagiarism is inevitable, because there are few original ideas around, and most games in the commercial world share some features with others. What matters is that those designing their games get into the content, and match their ideas or form of the game to the material in view. Therefore, the instructions given to the class must be clear. Worksheets setting out all the requirements for a game can be one way of doing this. A sample worksheet that I have used with classes on designing a game on rites of passage can be found at the end of this article.

WHEN TO USE GAMES

The first thing to be said is that games should be used as part of a structured programme of work. They are rarely 'stand alone' items, and their use should be educationally sound, making sense within the framework of the Agreed Syllabus and the school's own RE curriculum.

In particular, the use of a game needs to make reference to the topic within which it is embedded. Here there are three possible points at which a given game might be useful: at the start of the work to introduce it; in the main body of the work as an ongoing stimulus; at the end of a topic as a means of revising or summarising the work covered.

Games are rarely successful when suddenly released on a class. As with videos, the potential for the unproductive filling of time is enormous. Clear introductions and careful guidance are advisable.

As to which age group to involve there seems to be no limit. From play group to university and beyond, children of all ages love to play. If the teacher is young enough at heart there will be little resistance to the idea.

WHERE TO USE GAMES?

Here we need to address questions both of time and space. The teacher must decide beforehand when and where this gaming is to happen. They will also need to find time to prepare the material–be it dice, photocopies, cardboard, or a suitable (possibly borrowed) classroom with appropriate space on desk tops. Once a kit is made, subsequent playing is easy, but the first time is always costly in terms of time and resources.

How much time will the pupils have to play the game or to devise one? Will this include homework as well as lesson time? What space will they require in order to be successful?

Behind all this lies the question of overall planning. If this activity is to be a good one it has to sit neatly into the rest of the programme. *Plan ahead!*

HOW TO USE GAMES

Finally to some practical tips, borne of salutary experience. The keynote is organisation, or organised chaos will be replaced by pure chaos!

1 All the components for use in the games must be readily available. Even where pupils have been encouraged to bring their own counters or dice, the teacher must have spares for the forgetful! Count everything out at the start and everything back at the end!

2 If boards are used they are best mounted on cards, coloured in by talented and/or enthusiastic pupils, and covered in sticky-backed plastic if they are to be used repeatedly. The same applies to cards which need to be durable.

3 Keen students can be encouraged to use their computer expertise to enhance the presentation of game sets.

4 For all games it is essential that players understand the rules before play begins. This cannot be stressed too strongly. Printed rules can be handed out for study, but there is no substitute for carefully taking players through the rules–a large wall-chart size version of the game or an OHP can help here.

5 Some rearrangement of the classroom may well be required, especially where a large playing surface is needed. If possible, set out the room before the class arrives.

6 The dynamics of small groups will exercise the teacher. It may be necessary to carefully choose the membership of groups, either to avoid awkward chemistry or to involve students who might otherwise sit on the sidelines of the activity.

7 Needless to say the forward planning even with regard to a commercially available game should include checking that there are the materials available for making it up into class sets beforehand. Do use pupil assistance where you can– there are always pupils who enjoy this.

8 Play any and every game you intend to use beforehand, preferably several times. An intimate knowledge of it will assist you in confidently managing first time pupil players, who may need lots of assurance and encouragement. You cannot afford to be flustered and unsure in the middle of a noisy and busy classroom.

9 Do not worry too much about the noise, though do suggest that working at a whispering level might be to everyone's best interest. Enjoyable fun activities are often rather noisy! Be in control without being a killjoy.

10 When pupils are making their own game it is vital that careful planning is undertaken. In *Skills Challenge*[4] we have suggested a series of questions to be used to establish what is needed to produce the game: Who is it for? What knowledge does it use? What RE content (if any) do the players need to know in order to play the game? What RE will they learn in the process of playing? What is needed to make the

game once we have thought of the idea? Who in the team will do what? etc.

11 Planning suggests a timetable, and it can include the following:

–decide in groups what the aims are

–draft various proposals for the game itself

–detail the material requirements

–obtain the materials including scissors, tape etc

–decide if a prototype is necessary

–manufacture the game

–play the game (essential) !

–evaluation of the game.[5]

The final suggestion is important. It is very easy to forget to evaluate the game playing. Whether this is in the form of a class discussion, small group work with plenary feedback, a written essay, or teacher marking of the game, something should happen. Moreover this should enhance the value of the exercise. Give opportunity for constructive criticism of both form and content leading to improvements next time.

Like all really worthwhile things in life there is an element of risky living here, but the risks bring immense rewards–happy game playing!

FOOTNOTES

[1] Terence Copley & Adrian Brown, *Skills Challenge* (RMEP: Norwich, 1992).

[2] Adrian Brown, *'It's All In The Game'* RE Today, 10:1 (Autumn 1992) pp 16-18.

[3] See (2) and Jenny Pearce's report on a pilgrim game in a primary school in the same issue.

(4) Copley op cit.

(5) ibid.

DESIGN YOUR OWN RITES OF PASSAGE GAME

In what follows you have a free hand within the guidelines given. There are certain things that you MUST do and certain things that you MAY do if you wish.

YOU MUST:

1 Include in your game all *four* of the major rites of passage, *or*
2 Concentrate on *one* rite of passage, eg death, but make reference to *several* different religious traditions.
3 Your game must have enough RE content to justify its place in your RE work. You must concentrate on getting into it as much information as possible.
4 In total you have only *two* double periods and *two* homeworks.
5 Plan it in rough, in terms of:

   a RE content
   b The form of the game
   c What you will need to create it.

Divide up the jobs within your group as soon as you can. Then trust each other to get on with it in an agreed schedule.

6 Your game must have clear written rules, a title and list of names of those that are in your group.

YOU MAY:

7 Work in groups of two to four people.
8 Decide on whatever format you choose for the game, but you must bear in mind the time constraint. Don't be too ambitious!
9 Use what ever materials you like, but please note that I can only supply you with scissors, sellotape, glue, A4 paper and A4 card. You will need to put in a request for the amount and colour of card required.

10 Use whatever information you have in your notebooks, plus textbooks if you need more information.
11 Negotiate with your teacher anything not mentioned above.

In everything that you do it is vital that you PLAN ahead, are ORGANISED, and GET ON WITH IT QUICKLY AND SENSIBLY!

18 | SIXTH FORM GENERAL RELIGIOUS EDUCATION

Adrian Brown

SUMMARY

In this article I explore various models for delivering Religious Education to sixth formers, as well as addressing the issues of staffing and resourcing. Finally, I suggest a list of ideas and possible areas of study for post sixteen students. I hope this may be of some help as individual institutions develop their own appropriate ways of offering quality learning experiences in RE.

There are good reasons for providing Religious Education for post sixteen students. For example, it recognises the enduring importance of the religious dimension of human life. The spiritual, whether understood as a separate aspect or as an integrating feature, deserves to be explored with the sixth form age group in a way that treats it seriously and presents it appropriately.

Religious educators know that the key questions of Life, the Universe and Everything have remained the same even in the midst of changing educational fashions.[1] Yet, RE must strive to be constantly reformed in order to remain relevant in new circumstances.

Once a climate of expectation is present the RE component is highly valued by the clients. That should not be a surprise. RE addresses *The Big* and therefore *The Interesting* and *The Important* questions!

DIFFERENT MODELS OF DELIVERY

RE is something of a chameleon. For some it is a synonym for Moral Education. For others the 'R' in RE is paramount and understood in traditional, sometimes exclusively Christian terms. At this level it has to be seen to have a more adult focus. Whilst there may be continuity with pre-sixteen RE in some institutions, where at the very least you can build on a pre-sumed prior knowledge, an element of discontinuity–some-thing new–may be desirable. Students may have been turned off in Year 9. An encounter with the philosophy of religion, or a look at (and listen to) the spiritualities of ten significant rock musicians may turn them on!

There is a debate as to whether RE should find its place in an explicit manner–a module on 'God and the gurus' for example, or whether it is found as an implicit cross-curricular theme, such as the religious and moral dimension in science or history and politics perhaps. The danger with the latter, and arguably with all cross-curricular themes, is that they may be an appealing notion to the planner with the overview, but rarely have the qualities of focusing the mind of the student in the way that a head-on encounter can. Those familiar with the single sciences versus balanced science debate will see parallels here. The cynic may see implicit RE as a rationalisation of the shortage of specialist staff!

As to the content of the RE, much current thinking is locking into the notion of 'competences'. Here the student learns about and understands the content, identifies key life experiences and issues, explores meanings and values and evaluates the contri-bution made by religion.[2] The material will have at least the components of knowledge, understanding, experience and interpretation.

The context of situations in which the learning takes place will vary enormously.[3] For example it has been suggested that the cross curricular combination of RE and Art and Design could prompt a consideration of the 'nature of beauty–response to beauty and moral implications', or with Business and Secretarial Studies, RE may throw up issues such as 'honesty, business ethics, competitive society'.[4] Whether all would see these as core agendas for RE is another matter, but if RE is not always going to be quantitively well off, implicit mode representations such as these could be entertained and developed, and even made more explicit thereby.

STAFFING

Staffing is an issue that is central to the success of sixteen plus RE. Unless committed, informed and skilled folk are involved, the enterprise is doomed to failure. INSET may be necessary, but who pays for and delivers this? Preparation time–always at a premium–is needed, but will it get the priority it deserves? Continuity in the sixteen plus team is desirable from year to year in order that sufficient incentive is in place to develop and revise material in the light of experience. There is nothing like a one year tender to discourage staff from creating good work. If teams are set up to deliver RE on its own or as part of a wide ranging General Studies programme, it then becomes a collective interest and the responsibility for its improvement is shared. It may be that such a team could create active feedback mechanisms to enable pupils to contribute to improving the learning process.

RESOURCES

Some courses can function successfully with very little in the way of resources. However, appropriate bids will be necessary for materials, expenses of visiting speakers, reprographics etc. RE staff should not end up with the dregs of accommodation, and someone may have to firmly request that the rooms need television, blackout, tables large enough for games etc. Even Cinderella has a desire to go to the Ball, which is a legitimate desire!

IDEAS THAT WORK

Finally here is a list of some ideas that might suggest possible models, content and style for sixteen plus RE. Many of them have been well tried out and successful in a range of places, but inevitably some only work because the course is being taught by a particular individual to a particular set of people:[5]

– The Good Book Guide: a fresh look at the world's best seller.
– Science Meets Religion: warfare or welcome?
– Psychology And Religion: is faith nothing but my state of mind?
– Religion Through The Looking Glass: a critical but sympathetic look.
– Sex And Religion: two taboos together or it takes two to tango?
– An Examination Of Cults: religion on the fringe (or over the edge)?
– 'God Is Dead. We Have Killed Him': Nietzsche rules OK!
– An Introduction To The Philosophy Of Religion.
– Beginner's Guide To Ideas.[6]
– Fundamentalism Or Bust: Is there religion beyond the caricature?
– To Be Is To Shop: alternatives to consumerism.
– Van And It: a look at the spiritual pilgrimage of Van Morrison.
– Religion And Art: the dialogue between the two.
– Religion And Architecture: how they have influenced each other.
– Medical Ethics: a view from a number of religions (and none).
– Technology And RE.
– Personal Development: stages and dimensions.
– Sacred Texts: the role of Holy Books, religious and other.
– Guard Our Unbelief: passages for examining religious belief.[7]
– The Universe Next Door: an examination of world views .[8]
– Religion And Literature: mutual influences and illumination.
– Evil And Suffering: are there any answers?
– Games In RE: an invention and trial.[9]

- Music And Religion: where do they meet? An historical survey.
- Great Moments In The History Of Religion.
- Ten Great Religious Figures.
- Books That Have Changed Our Way Of Thinking: religious and other.
- Agnostics Anonymous: do I have to be an atheist or a believer?
- Life, The Universe And Everything: religious questions in Adams' work.
- The Big Questions.
- The Final Frontier, Death: a look at all the angles.
- So What Is Wrong With Church Today?
- 'I'm OK But My Body Is Killing Me': attributed to Jesus.
- God On The Box: what do we make of television coverage of religion?
- What Do Church Goers Actually Think? Surveying the religious.
- An Introduction To The Sociology Of Religion.
- Meet A Believer: a chance to meet guests from religious groups.
- God Is A Mathematician: statistical surveying in and out of religion... and many more besides.........

FOOTNOTES

[1] Adams, Douglas. *Hitchhikers Guide to the Galaxy* (Pan: London, 1979).
 This book, other novels and the BBC tapes and records provide a rich vein of theological issues to plunder. You could build a whole course around the issues raised!

[2] Brenda Lealman, editor *What Next* (CEM: Derby, 1992) ch. 5.

[3] Ibid p 15.

[4] Ibid.

[5] Some of the following titles are cited in *What Next* and used with permission.

[6] This being the title of a superb and unique resource for sixth form RE:
 Smith, Linda and Raeper, William, *Beginner's Guide To Ideas: Religion and Philosophy Past and Present* (Lion: Oxford, 1991).

[7] The title of an anthology of readings:
 Evans, J J, *Guard Our Belief* (OUP: London, 1971).

8 The title of the following book:

Sire, James, *The Universe Next Door* (IVP: Leicester, 1977). See also *Clash of Worlds* by Daniel Burnett (Monarch: Eastbourne, 1990).

9 Sixth formers enjoy playing games such as those in:

Copley, Terence and Brown, Adrian. *Skills Challenge* (RMEP: Norwich, 1992) Also see article 25, 'Using Games in RE', as well as devising their own to explore RE topics.

Further topics for use with sixth formers are developed overleaf. These were produced for a sixth form college by Nick Pollard in 1989.

SPIRITUAL AND MORAL VALUES: SOME SUGGESTED TOPICS

Nick Pollard

INTRODUCTION

It is my experience that in the right circumstances, most students are very keen to discuss spiritual and moral issues. Indeed, once a debate has been started it can be difficult to stop.

If one allows students to choose the questions they would like to debate, they will often happily consider issues such as: 'How can a God of love allow suffering?' or 'Is the Bible reliable?' It is however, harder to encourage students to discuss more foundational, epistemological questions such as: 'What influences have shaped my current world view? or 'What is the nature of truth?'

I would suggest that a 'Spiritual and Moral Values' course needs to give students the opportunity to address both types of question. The following outlines cover a range of topics which could be debated and may help to bring in both of these dimensions to post sixteen lessons.

THE MEANING OF LIFE

A review of some of man's attempts to answer the fundamental question, 'What am I doing here?' This review will explore two strands of mankind's search for meaning:

a) Philosophers, a look at the ideas of people such as:

Soren Kierkegaard   (theistic existentialism)
Jean Paul Sartre   (atheistic existentialism)

Friedrich Nietzsche   (nihilism)

Richard Dawkins   (evolutionism)

b) Popular culture as expressed in Rock'n'Roll. A look at the ideas expressed through the decades. The following comments may provide a starting point:-

–'50s: emergence of Rock'n'Roll from Pentecostalism, rejection of 'church' and the search for individual answers.

–'60s: drugs seen as a tool for individual and internal mystical fulfilment.

–'70s: 'the dream is over', punk rock expresses the mood of despair.

–'80s: the spiritual quest is resumed.

Consider the meaning of life according to the teaching of Jesus recorded in the gospels.

Open discussion of the positions expressed asking two specific questions of each of these 'answers to life':

1 Is it true?   (Does it have objective validity?)

2 Does it work?   (Is it subjectively meaningful?)

Extend the discussion into questions the students raise themselves.

HOW CAN CHRISTIANS BELIEVE IN A LOVING GOD, GIVEN A WORLD OF SUFFERING?

A critical assessment of the validity of the (partial) answer to the question of suffering given by historic Christianity.

Discussion is introduced at each stage as the orthodox Christian view is developed:

–Some suffering is due to man's selfish actions

–What would be the implications if God were to step in and intervene to stop man's actions?

–Other suffering does not appear to be directly due to man.

–The Bible's account of mankind's rejection of God and the consequences for the world.

–The Bible's description of God's 'ultimate' solution.

–A new suffering-free world.

– What are we waiting for?
– The Bible's description of God's 'meanwhile' solution.
– Being part of the solution, not part of the problem.
Discussion opened up to include any other questions students raise.

WHY DO CHRISTIANS BELIEVE THE BIBLE?

A consideration of the nature of the Bible; why historic Christianity has seen it as the inspired, reliable and trustworthy word of God; how recent scholarship has questioned this view.
A brief review of the Bible, its contents and its claims.
A more detailed consideration of the gospels asking two questions (and inviting discussion at each stage):
a) Is this reliable history?
   Were events recorded accurately?
   Do we have now what was originally written?
b) Are Jesus' words God's words?
   Did Jesus claim to be God?
   Did he substantiate that claim?
Open up for discussion of any questions that students raise.

19 | TEACHING MIXED ABILITY GROUPS

Janet King

SUMMARY

This article considers some of the problems and pitfalls associated with teaching mixed ability groups and examines appropriate teaching and learning strategies. At the end of the article there are some differentiated materials from a unit on 'The Life and Times of Jesus'.

The first school I taught in 'streamed' pupils. This system provoked a good deal of concern. There were few complaints from the teachers or parents of the pupils in the 'top' classes, but there were plenty from the parents of pupils in the lower groups and from the teacher whose job it was to teach them. The creation of large comprehensive schools and an emphasis on 'equality of opportunity' in the early seventies, however, resulted in most LEA schools choosing to move to mixed ability classes or mixed ability teaching groups. Although I certainly welcomed this change I soon found that this system too was not without problems.

PITCHING IT RIGHT

One of the major difficulties was how to pitch the material at the 'right' level when you may have a pupil with a reading age of seven years and another with a reading age of thirteen years all in the same class. With such a wide range of reading levels using written material can be a real problem. Some RE text books I have used proved to have a readability level of eleven years, another appeared to have a reading age of sixteen years.

165

Obviously for many pupils both text books were unsuitable, one being much too difficult for all the pupils in the class. Furthermore the simple text used previously with the 'slow learners' could hardly be used with the 'high flyers' and vice versa. A further difficulty was in deciding appropriate tasks to set the group. Most teachers find themselves in this same kind of situation today.

PUPIL DIFFERENCES

Within any class and more particularly in a mixed ability class, there will be marked variations in the standard of work produced by the pupils and the levels of attainment they reach. Pupils learn in different ways and at different speeds. They also experience different learning problems and difficulties and these can vary from subject to subject. In RE, for example, some less able pupils find handling religious concepts extremely difficult.

As any teacher knows, within a mixed ability class pupils will display a number of different needs. For example, some will have persistent learning problems; some an ingrained sense of failure. Others lack the ability to concentrate for any length of time while others, by comparison with their peers, perform badly across a whole range of subject areas.

We need a curriculum which is differentiated to meet individual needs while still reflecting the wider, basic aims of education. Identifying individual pupil's problems and learning needs, however, is a difficult and time consuming task. Equally difficult is finding appropriate and manageable ways of responding to those needs in a classroom situation.

SPECIALIST LANGUAGE AND CONCEPTS

Secondary teachers need to recognise that many pupils will not be familiar with the details, concepts and technical terms associated with their subject. RE is no exception. It also deals with values, attitudes and abstract ideas and requires a variety of skills. In common with many other subjects, RE also involves a new kind of literacy. The language of the specialism must be used in such a way as to make both the language and the specialism accessible to the pupil. The language must draw the pupil into the specialised area rather than exclude them from it.

A DIFFERENTIATED CURRICULUM

No one would pretend there are any quick fixes or easy answers to these problems, but any teacher interested in improving their pupils' performance–whatever the subject specialism–needs to consider the question of differentiation, especially when planning new courses or writing new units of work.

Religious Education is not tied to the National Curriculum framework of attainment targets and levels of attainment, but many LEAs are now building these into their programmes of study for RE. This may encourage continuity and progression, however, it also implies a differentiated curriculum tailored to individual needs. How can this be done?

THE CHALLENGES FOR THE RE TEACHER

With the best will in the world, it is very difficult for any teacher to be aware of the learning needs of every pupil they teach and even more difficult to do something about meeting those needs. For RE teachers this is an even greater problem since they probably teach most of the pupils in the school!

Tasks set can be open-ended, allowing space for pupils to respond in a variety of ways and at different levels. This approach could be used, for example, in a lesson about the Last Supper. Instead of reading or telling the story and then asking questions on the content or getting pupils to write down their own accounts of the events that night, the teacher might bring in a variety of articles connected with the events of that evening to use as visual aids to the Bible story. These could include bread and wine, a bowl of water and a towel. One or two slides of paintings depicting the events that night might be shown and then time given for pupils to reflect on the significance of the events. Given this kind of visual and verbal stimulation, pupils could then be invited to write a poem about 'The Last Supper'. The quality of the work produced will vary. Some may be difficult to read because of a pupil's problems with writing or spelling, but each pupil has the chance to respond at their own level and their level of ability can be assessed by the quantity, quality, complexity and style of their response. This kind of task offers two opportunities for differentiation, first in the way the content is presented and secondly it offers scope for differentiation by outcome.

Religious Education also offers opportunities for reflective work where pupils can be encouraged to respond to stimulus material in a variety of ways and at their own level. For example, a lesson on the Sabbath might include the lighting of the candles for Shabbat and the saying of the special prayer that accompanies this ritual. At the end of this demonstration pupils may be invited to express their feelings about this ceremony and what it meant for them. Pupils could choose their own way of doing this—for example they might choose to draw a picture, write a poem or a prayer or act out part of the ceremony themselves (provided this would not conflict with their own religious convictions).

One of the main problems with differentiation by outcome is one of progression. Pupils must be involved in the evaluation and assessment process and be offered help in re-drafting and improving the quality of their work and thus make progress.

GROUP WORK

Many active learning methods enable pupils to work together on a project in groups. Cooperation rather than competition can be encouraged in this context. This in turn helps to create a supportive working atmosphere in the classroom and encourages pupils to learn how to give and receive help from each other. It is important to match the task to be completed with the most suited working environment. Group work provides an excellent context to develop co-operative skills, but there will be other tasks that are more suited to pupils working alone.

Active and cooperative learning may need to be approached in stages if pupils are not already used to working in this kind of way. This can be done by putting pupils in pairs to work on a clearly defined task. For example, a unit with older pupils on 'Life and Death' could involve pupils preparing arguments for or against euthanasia in pairs. This could then lead on to work in a small group situation–for example two pairs of pupils working together to prepare a 'case' to present to the rest of the class.

DIFFERENTIATED MATERIALS

Another way of giving all pupils access to the RE curriculum is to prepare materials at different readability levels and targeted at different ability levels. I use the term 'readability' here to indicate the reading level of the material which is then loosely matched to the pupil's reading age. This covers three aspects of the reading process–comprehension, fluency and interest–which interact with each other to affect readability. I have used this approach with success. The main drawback is the time it takes to prepare such material, although once done it can be re-used. This approach also allows more time to be given to individual pupils because more pupils could cope with the tasks set without lengthy explanations. I also found that pupils were motivated and achieved a great deal of satisfaction from being able to work at their own pace and level.

The sheets at the end of this article should illustrate how this idea works. They are taken from a unit designed for twelve year olds on the 'Life and Time of Jesus'. The story of the healing of the paralysed man is written at three different reading levels. Sheet A has a reading level of about seven years, sheet B requires a reading age of nine to ten years and sheet C thirteen to fourteen years. It may be preferable to colour code these sheets rather than identifying them by letters. I allow pupils to select the sheet they feel is right for them, but guide them to another the next time if I feel they have a wrong choice or are just being lazy! The accompanying Fact Sheets are the same for all pupils as they contain only small blocks of text and illustrations. The Review Sheets are graded, with the questions and tasks on sheet C being the most demanding.

Known as 'DARTS', Directed Activities Related to Text offers teachers a variety of strategies for adapting text and making it more accessible to pupils. If the written material is no more than two years in advance of the pupil's reading age, DARTS activities may provide busy RE teachers with some suitable strategies for learning. DARTS are text based activities which are rooted in discussion. They include making use of modified text and problem solving activities. They also focus on reading for a specific purpose and offer opportunities to reflect upon the text. These activities or strategies include:

- labelling and segmenting longer passages
- underlining important words or sections
- filling in information from the text on a table/chart or diagram
- giving pupils extracts of text and inviting them to make predictions about the next stage
- asking pupils, in groups or pairs, to note down any questions they have about the text and then letting different groups quiz each other
- deleting key words in the text leaving pupils to fill in the gaps
- drawing up headings under which information can be summarised
- inviting pupils to arrange unsequenced material into the correct or logical order

The role of discussion in all of these activities is vital. However, I have tried a number of these ideas in my own lessons with mixed ability groups and found them useful ways of getting more children into the text. Their understanding has also been increased.

CONCLUSION

If one accepts the entitlement of access for all pupils to all areas of the curriculum, including Religious Education, then in common with the rest of the staff, we need to take some responsibility for improving pupils' reading skills and their ability to interact with the text. This task cannot be regarded as the sole responsibility of the English department or special needs teacher. It is a sobering thought that some pupils may leave school without the ability to read through Mark's Gospel satisfactorily. We must therefore provide RE materials which will allow pupils to engage with the text and gain some understanding of its meaning.

In conclusion, the following checklist suggests ways in which teachers can give pupils of varying abilities wider access to the Religious Education and curriculum:

– Use open ended questions which will develop pupils' thinking skills.
– Seek to provide texts at appropriate levels of readability so that every pupil will have access to the material.
– Use clear, straightforward active and positive language.
– Differentiate through conversation; when talking to individuals be selective in the language used and the questions asked, simplifying the content or stretching the pupils where appropriate.
– Be selective in your uses of technical terms and explain them.
– Make sure every pupil knows and understands what they are being required to do.
– Continually strive to bring out the best in each pupil.

JESUS HEALS A PARALYSED MAN

People heard that Jesus was back in CAPERNAUM. They all wanted to see him. They had heard that Jesus was making sick people well.

When they found out where he was staying, they ran to the house. Soon, it was full up. Even the SCRIBES and PHARISEES had come.

As Jesus was talking, four men came to the house. They had a man with them who could not walk. He was on a bed and his friends were carrying him. The men wanted to get their friend to Jesus. They knew he could make him well. They tried to get past the crowds, but they could not. The only way they could think of to get their friend to Jesus was through the roof! They went up the steps outside the house. Then, they made a hole in the roof and let their friend down through it to the room below where Jesus was.

When Jesus saw the faith these men had in him, he told the sick man that his sins were forgiven. This upset some people there. The scribes and Pharisees said it was BLASPHEMY. This means acting like God or saying you are God. 'Only God can forgive sins', they said.

Jesus knew what they thought, so he asked them if it was

easier to say: 'Your sins are forgiven', or 'Get up and walk?' No one could tell if the man's sins were forgiven, but so people would know that Jesus could do both things, he told the man to get up, pick up his bed and go home. The man did just as Jesus told him.

When the people saw what Jesus had done, they praised God. They said they had never seen this kind of thing before.

B

JESUS HEALS A PARALYSED MAN

News that Jesus was back in CAPER-
NAUM spread quickly. Stories were
going around about Jesus doing signs
and working miracles. This made him
the talk of the town.

As soon as the people around
Capernaum found out where he was staying, they ran to the
house. The whole town seemed to be there, even the local
SCRIBES and PHARISEES. The house was soon full up with
people in the doorway and even in the street.

As Jesus was speaking, four men arrived carrying a
PARALYSED man on a mattress. They were sure that if they
could get their friend to Jesus, he would heal him. They tried
everything to get through the crowds, but it was hopeless. The
only way they could think of to get their friend to Jesus was to
get on the roof and make a hole in it, so they could let their friend
down to the room below where they could hear Jesus talking.

When Jesus saw the faith these men had he turned to the man
on the mattress and told him that his sins were forgiven. This
caused quite a stir. The scribes and Pharisees were particularly
upset and said it was BLASPHEMY (ie acting like God or saying
you are God). 'Only God can forgive sins', they said.

Jesus knew what they were thinking so he asked them a question: 'Which is easier to say, your sins are forgiven or get up and
walk?' Jesus could do both things,

but no one could see if the man's
sins were forgiven or not. So in order
that they would know that he could
forgive sins, Jesus told the man to
get up, pick up his bed and go
home. Straight away the man
jumped up, picked up his bed and
made for home. When the people
saw what Jesus had done, they
praised God. 'We've never seen anything like this before,' they said.

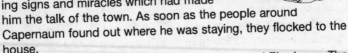

JESUS HEALS A PARALYSED MAN

News of Jesus' return to Capernaum spread quickly. Amazing stories had been circulating about Jesus performing signs and miracles which had made him the talk of the town. As soon as the people around Capernaum found out where he was staying, they flocked to the house.

Everyone was there, including local scribes and Pharisees. The house was soon packed out with crowds cramming the entrance and spilling into the street.

As Jesus was speaking, four men arrived carrying a paralysed man on a stretcher. They were convinced that if they could get their friend to Jesus, he would heal him. They tried everything to get through the crowds, but it was hopeless. Then they had an idea. They would get in through the roof! They set about making a hole in it right over the spot where they could hear Jesus talking below, then carefully lowered their friend, who was still on his stretcher, through the hole to the room below.

When Jesus saw the faith these men had, he turned to the man on the stretcher and told him that his sins were forgiven. This caused quite a stir, especially among the scribes and Pharisees who immediately accused Jesus of blasphemy (ie acting like or claiming to be God). 'Only God could forgive sins', they said.

Jesus realising what people were thinking, responded by asking them a question. 'Which is it easier to say,' he asked, 'your sins are forgiven or get up and walk?' Jesus wanted people to see that

he had the power to do both things, so he turned to the paralysed man, told him to get up, take his bed and go home! Immediately, the man got up, rolled up his mattress and made his way out through the crowd.

After seeing this, the people recognised the significance of what had happened and praised God. 'We've never seen anything like this before,' they said.

NOTES

SCRIBES were experts in the Law. They were also called lawyers, teachers or Rabbis.

The name PHARISEE means 'separate ones'. They saw themselves as a special or separate group who tried to work out all God's Laws in minute detail. They also added lots of rules of their own. They tended to think of themselves as very holy people and looked down on people who were not as religious as they were.

To be PARALYSED means that you have no use of your legs and possibly other limbs. The man in this story was obviously unable to walk and had to be carried to Jesus on his bed.

The word used for 'BED' in this story usually refers to a kind of quilt or mattress which could easily be rolled up during the day then just rolled out to sleep on.

FACT SHEET ON CAPERNAUM

Jesus moved from his home town of Nazareth to Capernaum soon after he started to preach and heal people. This was because the folk in Nazareth did not like what he was doing and they made trouble. Capernaum was a village on the north west shores of Lake Galilee, just 2½ miles from the place where the River JORDAN ran into the Lake. At the time of Jesus it was one of the biggest, richest villages in the area. It was on a main trade route and had a customs station and villa for Roman officials. Jesus made Capernaum his base for about twenty months. People called it 'his town'.

Little remains of Capernaum now, except for a small park area of ruins excavated in 1905.

The site is looked after by FRANCISCAN monks. An important find at Capernaum was the remains of a synagogue, dating back to 244 AD. Underneath were found the remains of an older synagogue thought to have been built by the Roman CENTURION whose servant was healed by Jesus.

Another important find was the remains of what is thought to be St Peter's mother-in-law's house with the ruins of a fifth century church built over the top. This kind of building was called an INSULUS. This was like a large apartment block, built in the local BASALT stone and plastered over. All the rooms were built around a central courtyard. Large family groups shared these buildings.

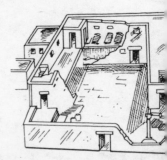

Most houses had steps leading up to a flat roof which
was sometimes used for
storage. Fruits like dates and
figs could also be laid out
there for drying.

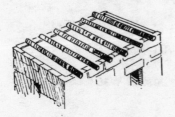

The roofs of the houses at
Capernaum were made by
placing wooden rafters or
palm branches across the
walls.

These would then be covered
with reeds or grass matting.
Covering this would be a two
inch layer of volcanic mud.
This would seal the roof and
give good protection from an
annual rainfall of only sixteen
inches.

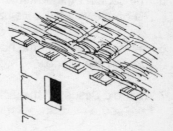

It would have been quite easy for the friends of the paralysed
man to make a hole in a roof like this.

REVIEW SHEET (A)

SECTION ONE:

CHOOSE THE RIGHT ANSWER:

1 At the right time of this story Jesus was living in:
　　NAZARETH　　CANA　　CAPERNAUM

2 It was near:
　　THE MEDITERRANEAN　　THE SEA OF GALILEE
　　THE DEAD SEA

3 How long did Jesus live there? Was it:
　　20 MONTHS　　2 YEARS　　ALL HIS LIFE

4 Why did everyone want to see Jesus? Was it because:
　　He had healed some people
　　He wore strange clothes
　　He was kind

5 Why couldn't the sick man get close to Jesus?
　　The house was full　　He had no money　　He was dying

6 How did he get into the house?
　　Through the window　　Through the roof　　Over the wall

7 What did Jesus tell the sick man to do?
　　Take some medicine　　Get up and go home　　Help his friends

SECTION TWO: Answer each question with a short sentence or with drawings.

a) What were the houses in Capernaum like?
b) Why was it easy for the men to make a hole in the roof?
c) Why did the four men want to get their friend to Jesus?
d) Why do you think Jesus healed this man?

REVIEW SHEET (B)

SECTION ONE: Use short sentences or one word answers only.
12 QUICK 'WHAT DO YOU KNOW' QUESTIONS

1   What town was Jesus living in at this time?
2   Where was it?
3   Why had he moved from Nazareth?
4   How long did Jesus live there?
5   Why was Jesus the 'talk of the town'?
6   How did the paralysed man get to the house?
7   Why couldn't he get close to Jesus?
8   How did he finally get into the building?
9   What was the first thing Jesus said to the man?
10 Which two groups of people were particularly upset by this?
11 What sin did they think Jesus had committed?
12 What did Jesus tell the paralysed man to do?

SECTION TWO: Use longer sentences and include some drawings.
4 QUESTIONS TO CHECK YOUR UNDERSTANDING

a) What were the houses in Capernaum built of?
b) Why did the four men bring their sick friend to Jesus?
c) Why was it easy for them to make a hole in the roof?
d) Describe what an insulus was like.

SECTION THREE: Write a short paragraph for each answer.
2 QUESTIONS TO MAKE YOU THINK

i) Why was Jesus so popular with the people?
ii) Why do you think Jesus healed this man?

REVIEW SHEET (C)

SECTION ONE: Short sentences or one word answers only required.

13 QUICK 'WHAT DO YOU KNOW' QUESTIONS

1 Name the town Jesus was living in at this time.
2 Where was it situated?
3 Why had he moved from Nazareth?
4 How long did Jesus live there?
5 Why was Jesus the 'talk of the town'?
6 How did the paralysed man get to the house?
7 Why couldn't he get close to Jesus?
8 How did he eventually get into the building?
9 What was the first thing Jesus said to the man?
10 Which two groups of people were particularly upset by this?
11 What sin did they think Jesus had committed?
12 What question did Jesus put to the people?
13 What did Jesus tell the paralysed man to do?

SECTION TWO: Use longer sentences and include some drawings.

5 QUESTIONS TO CHECK YOUR UNDERSTANDING

a) What were the houses in Capernaum built of?
b) What sort of people were the scribes and Pharisees?
c) Why did the four men bring their sick friend to Jesus?
d) Why was it easy for them to make a hole in the roof?
e) Describe what an insulus was like.

SECTION THREE: Write at least one paragraph for each answer.

2 QUESTIONS TO MAKE YOU THINK

i) Explain why Jesus had become so popular with the people.
ii) Why do you think Jesus healed this man?

20 | RELIGIOUS EDUCATION AND PUPILS WITH SPECIAL NEEDS

Carol Dunbar

SUMMARY

You are about to be faced with the final class of the week–a low ability group who would much prefer to discuss their social engagements for the weekend than matters spiritual! How can you survive the next forty minutes, given their limited ability in reading and writing, not to mention their short attention span? This article is an attempt to address practical issues concerning the teaching of Religious Education to special needs pupils, but first, a brief word on the concept of 'special educational needs'.

A DEFINITION

Since the publication of the Warnock Report in 1978, we have become accustomed to reading and talking about children who have 'special educational needs'. The 1981 Education Act gives the following definition: '..... a child has "special educational needs" if he has a learning difficulty which calls for special educational provision to be made for him.'[1]

It is argued that special educational needs may arise from personal disabilities, from environmental circumstances or, as is often the case, from a combination of the two. In addition to the major physical, mental and sensory disabilities, there is an increasing awareness of other circumstances and disabilities which can have an adverse effect upon school progress. For example, children can suffer from emotional difficulties, specific learning difficulties, behavioural problems, social and cultural disadvantages. According to Warnock, '... about one in six children at any time and up to one in five children at some time during their school career will require some form of special educational provision'.[2]

THE SAME GOALS

In any school pupils will come from different cultural and social backgrounds, bringing with them a wide range of abilities and needs. Differences will be identified in terms of their levels of skill and understanding and in their intellectual, social, emotional, moral and spiritual development. However, as indicated in the Warnock Report (1978), the goals of education are the same for all children – the difference lies in the help that individual children will require in order to progress towards those goals. Obviously, mainstream schools will vary in the type of provision made for such pupils, but it is fair to comment that, ultimately, having to deal with pupils who have special educational needs is an integral part of every teacher's work, irrespective of the curricular area. If we are to encourage pupils to regard Religious Education as something MORE than just another slot on the timetable, then we need to step outside the realms of using a watered-down version of the mainstream programme, complete with its seemingly simplified 'notes' and the 'read a story, draw a picture' syndrome and direct our efforts to delivering content in a more dynamic fashion. With that in mind, let us focus upon some of the practical issues.

A SENSE OF ACHIEVEMENT

Characteristic of many special needs pupils are feelings of failure, low self-esteem and a lack of motivation, each of which presents an impediment to learning. Therefore, these pupils need to be given the chance to develop self-confidence, to capitalise upon their strengths and to experience success. In any teaching situation, an atmosphere which is free from tension and conducive to instilling in pupils a sense of achievement is highly desirable; for pupils with special needs it is *essential*. Moreover, consideration needs to be given to the suitability of material being used and the method of presentation. More often than not, special needs pupils find abstract ideas extremely difficult to understand, so it is vital that, where possible, content is related to individual experience and is relevant to the pupil at a personal level. Enabling pupils to understand the religious concepts of sin, forgiveness, sacrifice, worship and prayer is not an easy task, but it is not impossible if such concepts are presented in a way which will allow pupils to relate them to their own experience. Take, for example, the concept of forgiveness. By using individual experiences of forgiving or having been forgiven as a starting point, the teacher can begin to explore the concepts of forgiveness with her/his pupils at a level which is appropriate to their understanding.

ACTIVE LEARNING

When working with special needs pupils, it makes good sense to adopt an experiential approach which promotes active rather than passive involvement in learning. As in other curricular areas, it is surprising what low ability pupils can do in Religious Education if the opportunities are provided. It is not uncommon to discover that a pupil who is not always capable of expressing him/herself through written work, can make a worthwhile contribution to informal discussions in class and to tasks which are of a practical nature. It may be argued that giving pupils the chance to share their views, listen to each other's opinions and to share their knowledge on a given topic, is a more valuable exercise than filling in the missing words in a passage or copying down notes from the chalkboard. Oral work can be stimulated in a number of ways:
–through effective teacher questioning;
–by using 'case studies' either real or imaginary;
–by brainstorming a topic or question;
–by forming 'buzz groups' whose task is to discuss with each

other a given issue and then report back at the end of the time limit. The points raised can then be discussed generally or by engaging in role play.

The delivery of Religious Education through the Creative and Expressive Arts has much to recommend it. Work which is creative not only contributes to emotional growth, but also involves thinking. Activities such as drawing, model making, listening to music and poetry, looking at paintings and acting out situations, can promote observational skills and can make pupils think about what they observe and the interpretations they place upon those observations. You might be pleasantly surprised at the diversity of responses elicited by a simple scenic poster and the request to think of a word (or biblical verse) which the scene evokes for the pupil!

Sadly, poetry writing is an area which is often neglected and yet special needs pupils are capable of expressing their thoughts and feelings in ways which might exceed all expectations–if they are given the opportunity. Space does not permit detailed discussion of how poetry writing may be approached, but the reader is recommended to beg or borrow any of the books produced by Sandy Brownjohn which offer a wide range of poetry writing techniques. From my own experience, one which proved highly successful when writing about the Christmas story was 'Time, Weather, Place, Person'.[3] The pupils had to provide information about each of these aspects and incorporate it into their poem. As a result, we had shepherds on windy hillsides at midnight and a grumpy innkeeper being forced out of his warm bed at one o'clock in the morning to show a young couple the way in the cold night air. Through this activity the story began to come alive for the pupils and they were encouraged to empathise with the people about whom they were writing.

ASSESSMENT

The merits of providing special needs pupils with opportunities to engage in activities which are creative and challenging are readily apparent. By such means, the ability to relate the lesson content to their own lives and to grow in moral and, hopefully, spiritual understanding will be promoted. It may be argued that how the pupils feel may be more important than how much they learn in terms of facts. Assessment should be constructive and should be concerned with behaviour outcomes. Through mainly formative assessment, teachers should provide pupils with opportunities which allow them to demonstrate their knowledge and understanding of Religious Education and the relevance which it has for their lives. Moreover, assessment techniques need to take account of individual abilities and should incorporate a range of approaches–through talking, role play, writing and so forth. Pupil participation in school-based activities which are linked to the community should be recognised. For example, pupils' comprehension of the term 'sharing' could be explored when they are invited to share their time and their talents with others. Fund raising, visiting the elderly, participating in carol singing and looking after the vegetable plot or wildlife garden in the school are valuable learning experiences which deserve acknowledgement. If indifference is shown to such work, how can we instil in our pupils a concern for others and for the world in which they live?

Teaching children who have special educational needs is both challenging and rewarding. Through the use of audio-visual material, information technology, poetry, music, drama, art, story, discussion and involvement in school activities such as Assembly or Religious Observance and visits to places of worship, we can try to ensure that Religious Education is recognised by the pupils as being dynamic and relevant to their preparation for life beyond the classroom... and yes...even what they decide to do at the weekend!

FOOTNOTES

1 *The Education Act* (HMSO: London, 1981) section 1 (1).
2 *Special Educational Needs (Report of the Committee of Enquiry into the Education of Handicapped Children and Young People* (HMSO: London, 1978) Chapter 3, para 17 page 41.
3 Sandy Brownjohn, *What Rhymes with 'Secret'?* (Hodder & Stoughton: Sevenoaks, 1982).

RESOURCE MATERIALS

Obviously, materials to be used with special needs pupils require careful selection. More often than not, teachers find themselves having to adapt commercially produced texts to suit individual ability levels. If the school is fortunate enough to have a Special Needs Co-ordinator, materials tailored to the individual's needs may be produced with her/his assistance. The publications listed are ones which contain ideas and techniques which have been tried and tested in the classroom. Although some of them may have been written with the primary sector in mind, the reader will find that they offer suggestions which can be adapted accordingly.

Finally, if the reader has a particular interest in teaching Religious Education to children with special needs, a journal entitled *Respect* is available by subscription from the following address: *Respect* 7 Elyham, Purley-on-Thames, Pangbourne, Berkshire, RG8 8EN. This journal contains useful classroom activities on various themes and provides articles, book reviews, and a list of modestly priced booklets which are designed to assist teachers in meeting the needs of their pupils.

BIBLIOGRAPHY

Brownjohn, Sandy. *Does it Have to Rhyme?* Hodder & Stoughton: Sevenoaks, 1980.
Brownjohn, Sandy. *What Rhymes with Secret?* Hodder & Stoughton: Sevenoaks, 1982.
Brownjohn, Sandy. *The Ability to Name Cats* Hodder & Stoughton: Sevenoaks, 1989.

Cooling, Margaret. *Christianity Topic Books 1-3* RMEP: Norwich, 1992/93.
Cooling, Margaret *REsource Banks Volumes 1-3* Bible Society: Swindon, 1993.
Corbett, Pie. & Moses, Brian. *Catapults and Kingfishers: Teaching Poetry In Primary Schools* OUP: Oxford, 1986.
Scher, Anna. & Verrall, Charles. *100+ Ideas for Drama* Heinemann: Oxford, 1975.

TOPIC: THE BIBLE

AIM

To enable pupils to recognise that the Bible is a collection of many different kinds of books.

ACTIVITY 1

1 Begin by identifying the number of books in the Bible and the names that are given to the two main parts.
2 Read aloud a selection of extracts from different books in the Bible and discuss with the pupils how each one might be categorised. Eg law, poetry, history, proverbs, letters etc.
3 Working in pairs or small groups, ask the pupils to choose a category and design an appropriate book cover. Allow time for discussion and rough sketches to be made; pupils should be encouraged to assess each others' designs.
4 Once the design has been agreed, the book cover can be made to the required specification–anything from matchbox size to A4 or larger! To make a display of 'false books' place each cover over a cardboard box of appropriate size.

ACTIVITY 2

1 Ask the pupils to think about a book which they have enjoyed reading and to identify the main characters and events in the

book. In the course of discussion, draw attention to the fact that it is only when the book is opened and read that the characters can come alive.

2 With reference to the Bible, ask the pupils to list some of the characters and events contained between its covers.

3 Write a poem which describes some of the Bible's contents. This may be written in pairs, or in a small group, or may be presented as a class poem.
Begin with the phrase:
'Between the covers of the book..'
End with the phrase:
'Waiting to get out.'
For example;

'Between the covers of the book.
There are lions and a whale,
Angels and shepherds,
Blind men and a new born King,
Waiting to get out.'

TOPIC: CHRISTMAS

AIM

To enable pupils to understand that there are 'invisible gifts' which we can give to others.

ACTIVITY 1

1 Informal discussion about giving and receiving presents.

2 Introduce the idea of 'invisible gifts'...money cannot buy such gifts and they may be more difficult to give than something which can be bought. Ask pupils if they can suggest what these 'invisible gifts' could be, eg love, kindness, thoughtfulness, obedience, peace, friendship, giving of one's time and so on.

3 Show the video or read the story of Papa Panov[1] to the pupils. Ask the pupils if they can identify the 'invisible gifts' which Papa Panov gave to each of the people he encountered.

Possible follow up activities might include:

a Make a bookmark, write on it the name of the invisible gift and decorate it.

b Ask pupils to make a list of the invisible gifts which they could give to those at home, eg tidying their bedroom, taking their turn at drying the dishes etc.

[1] This has been adapted from the original told by Leo Tolstoy: Mig Holder. *Papa Panov's Special Day* (Lion Publishing: Berkhamsted, 1976).

TOPIC: EASTER

AIM

To explore the feelings associated with the Easter Story through the medium of colour.

ACTIVITY 1

1 Invite pupils to give examples of colours which they associate with sadness, with joy, with anger, with peace, with loneliness, with fear, with jealousy etc.

Alternatively, show the pupils a variety of colours in turn; what emotional response does each colour evoke from them?

2 Recap on the main events of the Easter Story, focusing on the various moods and feelings of the different characters.

3 Ask the pupils to suggest colours which they would consider appropriate to Good Friday and Easter Sunday.

4 Divide the pupils into small groups and set each group the

task of designing a stained-glass window which would reflect the feelings associated with a particular part of the story.

5 The stained glass windows may be made using coloured cellophane and tissue paper, or simply drawn on white paper and coloured in with paints, wax crayons or felt-tips.

ACTIVITY 2

1 Discuss the association of certain colours with particular kinds of feelings, eg 'seeing red' meaning 'being angry'.
2 Select poems on the theme of colour to read aloud to pupils.
3 Either collectively or individually, have the pupils write their own colour poem:

Joy is....
A yellow canary
Singing a song
Ripe golden apples
And orange lollipops.

Peacefulness is...
A green meadow,
A clear blue stream gurgling along,
Looking at the white surf
Lapping over the brown sand.

We are grateful to Margaret Cooling for permission to use these topic outlines which draw heavily upon her work in the *Christianity Topic Book* Series (RMEP: Norwich, 1991/1992).

SECTION FOUR

DEPARTMENTAL ISSUES

21 ORGANISING A RELIGIOUS EDUCATION DEPARTMENT
Paul Bee

SUMMARY

Building a successful RE Department requires foundations to be laid before work can begin on erecting a super-structure and completing the building. Fundamental issues such as 'Writing a Policy Statement', 'Maintaining Morale', 'Allocation of Resources' and 'Creating a Departmental Identity' need to be addressed. This article focuses on these issues.

Religious Education teachers are often confronted by practical difficulties not faced by their colleagues when it comes to organising a department. Like Moses leading the people of Israel in the wilderness they are expected to 'wander' to the far corners of the school or campus to find the various rooms, usually unsuitable, in which they are expected to deliver their spiritual pearls. Whilst on their travels, if they are the Religious Education co-ordinator, they may like to consider the aspects of departmental organisation mentioned above. Then, should the 'Israelites' complain perhaps 'Moses' will have some of the answers!

To limit these 'desert wanderings' make a departmental base a priority, a room where most of the Religious Education can be delivered and which can act as a focal point of the department's activity and identity. This will make all other facets of departmental organisation considerably easier, especially the efficient management and use of visual aids and displays.

Even better, request an office too! Most departments in secondary schools will have one and if Religious Education is to be effectively organised then it will need a similar provision. This can then become the department's nerve centre.

Resources such as videos, filmstrips and worksheets can be safely stored and if properly labelled and arranged can be found by any teacher called upon to put their finger in the dike and teach some Religious Education. Over a period of eight years, twenty colleagues have assisted me in my department. Their willingness to help out and continued good will has been contingent to some extent on my capacity to calm their anxieties by providing them with all the resources they need for the designated scheme of work. So, ideally with an office, and a nearby classroom acting as a central base, building the department superstructure can begin.

LAYING THE FOUNDATIONS

Your second priority should be a Policy Statement setting out the aims and objectives of the department and outlining the department's policy on matters like homework, marking pupil's work and preferred learning styles. An example of a policy statement prepared by the Head of RS in a Nottingham school follows this article.

The Agreed Syllabus should be the quarry from which to hew your departmental aims. Keep them simple and short! Both you and the rest of the department will operate more effectively if you can easily call them to mind.

Homework is more problematic because it is likely to be determined by a whole school policy. If you intend to deviate from this then be clear about your reasons. If you want to build up a positive image of Religious Education with both pupils and parents, then set it regularly and mark it according to clear criteria. Make sure the rest of the department do the same. Stimulating and varied homework tasks will help sustain pupil interest and raise the credibility of Religious Education as an academic subject in the eyes of parents–people you are going to need to impress if you want young James to take an examination course!

Other things to include in your Policy Statement might be:

How do you intend to allocate resources? What percentage of the budget will go on books, audio-visual aids and artefacts? Departmental attitude to equal opportunities is an issue where the subject should be setting an example and you might try to grasp the nettle of the role personal faith might play in the classroom. Beware of the budding Billy Graham. The local minister might be overjoyed as numbers at confirmation classes triple, but an overtly confessional approach can do more harm than good with most pupils. Your aims and objectives will help but be alert. If you have a Policy Statement then nobody from the head down can have any doubt about your expectations.

BUILDING THE SUPERSTRUCTURE

In line with developments in other subject areas Religious Education syllabuses will become more prescriptive. This means the choice of syllabus content might be limited, but whatever your local circumstances a varied diet of topics in your own syllabus is vital. Breaking the work up into discrete half term units which reflect the educational needs and interests of the pupils and promote motivation may help to keep interest alive which is, perhaps, the teacher's most difficult task. Do not allow the work to die by dwelling on it too long. There is only so much mileage in Aborigine birth rites or the pilgrimage of the soul in Sikhism! When pupil curiosity is exhausted move on to something new. When bottom set Year 9 burst excitedly into your classroom after half term and ask, 'Miss, what are we doing today?' will you be able to whet their appetites with a tasty religious *hors d'oeuvre* or will you say 'We cannot do anything new, Gary, until we have completed the genealogies in Genesis, so sit down and pay attention'?

For example, a Lower Secondary course might include studying the following units: Religion and Nature, Moses, Signs and Symbols, Jesus: The Last Week, Birth Customs and the Bible Project. Support each topic with at least half a set of textbooks and a box of resources such as worksheets, slides, videos and handouts. At the top of the box have a brief outline of the scheme of work for that topic giving details of what you expect to be covered in the six or seven weeks available. I can guarantee that colleagues teaching only one or two periods will be most appreciative.

PUTTING ON THE ROOF

Having decided what you are going to teach and where this teaching is to take place give some thought to presentation and teaching methods. Religion should be a participative activity and Religious Education should reflect this. Involve the pupils in their own learning. This is not a subject where divine knowledge is passed on to bemused adherents via prophets and seers. Discussion, drama, quizzes and puzzles, art and craft, and creative writing should all play their part. If you are not familiar with these methods then make the effort to learn. Other departments can provide you with valuable expertise. Plug into the English department for discussion strategies, Art for poster work and cartooning and so on.

Once again pace and variety are essential. Not only must the whole syllabus move on, so must individual lessons. Keep activities short and sharply focused to enable pupil interest to be maintained. A double lesson can seem an eternity if you are ill-prepared or run out of ideas half way through. Conceal some tricks up your sleeve in case of emergency. A pupil in a GCSE class once remarked to me, 'In Business Studies I have to keep tapping my watch to see if it has stopped but in this lesson I don't know where the time goes!' Ah, if only they would all say that!

A GOOD PAINT JOB

Maintaining morale in the department can be taxing particularly if you are a one woman/man band. Members of your team may pass as frequently as English batsmen leaving the crease. In one year it might be a chemistry teacher filling in, the next it could be a linguist and so on. This can, though, work to your advantage. They will undoubtedly be pleasantly surprised by the quality of your organisation and the interesting subject matter they have been asked to teach. When it comes to needing support in the face of senior management pressure to cut Religious Education time and/or resources, having taught it these colleagues may become valuable allies.

Give members of your team encouragement and every opportunity to fulfil their role. Co-opt them to help in producing displays or organising visits. Consult them when departmental policy is reviewed and updated or resources allocated. Do all you can to make them conscious of being part of a team, a valued member of the department no matter how small their contribution. Who knows, they may enjoy it so much that they beat a path to the deputy head's door to be first in the queue for next year!

FOR SALE!

Among the many skills a Religious Education Co-ordinator will be expected to demonstrate, a sales-person might not be very high on the list but you underestimate its importance at your peril!

Start with your 'clients'. Prove to them that Religious Education is one of the most stimulating subjects in the curriculum by the range of strategies you utilise and the thought provoking nature of the material. Make the room you teach in look attractive by the way you arrange your displays or position your artefacts. In partnership with a colleague, who did the layout for me, I produced a printed workbook for our first two year groups containing thirty tasks to support the year's work. This has excited pupil interest alerting them to what's on the 'course menu' and it's something different. It has aroused parental interest too when displayed at Open Evening, provoking discussion about aims and intentions of modern Religious Education. Most schools have the necessary reprographic resources to make such a booklet feasible and, once the initial planning and formatting of the sheets has been done, they can be used again and again with only minor changes. If your artistic talents are as remedial as mine, then do what I did and ask for help!

Next concentrate your efforts and resources on recruiting some exam candidates. Swamp the Year 9 syllabus with all your very best topics. Arrange visits and invite visitors likely to provoke lively debate. Save your best audio visual material for this year – anything to make an impact and kindle an interest in the subject. National Curriculum is making it increasingly difficult for minority subjects like Religious Education to persuade sufficient numbers to opt for GCSE or Standard Grade, but the cause is not yet lost so do not be deterred. Ensure that what you offer is up to date and suited to pupil interests. You may think the eschatology of Mark's gospel is riveting, but I seriously question whether prospective candidates would share your passion. A mix of social, religious and ethical issues usually goes down well and most of the exam boards offer something along these lines.

Emphasise to pupils the value of the subject for careers, especially those which involve working with people, and highlight the general skills of empathy and understanding that Religious Education fosters. I usually give out a pack to each pupil which explains what the course covers, how it is assessed, its career value and the varied teaching strategies used in its delivery.

So check the following to see whether your department foundations are firm, your structure solid and your interior and exterior decor appealing. Do you have:

– a Policy Statement outlining aims and objectives and departmental practice on issues like assessment?
– a scheme of work outlining the main topics you want taught through the school?
– properly filed and labelled resources?
– a departmental base and/or office?

–lively and imaginative ideas for lessons?

–strategies for making part-time colleagues sense they belong to a team?

–a teaching room that reflects the exciting and varied work that pupils do in Religious Education?

If you do then I must arrange a visit because my department is still under construction! However, if you also feel that there is still a lot of building to be done, don't be discouraged. Achieving what has been described here is not a one year programme. Many schools require each department to outline their strategy for the next five years in a development plan, so this is a useful way of planning ahead and pacing your progress. A copy of my own policy statement for RE and five year plan follows this article, as well as the Departmental Development Plan, Statement of Equal Opportunities and Aims and Objectives of the Religious Studies Department at Bramcote Park School, Nottingham.

CHIPPING CAMPDEN HIGH SCHOOL RE POLICY STATEMENT

Paul Bee

1 AIMS AND OBJECTIVES OF RE

AIM:

To enable pupils so to understand the nature of religious beliefs and practices, and the importance and influence of these in the lives of the believers, that their own personal, spiritual development will be promoted.

OBJECTIVES:

Beliefs: Pupils should develop knowledge and understanding of religious beliefs through a study of ideas of God, key religious figures, sacred texts and the use of religious language and symbolism to convey beliefs.

Practices: Pupils should develop knowledge and understanding of religious practices through a study of worship, prayer, celebration, pilgrimage, rites of passage and the use of ritual in religious practices.

Lifestyles: Pupils should develop knowledge and understanding of personal, family and community religious lifestyles through a study of religious commitment, values and attitudes to a variety of life issues (page 3, The RE Cube).

2 WORK TO BE COVERED BY EACH YEAR GROUP

YEAR 7

Unit 1: Religious Belief (AT1)–a study of the importance of beliefs in human experience and the key beliefs of Christians and Muslims about God.

Unit 2: Sacred Texts (AT1)–an investigation into the base form and outline of the Bible and Qu'ran.

Unit 3 Religious Festivals (AT2)–a consideration of the significance of annual festivals in Christianity and Judaism.

Unit 4: Belief and Lifestyle (AT3)–an exploration into the variety of lifestyles to be found within religious and non-religious traditions with particular reference to the world environment.

Unit 5: Religious Developments in Britain (AT1)–a study of how, over the centuries, Christianity became established as the main religion in Britain and how Judaism became established in more recent times.

Unit 6: Places of Worship (AT2)–an exploration of a traditional church, a non-conformist church and a mosque to discover the meanings given by believers to the main features and to become sensitive to the reasons for specific requirements in dress, behaviour and attitude when visiting.

At the end of Year 7, pupils should be able to:
- explain in their own words beliefs about God held by Christians and Muslims and express some of their own views about belief in God.
- describe the structure of the Bible and explain how its text was transmitted over the centuries; explain the importance of the Qu'ran to Muslims.
- describe and explain the significance of the main festivals in the Christian and Jewish calendars.
- discuss religious and moral principles concerning humanity's relationship with the environment.
- discuss two significant periods of movements in the development of Christianity in Britain and the circumstances in which Judaism became established in the twentieth century.
- identify the main features of a church, a chapel and a mosque and explain the meanings given by the believers to symbolic features.

YEAR 8

Unit 1: Religious Symbolism (AT1)–an exploration of the way humans have used religious language and symbolism to convey religious belief.

Unit 2: Tensions in Belief (AT3)–a study of Judaism in order to understand issues facing people with religious commitment in contemporary society.

Unit 3: Key Religious Figures (AT1)–an opportunity for pupils to study the beginning and development of Christianity and Islam and the way in which Jesus and Muhammad influenced their formation.

Unit 4: Varieties of Worship (AT2)–an investigation into varieties of worship and meditation within Christianity and other world faiths.

Unit 5: Leadership in Religion (AT1)–a study of leadership in religious communities and how it is recognised and exercised.

At the end of Year 8, pupils should be able to:
–appreciate and understand the role of religious language and symbolism as pointers to beliefs and values.
–identify and discuss some of the dilemmas faced by Jews in living according to the rules of their faith and give appropriate examples.
–explain how Jesus and Muhammad influenced the formation of Christianity and Islam.
–identify the meaning given to ritual actions in worship and meditation, including the place of silence and stillness, and explain the feelings and attitudes expressed by believers.
–give examples of how leadership is exercised in religious communities today and the responsibility that leaders have as guardians of the faith.

YEAR 9

Unit 1: Religious Commitment (AT3)–an investigation into what it means to be committed to a faith and the obligations that arise out of that commitment.

Unit 2: Religious Leaders (AT3)–an investigation into the lives of contemporary religious figures in Christianity, Hinduism and Islam and how they influenced and made an impact on society.

Unit 3: Codes of Conduct (AT3)–a consideration of the codes of conduct of different religious traditions.

Unit 4: Rites of Passage (AT2)–a study of the significance for believers of coming of age ceremonies.

Unit 5: Belief and Practice (AT3)–an investigation of the significance of fasting and pilgrimage as expression of faith within Christianity and Islam.

At the end of Year 9, pupils should be able to:

–discuss the obligations of commitment for Christians and the attitudes and behaviour that result from their faith.

–describe the life of two contemporary Christian leaders and two leaders from other religions, showing their influence and impact on society.

–explain some of the consequences for believers of keeping religious codes of conduct.

–explain the significance of fasting and pilgrimage as examples of the relationship between belief and practice within Christianity and Islam.

3 GUIDANCE ON DIFFERENTIATION

Differentiation is normally achieved by outcome not task. Pupils respond at their own level to the stimulus material. Care is taken to ensure that the language used in the description of the tasks is accessible to all across the whole ability range. For lower sets simpler texts and tasks where possible are employed. When appropriate a choice of lesson activities is given to suit the pupils' varying aptitudes and interests.

4 GUIDANCE ON TEACHING AND LEARNING STYLES

Activity based learning is favoured where pupils interact in pairs or small groups to complete a given task. Co-operation, initiative, tolerance and empathy are fostered through drama, role-play, art, discussion, puzzles and creative writing. Each lesson should contain at least one pair or group activity, more if circumstances allow.

Teaching is open ended and non-dogmatic, aimed at presenting the beliefs and practices of the world's major religions as being of equal value. Pupils are left to judge for themselves the merits of their respective truth claims, and find their own, 'faith for life'. The classroom is not to be seen as a platform for an individual teacher's own convictions, although these may be a useful resource in discussion activities.

5 ASSESSMENT ARRANGEMENTS

A variety of assessment methods are employed to test knowledge, understanding and the ability to form an opinion supported by evidence and argument. The most common is a formal end of unit test which assesses what pupils have learned in the preceding weeks. These occur half termly. Formative profiles are also used half-termly to assist pupils in self-evaluation and target setting. These provide valuable feedback to the teacher on the strengths and weaknesses of the unit of study.

6 HOMEWORK

It is the department and school policy to set homework weekly to all groups. Pupils are asked to spend twenty-five to thirty-five minutes on a task which asks them to interpret religious beliefs and ideas through creative writing or art, or asks them to research relevant information for a forthcoming lesson. In years 7 and 8 formatted sheets are provided to give the homework structure and direction. Failure to do homework results in a lunchtime detention.

7 MARKING POLICY

Pupils' work is marked weekly whenever practical (although large numbers of classes with limited contact time means this is not always possible). Poor grammar and spelling are corrected. Positive comments are made on completed work to recognise effort and to prompt motivation for further tasks. Grades are awarded as follows:

A = Very good effort
B = Good, expected standard reached
C = Barely satisfactory
D = Work completed but not presented
E = Work not completed or presented

8 ARRANGEMENTS FOR RECORDING ATTAINMENT

There are no 'levels' in RE so there can be no attainment score. Descriptive judgments are made based on evidence accumulated through the year. End of unit tests are one method of recording attainment, another is the completion of a Record of Attainment sheet. Pupils are judged against a range of criteria such as willingness to join in discussion, quality of written work and sensitivity to others' feelings.

9 ARRANGEMENTS FOR REPORTING TO PARENTS

In line with school policy full written reports including effort and attainment grades are given annually. Effort grades are given termly on an A-D scale to reflect the level of effort shown by each pupil.

10 GUIDANCE ON CROSS-CURRICULAR LINKS

In co-operation with IT some pieces of work are done on the computer. This is at the discretion of the class teacher. Links with other humanities subjects and English are also encouraged.

11 ALLOCATION OF RESOURCES

Each unit of work is supported by a minimum of a half set of textbooks. The emphasis on activity based learning means that up to a third of the department budget is spent on consumables: paper, pens, sugar paper, glue-sticks, photocopying etc. The majority of the remainder is spent on replacing old stock and buying books for new units of study. Audio-visual resources are a high priority–recording of ITV/BBC programmes is a considerable help in this respect.

BRAMCOTE PARK SCHOOL, NOTTINGHAM RELIGIOUS STUDIES DEPARTMENT DEVELOPMENT PLAN

Maureen Collins/Mike Philips

A priority for the future of the department must be that the 'reasonable period of time' for the study of RS (required by the 1988 Education Reform Act) be assured within the curriculum time. This has been defined as at least one hour each week for all pupils. It is also crucial for the maintenance of RS as an academic subject that 'public examinations are available to all pupils 14- 18', as required by the Nottinghamshire Agreed Syllabus. Obviously we would like to see thriving 'A' level and GCSE groups, with good results. This would necessitate the building up of resources and specialist staffing. We consider having properly trained and committed staff as very important.

We would like to see the RS room urgently refurbished–re-carpeted, desks replaced, new display panelling, curtains, white board etc. The department would greatly benefit from its own TV, video and slide projector. We would also like to see the phone that is in the science office moved to the RS office–

where it would be easily available to both departments and frequently used.

Some of the areas we hope to develop are cross-curricular themes, including the RS content of the PSE programme, and cross-curricular links with IT, HE, Art, Music etc. We aim to develop field work and the use of visitors in schools, as well as primary liaison.

Overall we want to see the department build on its present good foundation. Its status, resources and staffing need to be steadily taken forward–to the benefit of the pupils, both academically and in the personal/social area.

1993/1994

1 Make a detailed evaluation of the existing syllabus for Years 7-9 in the light of the Agreed Syllabus.
2 Draw up a detailed Programme of Study for Key Stage 3. Select appropriate content and Attainment Targets. These are to be implemented in three phases.
3 Evaluate the existing 'A' level syllabus. Seek to enlarge 'A' level groups through liaison with Bramcote Hills.
4 Research cross-curricular initiatives.
5 Explore the greater possibilities of using Information Technology in Religious Studies.
6 Evaluate all existing extra-curricular activities, field courses etc and suggest more appropriate ones if necessary. Changes to be implemented over two years.
7 Do a complete appraisal of all forms of teaching resources–including the libraries at Bramcote Park and Parkview. New resources to be introduced over three years.

1994/1995

1 Implement phase 1 of the Programme of Study for Key Stage Three. Evaluate changes and suggest improvements.
2 Make any necessary changes to 'A' level syllabus following on from last year's evaluation.
3 Develop cross-curricular initiatives. Evaluate at the end of year, also suggest improvements.

4 Develop the greater use of Information Technology. Evaluate and suggest improvements.

5 Make a full appraisal of all forms of assessment used by the Department.

6 Take action on phase 1 of changes to extra-curricular activities, field course etc.

7 Following appraisal introduce new resources in Year 7.

8 Evaluate Staff Development Plan.

1995/1996

1 Implement Phase 2 of the Programme of Study for Key Stage Three. Evaluate and suggest improvements.

2 Make any necessary changes resulting from evaluation of Phase 1.

3 Evaluate any changes to the 'A' level syllabus.

4 Take action on any changes to GCSE syllabus suggested at national level.

5 Implement improvements in the use of Information Technology.

6 Make any changes to the assessment procedures following from last year's appraisal.

7 Take action on Phase 2 of any changes to extra-curricular activities etc.

8 Introduce new resources for Year 8.

1996/1997

1 Implement Phase 3 of the Programme of Study for Key Stage Three. Evaluate and suggest improvements.

2 Make any necessary changes from evaluation of Phase 2.

3 Introduce new resources for Year 9.

BRAMCOTE PARK SCHOOL, NOTTINGHAM AIMS AND OBJECTIVES OF RELIGIOUS STUDIES

Maureen Collins

In accordance with the 1988 Education Reform Act, we aim 'to promote the spiritual, moral, cultural and mental development of pupils' and to 'help prepare such pupils for the opportunities, responsibilities and experiences of adult life'.

Other aims of our department are to:

1 Allow pupils to become acquainted with Christianity and some of the other principal religions of our society, through the study of contemporary religious beliefs, practices, insights, attitudes and experiences.
2 Encourage pupils to recognise a spiritual dimension in human experience and to raise questions about the meaning of life, considering religious answers and beliefs.
3 Consider a number of religious issues and help pupils reflect critically upon their own stance towards them.
4 Enable pupils to appreciate the diverse and sometimes conflicting beliefs and values which arise from religious involvement.
5 Encourage development of respect for and empathy with the major religions and non-religious life stances.
6 Help pupils reflect upon a range of life experiences and the questions they raise.
7 Help pupils develop lively, inquiring minds, with the ability to argue and question rationally.

Some of the objectives to achieve these aims are:

1 Pupils will study Christianity, Judaism and Sikhism, and be introduced to Hinduism, Islam and Humanism.
2 Pupils will be encouraged to think about the nature, unique-

ness and worth of humans and the ultimate questions humans ask and how they answer them.

3 Pupils will be asked to give their 'reasoned' opinions on issues such as baptism, abortion etc.

4 Issues are considered over which people in religions may disagree, eg baptism, communion, family issues, marriage.

5 Pupils are encouraged to respect the opinions expressed by others in the classroom, then to extend this respect to the ideas presented in the religions.

6 Through study of rites of passage and moral issues, pupils will reflect on questions such as 'Why am I here?', 'Is there a God?', 'What happens when I die?'

7 Regular class discussion, as well as written work, encourages pupils to think through ideas and express themselves clearly.

BRAMCOTE PARK SCHOOL, NOTTINGHAM RELIGIOUS STUDIES EQUAL OPPORTUNITIES STATEMENT

Maureen Collins

The Religious Studies Department fully participates in the School Equal Opportunities Policy—we seek, through content and approach, to create an atmosphere in which the opinions and beliefs of all are treated with respect. We try to encourage all pupils to express themselves, and try to develop self esteem in all pupils—both in the things they can do (be this written or artistic work) and in themselves as thinking, feeling human beings.

Through RS we seek to extend the pupils' own cultural experience—by getting them to explore the religious practices and beliefs of the faith predominant in their own community. We also draw attention to the diversity of faiths and cultures represented in Nottingham, and try to present these as a positive and interesting area of study. In both these topics we sometimes meet intolerant attitudes, as well as overt racism and insult. The aim of the department is to challenge these attitudes in a way which will make the pupils see for themselves why their attitudes are inappropriate and help them move towards a greater understanding of the rights and feelings of others. Studies of world faiths aim to help pupils to understand the religion through the eyes of a member of the religion. This is encouraged by the use of videos and books by faith members, as well as artefacts and visits. We hope that if pupils are at least familiar with and know the reason for items of dress and customs that seem strange to them, there will be less likelihood of insulting comments when they come across them in life.

We also spend time on moral issues within the RS curriculum, and aim to encourage pupils to clearly express their own opinion—including a reasoned argument for it, but also to listen to, and try to understand, the reasons for opposing views. We try to encourage an environment where all views are treated with respect, and encourage a realistic understanding of why particular views are held. Pupils do not have to say what they think the teacher wants to hear, but all views must be expressed politely and without insulting others. A conflict is acknowledged to exist where certain cultures might have ideas which this policy might deem sexist etc, but the department aims to show that one can understand the reasons for a belief without having to agree with it.

Overall the RS department aims to give all pupils a sense of self-worth, as well as an understanding of, and respect for, people who are different from themselves.

22 | DEPARTMENT MEETINGS AND PLANNING INSET

Paul Bee

SUMMARY

Departmental meetings and INSET are often neglected in Religious Education yet the demanding nature of the subject and the way it is often staffed piecemeal should make them 'holy writ'. Where most of the people teaching the subject are likely to spend only a small amount of time in the department, the need for good communication and training in specialist skills is proportionally higher. I shall suggest some way of organising departmental meetings and INSET concentrating on the practicalities. Every school's circumstances are different, but most of these ideas will be relevant in any situation.

DEPARTMENTAL MEETINGS

If your department is made up of you and a few colleagues from other departments who contribute a few lessons, there may be as much chance of holding a scheduled department meeting as there is of finding the Holy Grail! Your team will be needed elsewhere when you want to convene a meeting. Anticipate such difficulties early in the term by finding a mutually convenient time when you can all meet.

Organising a successful meeting involves much more than a chat over a cup of coffee about why 9F are failing to grasp mediaeval mysticism. Starting with refreshments is a good idea as it helps people relax and shows you appreciate that they have made the effort to attend. Chocolate biscuits would certainly be an incentive for me to attend any meeting!

PREPARATION

Thorough preparation for the meeting should be your first priority, especially if you are planning significant changes in the way your department operates. Think through your objectives for the meeting. Are you holding it because it is on the calendar or because important departmental matters need to be discussed? Hopefully it is the latter, which means you need to know what you want discussed and why. Distinguish between major and minor issues so that you are not sidetracked into spending too long on something relatively unimportant. You might specify on your agenda how long you intend to spend on each item: eg purchase of new resources (ten minutes), matters arising from the senior staff meeting (ten minutes), new modules in Years 10 and 11 (thirty minutes). Routine information might be communicated in a more informal way—a chat at break or lunchtime perhaps, leaving major items for official after-school meetings when they can be allocated more time.

The key to a successful meeting is a properly prepared agenda. It should be more than just a list of items and might also include a list of people expected to attend, a note of what kind of meeting it is to be and a note drawing people's attention to accompanying documents which should be read or brought to the meeting. Publish in advance so that colleagues will have had a chance to think about what is going to be discussed before they arrive. That way they are more likely to take an active role in the proceedings.

No matter how well organised you are, it is highly unlikely that in the special staffing circumstances that Religious Education endures, all your team members will be able to come. Inform absent colleagues about what was discussed at the meeting, in this way including them and making them feel part of the operation. They may have to be absent in body, but you want them to be with you in spirit.

Finding a suitable location may be a problem. If it has to be a classroom then organise the chairs and tables so that every one can make eye contact. Sitting round in a circle is a good idea or if you have to go through a document or people have to write as well as talk, sit around a table. Ensure that you have everything you need before the meeting starts. A five minute hiatus while you rummage through the stock cupboard for 'Tibetan Buddhism and the meaning of Life: a Discussion Document' does not send the best of messages about how seriously you take the meeting yourself!

Part of your preparation work will involve foreseeing possible difficulties. Is your meeting predestined, that is you will not be deflected from your policy course which has been mapped out since the beginning of the world? Or are you willing to compromise if impressive counter arguments are put up by colleagues? Thinking about how much ground you are willing to concede might be usefully considered beforehand.

As the chair of the meeting you have a crucial role and only experience will help you acquire the skills necessary for driving the Religious Education juggernaut through the contra-flow of the agenda. Flexibility is important and you will have to drive purposely and sensitively as the meeting progresses.

OUTCOMES AND EVALUATION

Meetings should have outcomes, decisions should be made. The chair should ensure that there is a tangible outcome to the deliberations. Progress should be measurable. This means you will have to keep a fairly firm hold on the steering wheel so that your precious cargo negotiates unexpected lane changes and reaches its destination. Your communication skills will be needed and as the 'expert' you will need to be conversant with the arguments and have the information at your fingertips to support what you say. Persuading colleagues to adopt new learning styles might, for example, be a contentious issue. Your soothing words will reassure them that mayhem will not be unleashed when 8D are asked to enact a Jewish seder meal!

Some record needs to be kept of the meeting in the form of minutes. This makes it clear what was discussed and decided at the meeting leaving no room for doubt and it can be used as a means of informing people who were not present of the main points of discussion. Minutes should be concise and reflect the major contributions different people made to the meeting.

Finally some evaluation of the meeting is helpful to analyse how well you did in your capacity as organiser and chair. Ask yourself: were my objectives for the meeting achieved and if not, why not? Could I have done anything to prevent any difficulties that arose? Will I have to organise the next meeting differently as a result of what I have learned this time? Ask the people who came to the meeting! Did they feel that they had an opportunity to contribute. and think that the session was valuable? Like all good teaching, the secret lies in the preparation. The better prepared you are the more productive the meeting will be. Do not leave it to fate. Colleagues will be more willing to give up their precious time in future if their previous experience was a good one and whatever else you do, do not forget the chocolate biscuits!

INSET

When the INSET cake is cut Religious Education can often be left without a slice, or worse, even the crumbs that fall from the table. If money has to be bid for, ensure that the Religious Education bid does not fall by the wayside. With 'hard' curriculum subjects such as English, Maths and Science demanding so much INSET time the Religious Education case needs to be persuasively argued and evidence of proper planning of prospective INSET time needs to be shown.

TARGET NEEDS

To plan effective INSET the members of your department need to be consulted first, so that their needs can be catered for. You want to support every individual by encouraging them to reach their full potential. This will lead to an increasingly effective department and more job satisfaction amongst colleagues. First discover what INSET your team members have had over the past year or two. Did it have any impact on their work in school? When time is at a premium ill-targeted INSET should be avoided and such an evaluation may shed light on the best way to use future sessions.

The lack of INSET opportunities could pitch you into a frenzy of planning regarding the possibilities for your next allocation. Beware of trying to do too much and spreading your net too widely. Solomon's Temple was not built in a day, so do not expect to train your team in assessment developments, learning styles, exam work and the social teaching of Hinduism all in one go! Work out your priorities. Think too about the needs of your team. For example, fairly frequent staff turnover would mean that the team rarely stays together for more than a year. How are you going to target your INSET? Will it aim at improving team co-operation or developing specific Religious Education teaching techniques? Will it be task centred or person centred? Once the INSET is over, consider methods of evaluation to ensure that INSET in the future will be worthwhile.

Finally, you have to decide the type of INSET you want. Some INSET could take place at regularly held department meetings. Here you might consider issues relating to a new Scheme of Work or phasing in a new syllabus. By working collaboratively in this fashion, misunderstandings about the nature and aims of a particular section of work can be kept to a minimum. 'Mr. Jones, would you like to do "Death" with Year 11 next term? I have a video about cremation you may find helpful,' is the more usual answer given to a colleague when they ask you what they have to teach next year. Better to have discussed the topic together at a departmental meeting.

SCHOOL BASED INSET

A more attractive option may be school based INSET when you can be sure of getting your whole team together. Some of the 'Baker' days in schools are usually set aside for departmental planning and review. Who knows, you may be successful in shoe-horning your team members out of their other departments to spend some time on INSET with you, especially if they are going to be rewarded with a meal at a local restaurant for giving up their time! If you believe you lack the expertise needed to lead such a day then try to recruit people from outside, such as advisory teachers or people from educational institutes. Planning how the time will be spent on such a day is vital. If you are expecting your colleagues to give up time for INSET then you must guarantee that it is well organised and stimulating.

Using external courses may provide your team with the training it needs, but with local authorities cutting back their services, these can be as rare as they are expensive. Lack of funds will probably mean that only one of your team can attend a course. Do you go and then cascade your discoveries on to your expectant team when you return or do you send a team member? If so, whom? Sending a less experienced colleague is likely to be best, because it will foster team spirit in the department and hopefully improve their expertise. With any luck they will come back so enthused that they think the land of milk and honey is the Religious Education Department and not that holiday in the Bahamas they are contemplating.

The chief concerns in Religious Education, at the time of writing, are methods of assessment and learning styles appropriate to promoting an exploration of life's spiritual dimension. Either of these would make fitting INSET topics as would using Information Technology, teaching world religions or recruiting and using visitors. The important thing is to be crystal clear about the purpose and intended outcomes of the training. As the writer of Proverbs might have observed, 'Train a teacher in the way he should go, and when he is old he will not turn from it' (with thanks to Proverbs 22:6).

FOOTNOTE

[1] Richard Kemp and Marilyn Nathan, *Middle Management in Schools: a Survival Guide* (Blackwell: Oxford, 1989).

23 | USING SCHEMES OF WORK TO PLAN TOPICS FOR ELEVEN TO FOURTEEN YEAR OLDS
Janet King

SUMMARY

Most RE teachers with a full teaching timetable find themselves spending a large amount of their time with their lower secondary pupils. Judging from a quick survey of teachers who attended a course at Stapleford House on 'Active RE', the time allocated to RE lessons with these pupils varied from thirty-five minutes a week to two hours! The amount of time you have will obviously affect your teaching programme and choice of topics. This article raises a number of issues which will affect your topic planning. It also stresses the importance of planning ahead, developing concepts, attitudes, skills and knowledge and provides two different planning models. The quality of classroom experience is another issue explored and a check list for planning study units is given.

MAKING A START

Imagine it is your first RE lesson with a Year 7 class. They arrive at the right room (eventually), eager and excited about their first encounter with the RE teacher. What will he/she be like? What will they do? You have a one-off opportunity to dispel any negative attitudes and show them that RE is a dynamic subject which looks at real life issues which have relevance for everyone of them. You pull out all the stops. The pupils respond positively and you finish the lesson feeling that you really achieved something. Great! The only thing is, you have another three classes to teach before 3.30pm, and tomorrow you have to do it all again. It is hard to be dynamic more than once a day. If you are going to interest and excite your classes all year, you definitely need a carefully planned, well-organised teaching programme which employs a variety of teaching strategies and which can draw on some good materials and resources.

PLAN AHEAD

Begin by identifying and choosing your topics or study units. *Starting Out with the National Curriculum*[1] cites a number of central issues and concepts that appear, to different degrees, in most post '88 syllabuses. These include topics such as beliefs about God, founders of religions and cross-religious concepts like transcendence and community.

When making your choice of topics for lower secondary pupils, have the relevant agreed syllabus, your current scheme of work and programmes of study to hand. These documents and the resources at your disposal will dictate to a large extent the content to be included in your teaching programme. You are unlikely to have the time or the money to resource an entirely 'new' scheme for all pupils, so you will need to 'cut your coat according to the cloth'. This is not to say that there will be no room for manoeuvre, just don't expect to change everything overnight or the only thing that will change will be the health of the RE teacher! So be realistic and plan ahead.

Once you have selected the topics, decide when you are going to teach each unit and the order they should come in. At this stage of the planning, I find that it is useful to have a supply of sheets to hand such as the sheet which is provided on page 224.[2] When you are happy with the topics selected, check carefully to make sure there will be progression and continuity for the pupils as they move through the programme. This can be done by increasing the level of demand by reference to Statements of Attainment or level descriptors and introducing students to harder content.

DEVELOPING CONCEPTS, ATTITUDES, SKILLS AND KNOWLEDGE

The next step may be to identify the concepts, skills and knowledge you want to communicate and develop. This process has been described by the Regional RE Centre (Midlands) Westhill College in *Assessing, Recording and Reporting RE: A Handbook for Teachers*.[3] They have given their formula the title 'CASK' and claim that using this (in the right order) will make programmes of study more specific and that it will help to focus the direction of the topics and units of work. They say that planning in RE means:

> 'First C' identifying the CONCEPT(S) we hope to develop through a topic or unit. This will enable us to be clear about the key idea which supports the learning experiences.
>
> 'Second A' considering the ATTITUDES we hope the learning experience will promote. This is of great importance in RE since we find ourselves dealing with personal, sensitive and sometimes controversial issues.
>
> 'Third S' deciding if there are particular SKILLS which pupils need to develop to help them to assimilate the concepts and attitudes we are considering. In some cases it will be necessary to give time to children to develop general educational skills, for example, giving reasons for an opinion; but these should always be related to and based on RE content.
>
> 'Fourth K' selecting from the wide range of content which is available to us in RE, the KNOWLEDGE (or information or content) which will best help to develop the concepts, attitudes and skills we have identified.[4]

PLANNING MODELS

When writing new study plans in the past I have used two different methods of planning. The first is the circular model. The example below, based on the Westhill model, has been developed by Dillington College.[5]

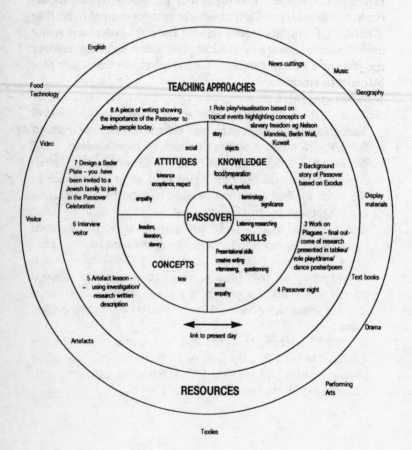

This method of planning has advantages. It is visually stimulating and quick and easy to read. The various headings indicate areas that need to be considered at the planning stage which include identifying attitudes to be fostered, concepts and skills involved in the topic and the main body of knowledge to be imparted. Teaching approaches are also set out and the outer ring provides space for listing resources. The area outside the circle can be used to indicate possible cross-curricular links. The disadvantage of this model to my mind is that there is not enough room to write in some of the information I would like included in a plan of this sort. Also, there is no space given for listing attainment targets, assessment arrangements or homework details, although it could be adapted to include space for this.

The other planning model I have used is the column approach. This method is developed by Westhill College as the example on the following page shows.[6]

Planning form for RE Topics

Key Stage:	TOPIC:		Attainment Targets:
Planning Programmes of Study:	**Assessing** Statement of Attainment:	**Teaching** Content/Knowledge:	
	Evidence ….	Questions to raise:	
Concepts:	Techniques:	Learning activities:	
Attitudes:	Tasks:		
Skills:			

Both these models offer scope for including information on attainment targets, programmes of study, teaching strategies and assessment. Personal preference will determine which, if any of these planning approaches you choose to use or modify for your own planning purposes.

A CONCEPTUAL APPROACH

This approach to Religious Education focuses on a concept, such as 'commitment' and then relates this to a particular religious belief. In this way RE becomes more than passing on a body of knowledge, as it requires pupils to understand certain concepts and beliefs. This approach is explained more thoroughly in several of the units of work which follow this article.

THE QUALITY OF CLASSROOM EXPERIENCE

Any planning activity should take into account the kind of experiences being provided for the pupils. This means giving careful thought to the purpose of the whole unit and of individual lessons, the teaching methods to be employed and the choice of learning styles. There needs to be a balance between the amount of oral work, writing tasks, reading and practical work set. Assessment procedures and homework are other major considerations. It is also very important to give time and space to evaluating each topic and individual lessons so that the programme can be modified and improved.

A CHECKLIST FOR PLANNING STUDY UNITS OR TOPICS

The following checklist attempts to summarise some of the main points which need to be considered when planning a topic or study unit:

- Consult your LEA Agreed Syllabus, appropriate national guidelines or other relevant syllabus.
- Look at your current scheme of work.
- Seek help from local advisors/inspectors and other Department Heads. Consider the resources at your disposal.
- Select your topics or themes.
- Link these with your Attainment Targets, Attainment Statements and Programmes of Study.
- Identify appropriate concepts, attitudes, skills and knowledge.
- Select and prepare new resources.
- Look for opportunities to make cross-curricular links.
- Plan your assessment arrangements.
- Identify a variety of suitable teaching methods.
- Plan a range of learning activities.
- Include details of your Programmes of Study in your departmental handbook.

FOOTNOTES

[1] *Starting Out With The National Curriculum* (NCC, York, 1992), p 57.
[2] *Assessing, Recording and Reporting RE: A Handbook for Teachers* (Westhill College: Birmingham, 1991).
[3] ibid.
[4] ibid, p 22.
[5] *Religious Education for Non-Specialists,* (Dillington College: Ilminster, 1991).
[6] Westhill op cit p 67.

ACKNOWLEDGMENTS

Two example study units for lower secondary pupils follow this article. These were developed to meet the requirements of the Oxfordshire Agreed Syllabus by Sue Hookway, Head of RE at Gillott's School, Henley.

THE CONCEPTUAL APPROACH

The following two examples are based on Programmes of Study in the Oxfordshire syllabus. They are 'skeleton' in nature, that is not all the teaching material will be reproduced in detail, though there will be information as to where it can be found.

The examples are set out in the following format;

a *Statement*–taken from the new syllabus to show its requirements relating to the topic.

b *Concept*–contained in the topic to be covered.

c *Experience*–from the children's own world to help them to engage with the concept.

d *Content*–material to be delivered with the topic.

e *Belief*–embedded within the taught material.

f *Biographical illustration*–an example taken from the life of a believer to illustrate the belief.

g *Understanding*–a task to assess the understanding by the pupils of what has been taught.

h *Reflection*–on what the learning has meant to the pupils in their own lives.

In these examples, the belief is presented after the content because:

i   After exploring the general concept in their own experience, it is a natural link for pupils to go to the content in which that concept is contained.

ii   It is a way of grounding the abstract (the belief) in the concrete (the content). Having learnt about the concrete, it will then be easier for them to understand the belief, especially when it is then illustrated in the biographical examples.

iii It is easier to engage the children's interest in the concrete; their own interest can then lead into teaching the actual belief.

EXAMPLE 1–HOW RELIGIOUS PEOPLE EXPRESS THEIR BELIEFS

Keeping a special day–Sunday.

a *Statement:* 'Pupils should be taught about and understand how personal commitments have effects on the actions of individuals and others.'[1]

b *Concept:* Commitment.

c *Experience:* Think of one thing, person or group they are committed to, eg club, hobby, friend. How does this commitment effect their behaviour? eg how they spend their time.

d *Content:* Seventh day of rest; Genesis 2:1-4, Exodus 20:8-11.

e *Belief:* Resurrection. Sunday, a day of rest and worship. For Christians, Sunday became the day of rest because 'Jesus rose on the first day of the week. The first day symbolises the new beginning, or new life, offered to people who believe in Jesus.'[2]

f *Biographical Illustration:* Eric Liddell. Account taken from *The Flying Scotsman; a biography.* Sally Magnusson, 1981, chapter 2. Pupils prepare a news item to be broadcast from the Olympic Games.

g *Understanding:* Write an imaginary letter home from Liddell explaining:
  i The reasons for his decision.
  ii His feelings about the decision.

h *Reflection:* Has what they have learnt altered their views about the ways Sundays are spent? Is there one day in the week that is more special for them than the others? Why?

EXAMPLE 2–RITES OF PASSAGE

Commitment Ceremonies–Confirmation, Believer's Baptism.

a *Statement:* 'Pupils should be taught about the rites of passage in religions. Any study should include:
  i Knowledge of what happens in the ceremony.

   ii Understanding of the symbols and the meanings of the promises made.

   iii Understanding why there is a diversity of practice within different traditions.

   iv Evaluation of the importance of the ritual and issues arising out of the study.'[3]

b *Concepts:* Initiation, Ritual.

c *Experience:* Write an account of when they joined something new, eg Scouts/Guides, new school, team. What did they actually do to join?

d *Content:* Confirmation; laying on of hands, wearing of special clothes, repeating of vows.

Believer's baptism; immersion in the water, statement of faith.

e *Beliefs:* Salvation, the Holy Spirit.

f *Biographical Illustrations:* Sarah's confirmation and Anne's Baptism accounts, as told in the Lion Publishing book, *Christianity Explored*[4] and Chris's Baptism as related in The Westhill Project 5-16: Christianity 3'.[5]

In groups the pupils should explain:

   i The reasons they gave for taking part in the ceremonies.

   ii What happened in the ceremonies.

   iii The meaning of the symbolism.

   iv Why they took part in different ceremonies.

g *Understanding:* In spite of outward differences, what was in essence the same about both the ceremonies? Make a Venn diagram to show the similarities and differences.

h *Reflection:* Think of all the occasions in every day life when they make a new start. What things symbolise that new start? For example, new subject–new book, new day–waking up, new page to write on. How important are new beginnings and why?

FOOTNOTES

[1] *Oxfordshire: The Agreed Syllabus,* (Unpublished: Oxford, 1992) p43.

2 Brenda Courtie and Margaret Johnson, *Christianity Explored* (Lion Publishing plc: Oxford, 1990) p164.

3 Oxfordshire op cit p44.

4 Courtie op cit pp156-157.

5 Garth Read et al, *The Westhill Project RE 5-16: Christians 3* (Mary Glasgow Publications Limited: London, 1987) p51.

6 John Rudge, *Assessing, Recording and Reporting RE: A Handbook for Teachers* (Westhill College: Birmingham, 1991) p67.

24 | ASSESSMENT IN RELIGIOUS EDUCATION

Fred Hughes

SUMMARY

This article begins with a brief explanation of the two frequently used terms–'Assessment' and 'Attainment Targets'. It then summarises the attainment targets designed by the Westhill Project and the FARE Project (Forms of Assessment in Religious Education). The wide variety of ways in which pupils' work in Religious Education can be assessed are explored and the possibility of using ten levels to assess and record pupils' achievements in the attainment targets is discussed. Finally, guidelines for assessment are suggested.

DEFINING ASSESSMENT AND ATTAINMENT TARGETS

Assessment refers to the task of making a judgment on progress and achievement based on evidence.[1] The main purposes of assessment are: formative, diagnostic, summative and evaluative.[2] *Formative* assessment is meant to assess achievement in a way that helps towards the next steps in learning. It guides and motivates. *Diagnostic* assessment is meant to clarify any learning difficulties and to identify areas that need particular attention through appropriate remedial help. Both of these kinds of assessment look backwards and forwards.

Summative assessment is about pupil achievement and occurs at the conclusion of a course or component. In *evaluative* assessment the focus is more on the quality of learning experiences offered than on students' achievement. In both of these kinds of assessment the focus is more backwards than forwards, though of course there can be some implications for the future.

Attainment Targets are broad learning objectives for a subject. They are often stated in terms of knowledge, understanding and skills to be developed.

Every thoughtful Religious Education teacher knows how difficult it is to mark or assess some kinds of Religious Education work. For example it can be difficult to judge the religious value of drawing, models, drama and role play. Publications on assessment in RE can seem of limited value to the busy teacher if they can not be related to such practical issues.

This article seeks to relate some recent developments and documents to the work of secondary Religious Education teachers. Some of the difficulties arise because teachers are unsure of just what they should be looking for. If we can clarify what objectives or targets are appropriate, that should help to give usable criteria for assessment.

ATTAINMENT TARGETS

The Westhill Project was supported by about thirty English local education authorities and based at Westhill College, Birmingham. It published its first handbook in 1989.[3] This handbook describes ten attainment targets, grouped into three profile components. This was later reduced to three attainment targets:
– Reflecting, responding and expressing
– Awareness of life experiences and the questions they raise
– Understanding religious beliefs and practices[4]
Seven local education authorities in the south west of England (plus Guernsey) were involved in the FARE Project between 1989 and 1991. It was based at Exeter University. The main report (1991) describes two attainment targets:
1 Reflection on meaning
2 Knowledge and understanding of religion
The attainment targets proposed by both of these projects

indicate that RE is concerned both with grasping the facts of religious belief and practice and with developing a capacity for personal reflection and response. These are sometimes called the cognitive and affective aspects (though clearly these aspects are not entirely separate in the lives of individuals). This distinction can be useful when a particular piece of pupil work is being assessed, such as a piece of written work, a dramatic presentation or a model. This basic distinction may be more useful when considering an individual piece of work than the complex description of ten levels given for example in the FARE Project Main Report.[5]

DIFFERENT KINDS OF ASSESSMENT

In the past, some Religious Education has relied too heavily on tightly prescribed pupil tasks which require reading and writing to develop and demonstrate knowledge and understanding. This approach, valid in its place, is too limiting if over used. First, over reliance on reading and writing hampers progress for the pupils who have particular difficulty with them. Also of course, cognitive and affective development are not entirely dependent on ability in reading and writing. Second, over-structuring the responses required from pupils can drown creativity and impede the development of some skills which need a wider range of activities. Third, over-reliance on assessment of written work results in potentially misleading assessment. This is because it fails to take account of the fact that some significant learning and achievement in Religious Education can occur through activities other than reading and writing.

Some Religious Education teachers now employ a wide range of pupil activities and a wide range of assessment methods. Group work and peer group assessment is one example. Pupil self-assessment is another and can be used for written work as well as many other kinds of work. This is sometimes related to a whole school profiling scheme. Another example is the use of questionnaires at the beginning and end of a component or of diaries kept over a period of time. Some of these may give more evidence about pupils' knowledge and understanding than reflection and response or vice versa. This shows the importance of using a range of means of assessment over a period of time if an accurate picture is to emerge.

Constant use of assessment sheets, by teachers and/or pupils, is likely to be burdensome and possibly distracting from the progress needed. On the other hand, moderate use of such sheets can stimulate valuable reflection and inform the assessment process, so examples are included at the end of this article.

The FARE Project Main Report gives twelve examples of different forms of assessment for Key Stage 3 and sixteen for Key Stage 4. All these were used by teachers during the life of the project. Readers wanting further ideas to consider trying themselves are referred to these examples.[5]

TEN LEVELS?

There have been attempts to demonstrate how pupils' achievements in Religious Education can be assessed according to ten levels of achievement.[6] Most Religious Education Agreed Syllabuses do not expect teachers to assess pupils' achievement on a ten level scale. Two of the notable exceptions to this are the Kent and Suffolk Agreed Syllabuses. Some people doubt whether this degree of precision is desirable or can actually be done with accuracy. The model syllabuses acknowledge this.[7]

Even if these misgivings can be overcome, there is the important question of whether or not Religious Education teachers have available the necessary time to operate such a sophisticated system, especially if they teach three or four hundred pupils a week (or even more!) Perhaps teachers do have the necessary time if they are expected to assess pupils according to these levels only once a year.

The FARE Report acknowledges that pupils' achievements in the two attainment targets may not progress at the same rate and suggests that in such cases achievement should be reported separately and not aggregated. Avoiding aggregation relieves teachers of an extremely difficult task, but it increases the need to explain carefully to parents and others what precisely is being reported.

PRACTICAL APPLICATION

In summative and evaluative assessment, it is crucial to refer to the relevant attainment targets. With these in mind, judgments can be made about pupil achievement over a substantial period of time and about the quality of a course which aspires to enhance the development stated in the targets.

The weekly, if not daily, concern of practising teachers is with formative and diagnostic assessment. These are intended to give frequent indications of pupil achievement and short term goals. Attainment targets sometimes help but may not be specific enough to guide assessment of particular pieces of work.

Dilemmas and hesitations easily arise when assessing particular pieces of work. Some RE teachers avoid grading most work on the grounds that giving grades can be de-motivating, controversial, insensitive and more precise than is justified. For those who provide only comments and those who give grades it is enormously helpful to be clear about the learning objectives for pupil tasks.

Among valid intentions for a task might be one or more of the following:
1) to help the pupils increase their knowledge and understanding in some specific area, including sometimes increasing their understanding of concepts (eg creation, prayer, miracle).
2) to help them think about an issue (eg the ordination of women priests, abortion) by grasping various arguments.
3) to help them reflect on, form and express their own beliefs on a religious matter (eg belief in God, life after death etc).

With such objectives in mind, the teacher can set appropriate tasks and use the objectives when assessing particular pieces of work. It is possible to design more detailed assessment criteria. Sometimes it is uncertainty about how to assess work which makes the teacher realise that the learning objectives were not clear to the teacher and therefore not to the pupils either. If the teacher adopts the practice of explaining to pupils the point of the task, this exerts a helpful discipline on the teacher.

This means that crucial questions need to be asked: 'What was the teacher looking for?' or 'What did the teacher hope the pupils would achieve?' and 'How well has this pupil responded to the task set?' and 'What evidence is there to show the extent to which this pupil has achieved the learning objectives?'. It is unfair to set tasks without deciding their educational purpose and sharing this with the pupils or to assess their work by different criteria or no criteria at all. The pupils are helped when teachers are open and specific about objectives and when they have some clear reference points when assessing work.

The following assessment, marketing and reporting policy illustrates some of these points. It has been written by Maureen Collins for Bramcote Park School, Nottingham. The policy is followed by a selection of attainment and assessment record sheets taken from the non-statutory guidance of the Gloucestershire Agreed syllabus of Religious Education.

FOOTNOTES

[1] *RE, Attainment and National Curriculum* (RE Council of England and Wales: Lancaster, 1991) p 50.

[2] P J Black, *National Curriculum Task Group on Assessment and Testing–A Report* (DES: London,1987) paras 23-29.

[3] *Attainment in RE: A Handbook for Teachers* (Westhill College: Birmingham, 1989).

[4] *Assessing, Recording and Reporting RE: A Handbook for Teachers* (Westhill College: Birmingham, 1991).

[5] *Forms of Assessment in Religious Education, FARE Project Main Report* (University of Exeter: Exeter, 1991) The Key Stage 3 examples are on pages 187-239, and the Key Stage 4 examples are on pages 241-296.

6 Forms of Assessment in Religious Education, FARE Project Main Report (University of Exeter: Exeter, 1991) pp 23-32.
7 *Model Syllabuses for Religious Education* (School Curriculum and Assessment Authority: London, 1994).

BRAMCOTE PARK SCHOOL, NOTTINGHAM RELIGIOUS STUDIES– ASSESSMENT, MARKETING AND REPORTING

Maureen Collins

The Religious Studies Department would rather not 'assess for assessment's sake', but realises that clear records of how a pupil is progressing are important for the following reasons:

a) to encourage the child when they show improvement.
b) to identify problems where improvement is needed.
c) to help the child see their realistic position so that they can set targets for their own progress.

Although 'marks' are sometimes essential, it is felt that comments in the pupils' books are more constructive because the route to improvement can be made clear. A number or letter mark may have very little meaning to a pupil. The comment should encourage and motivate the pupil wherever possible. Pupils' books are marked regularly with appropriate written comments.

In Lower School, where a mark is given it will usually be out of ten. Each term a piece of work is selected as an 'assessment' and a differentiated mark scheme is produced for this. Special care is taken with the marking and recording here, and marks out of twenty are passed to the Head of Department.

In Years 10 & 11, GCSE folders are marked regularly with comments. Essays and practice exam questions are set, and marked out of twenty. Course work is set and marked as defined in the MEG RS Syllabus.

In Years 12 & 13 files need to be checked from time to time to make sure that pupils' work is up to date. Collation and research of information needs to be checked. Regular homework, including exam style essays are set and marked. The writing of the extended essay is carefully monitored.

In all years homework is set, and marked, regularly. Pupils are encouraged to achieve their personal best in presentation. Non-written work such as drama, discussion or posters can also be assessed and their own assessment scheme developed. Staff keep their own record of marks given, but assessment marks are passed onto the Head of Department, who, therefore develops an overview. Each pupil in each class has an assessment record sheet for Years 7, 8 and 9 which contains negotiated statements and sets targets for improvement. This can be used by staff in records of achievement and reporting.

Staff are expected to write reports, following the Records of Achievement and Pastoral guidelines. They should be clearly understandable to parent and pupil. They should be positive; giving encouragement and targeting specific areas for improvement. Homework, behaviour and attainment should be made clear—albeit in positive terms! The following qualities are particularly relevant in RS: understanding, maturity and appreciation/tolerance of others' views.

This document fully backs the rewards system and every opportunity is taken to give credits when they are due. It is felt important to reward effort, as well as attainment and helpfulness (especially unsolicited!).

R.E. Record of Attainment Class .... Study Unit	Willingness to join in discussion	Readiness to listen to others	Readiness to bring items for display	Interest in asking & answering questions	Quality of written and practical work	Ability to concentrate	Sensitivity to others' feelings	Research skills	Recall of things seen & heard	Ability to reflect on new ideas	Assessment activities	End of unit assessment sheet

Thinking about my work

Study Unit: ....   Name: ....

What do I remember most?	What did I do best?	One thing I have learned that I didn't know before
What did I find the hardest thing to do?	**What did I enjoy best and why?**	**What did I not enjoy and why?**

A picture of something I will always remember from this unit

How well did I work?

....

Study Unit: .... Name: ....

	!	?	*
I think I worked well during this unit			
I was tidy and neat in all my work			
I helped the people I was working with			
I listened carefully when my teacher told me what to do			
I listened carefully when other children were talking			
My finished work in this unit was . . .			

Key

! Not very well/Not very good

? Some of the time/Quite good

* Very well/Very good

My Standard of Work Report

· ·

Study Unit: .... Name: ....

A = **Excellent**   I worked as hard as I possibly could
B = **Good**   I did work very hard
C = **Satisfactory**   I put in an average amount of effort
D = **Poor**   I believe I could have worked a lot harder
E = **Very weak**   I did not really try at all

1 The things I did for this unit were

_____

I would give myself the following grade for effort

_____

My group gave me the following grade for effort

_____

2 I did these things at home

_____

I would give myself the following grade for homework

_____

3 What I think about the final presentation of my work

_____

I would give myself the following grade for my finished work

_____

4 My mark in the test was   _____

Comment

_____

5 What I enjoyed most about this unit was

_____

_____

6 This unit could have been better if

_____

_____

My Study Unit Review

....

Study Unit: .... Name: ....

My comments about this Study Unit

What I liked best

_____

_____

Why?

_____

_____

What I did not like

_____

_____

Why?

_____

_____

What I did well

_____

_____

New things I learned

_____

_____

Looking through my work I need to

_____

_____

For this unit I would give myself

My poorest work 1 2 3 4 5 6 7 8 9 10 My best work

Study Unit Review

....

Study Unit: .... Name: ....

Group: .... Date: ....

organisation and attitude:

	always	usually	sometimes	rarely
1 I worked to the best of my ability				
2 I brought the necessary equipment				
3 I took great care with presentation				
4 I completed homework with care				
5 I worked well by myself				
6 I worked well with others				

pupil comment:

I enjoyed most of all

I have improved at

I am most pleased with

I found difficulty with

In the next unit I hope to

general comments by pupil:

pupil signature ————————————

teacher comment on skills:

	very capable	coped adequately	needed some help	needed considerable help
1 Finding information				
2 Creative writing				
3 Discussion skills				
4 Using religious terms and language				
5 Knowledge of religious practices and beliefs				
6 Forming and supporting an opinion				
general comments by teacher:				

a target area for consideration in the next Study Unit could be:

————————————————————————

—————————————————————— teacher signature

R.E. Annual Review

••

Name: .... Date: ....

Class: ....

1 STUDY UNITS covered this year

_____

_____

2 Which aspects of the work gave you most satisfaction?

_____

_____

3 Which aspect of the work gave the most difficulty?

_____

_____

4 Did you find it easy to join in discussions? Why/Why not?

_____

_____

5 What useful information and ideas did you gain?

_____

_____

6 How did you cope with the homework tasks?

_____

_____

7 How well did you work in groups?

_____

_____

8 Comment on your grades and marks

_____

_____

9 What do you need to give greater attention to?

_____

_____

10 Comment on your feelings about R.E. next year

_____

_____

25 EXAMINATION WORK
Clive Tougher

SUMMARY

This article recognises the problems some schools face in making Religious Studies a viable examination option, but suggests that the time may be right to press our case. It also sets out a plan of action for establishing or strengthening an RS Examination Course and looks at ways of delivering it.

Speaking to the SACRE Forum in Birmingham in March 1993, David Pascall, then chairman of the English National Curriculum Council, commended the use of GCSE as an effective way of delivering Religious Education. He suggested that it would encourage better motivation and raise standards among the pupils, and might ultimately help to create more specialist teachers in Religious Education. In Scotland the increasing use of the certificated short courses offered by the Scottish Examination Board to replace 'general RE' indicates he may be correct in this Judgment.

In England, Wales and Northern Ireland national GCSE examinations, designated as Religious Studies, have been provided for many years by a number of different boards. In Scotland, the Religious Studies Ordinary Grade examination has been phased out alongside the introduction of the new Standard Grade exam. Some schools have enjoyed a steady flow of entrants but many more have been squeezed by a competitive 'optional system' only to see enthusiastic pupils channelled into more 'important' or 'useful' subjects.

It is important to offer examination courses in RS to students in their final years of compulsory schooling for the following reasons: Firstly, as long as the secondary sector of our schools remains geared to the awarding of some kind of national recognised qualification or assessment, it is clear that the esteem of a subject will be related to the quality and numbers of the candidates who take part. Secondly, a well-constructed programme of study during a pupil's final years at school provides a valuable starting point for entry into the adult world. Last, but by no means least, it challenges all Religious Education teachers to be as professional and as rigorous as any other subject on the school curriculum. Increasingly, assessment is at the top of the educational agenda providing an opportunity which Religious Education teachers should seize. National policy is clear that Religious Education should have a significant place in the school curriculum, but the responsibility rests with local teachers to deliver it.

The following suggestions for implementing examination work may provide a new base for the school Religious Education programme, or a means of strengthening an established course:

PLAN OF ACTION

1 Carefully scrutinise the examination courses on offer. Most Boards have subject officers who will be able to answer enquiries. Base your final decision on staffing expertise and the social and cultural character of the school catchment area. The following are questions to be answered when deciding between the available options:
   – Which religion/religions are to be studied?
   – Does it involve a study of texts or a religion?
   – Does it concentrate on moral/ethical issues?
   – What is the role of coursework?
2 Discuss the programme and all the options available with colleagues who will be teaching the course to gain their support.
3 Submit the proposed course of study, with supporting arguments, to the Head and School Curriculum committee.

4 If the initial reply is sympathetic, arrange a meeting with the Head to discuss staffing requirements, timetable allocation, adequate resources.

5 Examine the implications of the proposed examination course for the overall school Religious Education programme, including timetable space, out of school fieldwork, internal assessment etc.

6 At least six or seven months ahead prepare the final scheme for implementation, giving adequate time to finalise planning and anticipate possible snags.

7 Use school communication network to inform governors, parents and other non-Religious Education staff.

UNDERSTANDING EXAMINATION CRITERIA

The successful delivery of Religious Studies depends, to a large extent, on the teacher's ability to understand the criteria which govern the structure and organisation of the course. According to the current national criteria for GCSE Religious Studies (applying to examinations sat from summer 1996 onwards) any syllabus must demonstrate the candidates' knowledge and understanding of:

1 The key elements of religion(s) studied including beliefs, practices, sources of authority and organisation;

2 The effect of religion(s) on individual or corporate moral behaviour, attitudes, social practices and lifestyles.

They also require candidates to produce evidence and arguments to support and evaluate points of view.

At the time of writing the exam boards are just publishing their new syllabuses which conform to these criteria. At the same time there is still heated debate as to whether the new criteria represent an educationally adequate approach to Religious Studies. No doubt this debate about the new criteria will continue for some time.

All examination syllabuses must conform to the national criteria and assessment objectives. GCSE places greater emphasis on understanding and evaluative skills than GCE/ CSE did. The introduction of an element of course work marked a move away from the examination-led syllabus. It is to be hoped that this will not be lost in future changes.

The Scottish Standard Grade Examination consists of four units which all pupils have to study. The 'Christianity' and 'Second Religion' are based on the study of key concepts. The 'Issues of Belief' and 'Issues of Morality' units are designed to help pupils appreciate the relation between belief and practice. The three assessable elements in the exam are identified as K, U and E (Knowledge, Understanding and Evaluation). There is also an Investigation which every student has to complete and which parallels the requirement for GCSE coursework. The purpose of this is to encourage students to grapple with a religious issue rather than to generate vast amounts of information. The topics chosen must therefore relate to issues of belief and morality.

At the moment there are variations among the examining groups and boards–for example, coursework weighting and the number of assignments. It is also worth noting that in response to the demands of the National Curriculum several examination boards are submitting both long and short course syllabuses for examination in 1996. From that date all coursework will be standardised at 20% of the marks awarded. The revised criteria for GCSE Religious Studies also require that candidates be entered for one of three tiers of assessment according to ability. All examination syllabuses will continue to test the extent to which pupils are able to show what they know, what they understand and what they are able to evaluate on the basis of argument.

The significance of these three terms, in this context, needs to be clearly understood.

KNOWLEDGE

Candidates must be able to do more than select and present relevant factual information in an organised manner. This means that pupils must demonstrate the ability to select information relevant to the task and then organise and present that material as a coherent whole.

UNDERSTANDING

Pupils must be able to show an ability to explain why things are done in a certain way; analysing, interpreting and applying facts, ideas and beliefs. They must also be able to differentiate their own response from that of others and appreciate the differences.

EVALUATION

This requires pupils to make informed and sensitive judgments, on the basis of evidence and argument, about issues of belief and practice arising from the study of religion. They are required to assess the arguments, defend a judgment and present valid reasons for their own opinions.

EXAMINATION WEAKNESSES

Examination Board Reports have highlighted the fact that pupils tend to do better in answering questions on Knowledge and Understanding than on Evaluation. Many pupils find it difficult to formulate coherent arguments and give reasons for or against belief and practice. They can often state a point of view but then fail to develop their ideas, support opinions or reach a judgment based on reasoned arguments.

The coursework/investigation element has also proved contentious in that some less able pupils appear unable to deal with it, while other pupils receive an unfair amount of help with it. Coursework 'cheating' is also difficult to identify and deal with unless the work is classroom based and under direct supervision.

MONITORING THE PROGRAMME

Once your programme is in place, you will need to hold regular departmental meetings to monitor progress and maintain careful liaison with your chosen examination board in order to become familiar with their requirements. Most of them hold periodic meetings to assist teachers with this. It is also important to keep the Head briefed on progress by providing concise, informative reports and you must keep precise records of pupil performance, especially in relation to coursework and internal assessments. Finally, monitor performance in 'mock' examinations as a basis for examination entries. On completion of the course and receipt of external examination results, arrange a department meeting to evaluate progress.

SETTING K, U AND E TASKS

Some teachers have experienced difficulty in setting appropriate K, U and E tasks. Examining Boards have been quick to point this out. The following lists provide some opening statements and leading questions which may prove useful starting points in setting pupil exercises.

KNOWLEDGE

Imagine...
Write an account of...
Identify...
Describe...
Name...
What is...?

UNDERSTANDING

Explain the significance of...
Why...?
What reasons...?
Comment on...
How does...?
Explain the purpose of...

EVALUATION

Give your opinion on...
How relevant is...
What arguments...
Consider...
What do you think...?
How would you justify...?
Do you agree...?

EXAMINATION BOARD ADDRESSES

- –Northern Examination and Assessment Board: Devas Street, Manchester M15 6EX
- –Northern Ireland Schools Examination Council: Beechill House, Beechill Road, Belfast BT8 4RS
- –Midland Examination Group: Purbeck House, Purbeck Road, Cambridge CB2 2PU
- –Scottish Examination Board: Ironmills Road, Dalkeith, Midlothian, EH22 1LE
- –Southern Examining Group: c/o Associated Examining Board for GCSE, Stag Hill House, Guildford GU2 5XJ
- –London and East Anglia Group: c/o London Regional Examining Board, Stewart House, 32 Russell Square, London WC1B 5DN
- –Welsh Joint Education Committee: 245 Western Avenue, Cardiff, CF5 2YX.

26 | RECORDS OF ACHIEVEMENT
Fred Hughes

SUMMARY

This article begins with a brief history of some recent developments concerning Records of Achievement and then relates these to Religious Education. It concludes with a discussion of questions raised by profiling methods.

RECENT DEVELOPMENTS

The Department for Education published circular 14/92 in December 1992. It was entitled 'Reports on Individual Pupil's Achievements' and referred to new Regulations which came into force on 4th January 1993. They apply to all registered pupils in county, voluntary, maintained special and grant maintained schools in England except pupils in nursery schools or nursery classes.[1] These developments were not altogether new or unexpected. For several years many local education authorities and schools have been developing their own arrangements for profiling and records of achievement.

The key changes required by the new Regulations are as follows:

1 Schools have to provide more detailed information for parents about their children's school progress and about their children's contemporaries' performance in the same school and nationally. This was a commitment made in the Parents Charter.[2]
2 Compulsory provision by schools to school-leavers of a National Record of Achievement (NRA).

3 Compulsory transfer of records of attainment when a pupil moves school.

The NRA is summative. This means it is issued to pupils around the end of National Curriculum Year 11. However it is intended to be the product of a process of review, negotiation and planning and based on a portfolio of collected evidence of past achievements. The NRA is a summary of achievement in a national format. A leaflet for pupils says the NRA is 'presented in a prestigious burgundy folder'![3] Readers who have seen it will appreciate this description.

The NRA is meant to strengthen pupils' self-confidence. Another audience is prospective employers and the NRA is meant to help ensure applicants are given credit for all their strengths and achievements. The intention was to record achievement increasingly in terms of attainment on the ten level National Curriculum scale. General Certificate of Secondary Education results were due on this scale from summer 1994 but a decision in spring 1993 removed this, and the government accepted the recommendation of the Dearing Report[4] that the A*-G scale should be retained for GCSE examinations.

PROFILING, RECORDS OF ACHIEVEMENT AND RELIGIOUS EDUCATION

The requirements about reporting pupils' achievements are too many to report here. However, Religious Education is involved in the process in a number of ways.

First, the mandatory reports to parents must include 'brief particulars of a pupil's progress in subjects and activities studied as part of the school curriculum and the results of any public exam entered...'.[5] Similar statements must be contained in reports to school leavers (NRA).[6] Religious Education is included in this because it has to be provided for all registered pupils at maintained schools, except where parents request that their children be withdrawn.

Circular 14/92 explains what is meant by 'brief particulars' of a pupil's progress. It says ' "brief particulars" are likely to take the form of a short commentary on the pupil's progress in the subject or activity concerned, highlighting strengths and particular achievements and identifying any particular weaknesses' .[7]

In order to give meaningful commentaries and statements of achievement in reports to parents and school leavers, teachers, including Religious Education teachers, need to give careful attention to assessment and record keeping throughout each school year. Some profiling systems are designed to provide such information.

Where pupils take GCSE Religious Studies that has to be included in reports to parents and new school leavers. This is because the new Regulations say that results of public examinations have to be included.

Secondly, although the National Record of Achievement is summative, it is meant to draw on a record of achievement built up during the secondary school years. Many schools developed a profiling system in the 1980s. Religious Education was often included and frequently still is. Through the profiling system pupils and teachers review achievement and negotiate agreed targets for future learning. A key aspect of this process is that pupils, in dialogue with teachers, agree a record of achievements, including grades and targets for future learning. Opinions vary as to whether these pupil-teacher interviews or discussions are appropriate strategies or unrealistic dogmas.

DEBATING THE ISSUES RAISED BY PROFILING AND RECORDS OF ACHIEVEMENT

Benefits

The supposed benefits of profiling may be summarised as follows:
- Profiling provides a detailed, ongoing and comprehensive picture of each student by recording information about a broad range of their activities both inside and outside the institution.

This is intended to give a more accurate picture than may be the case with more traditional and occasional teacher-written reports for parents, employers etc.

- It helps students to make progress in their learning by identifying targets and by relating regular reviews of students' achievements to the targets.
- The conversations between students and teachers, necessitated by the profiling process enhance the student-teacher relationship and this can pay dividends in terms of the students' learning achievements.
- Profiling enables students to express their views about their performance and about appropriate learning targets and grades.

The potential benefits for students are claimed to be in terms of their increased motivation and interest, because they are more involved in decisions which intimately affect them both during and after their course.

- Profiling also has advantages for those responsible for managing and implementing the curriculum, because it provides fuller and more accurate information on student performance than has previously been available. Profiling can also be a means of developing teaching methods.

Questions

A number of issues have arisen through the experience of schools which have been using profiling. In order to help provoke thought, I have expressed them as questions without assuming particular answers. Some of these are set out below:

1 How detailed should any profile system be? When something is currently fashionable it is possible to launch initiatives that soon become unworkable. Schemes which are over elaborate at the design stage and impossible to implement in practice are useless.

2 The availability of time is a crucial aspect. Will profiling interrupt teaching time? Is it essential to give time to profiling interviews or could these be optional? If the pressures on staff

time are too great will the intended benefits for student-teacher relationships be lost?

3 Where teachers invite students to say what grade they think is appropriate for a piece of work, are students usually reluctant to suggest a high grade–because to do so seems arrogant or proud? Is the student/teacher interview ever a fair match? At the end of the day, when there is disagreement about a comment or grade, will the teacher's view always prevail? Where there is a difference of view would it sometimes be right to record both the student's and the teacher's perceptions?

4 To what extent can profiling deliver its intention of providing more accurate (truthful?) records of achievement? Sometimes it is regarded as important to record only positive statements about achievement. Can such a policy be justified? What is the appropriate relationship between formative profiling and summative records of achievement? Once recipients of records of achievement know the policy has been to make only positive statements will they be eager to 'read between the lines' and 'wonder what has been filtered out'?

5 Is profiling a long-winded system? Is a longer statement necessarily more informative? Might teacher statements about achievement be more succinct than student statements and therefore more likely to be read?

6 Does profiling suit some subject areas or methods of approach better than others? Is profiling particularly helpful in Religious Education, because the development of students' viewpoints is an integral part of it, which means that self-assessment and dialogue with the teacher are highly appropriate learning activities?

7 Does reducing students' achievements in Religious Education to specific statements diminish the profound nature of Religious Education or enhance it because achievement is taken seriously?

8 Should different subjects have the same style profile documents in order to aid comprehension? Alternatively, do dif-

ferent subjects have differing rationales and therefore require profile documents designed for each subject?

9 What factors influence the selection of appropriate targets for pupils' future learning? Is review of progress related to targets a valid and necessary part of the learning process or can it be seen as a means by which teachers seek to control students?

CONCLUSION

It is important for Religious Education teachers to be flexible in the assessment procedures they use. Using a variety of assessment methods helps teachers obtain a range of evidence about achievement, and helps to keep teachers and pupils motivated and alert.

FOOTNOTES

[1] Recent developments in Northern Ireland, Scotland and Wales are detailed in the relevant circulars of which the following are examples. In Northern Ireland, two of the relevant departmental circulars are *Recording and Reporting Individual Pupils' Achievements* (circular 1991/39) and *Annual Reports and Records of Achievement* (June 1992). In Scotland, the Scottish Education Department Circular 7/92 *Guidelines on Reporting 5-14* was published in November 1992. In Wales, the Welsh Office Circular 69/92 *Reporting Pupils' Achievements* was published in January 1993.

[2] *The Parents Charter: You and Your Child's Education*.

[3] *National Record of Achievement—Introduction for Young People* (NRA Unit: London, 1992).

[4] *The National Curriculum and Its Assessment* (School Curriculum and Assessment Authority: London, 1993).

[5] *Reports on Individual Pupils' Achievements* (Department for Education: London, December 1992) Circular 14/92, p8, para 13.

[6] ibid p15, para 16.

[7] *Reports on Individual Pupils' Achievements* (Department for Education: London, December 1992) Circular 14/92, p8, para 13.

ACKNOWLEDGEMENT

Thanks are expressed to Tony Comber, Co-ordinator of Vocational Education, Churchdown School, Gloucester for his advice and for his support in providing Fred Hughes with opportunities to explore the development of the profiling system in Churchdown School.

BIBLIOGRAPHY

REVIEW OF RESOURCES

The following bibliography aims to provide teachers with a brief summary of some Religious Education resources. This is not a comprehensive list—the sections for 'Stories and Anthologies' and 'Biographies' in particular, represent only a small proportion of the books available. The reviews are intended to be descriptive rather than critical. The material, produced during or since 1988, has been categorised under these headings:

Books on Christianity
Books on Other World Religions
Issue or Theme-Based Books
Stories & Anthologies
Biographies

TEXTBOOKS ON CHRISTIANITY

According To Matthew

by RICHARDS, Clare
Nelson Blackie 1989
ISBN: 0 216 92620 3
AGE: Upper Secondary Pupils
Within the framework of four themes: the law, the prophets, the promised deliverer and the community, this book looks at Jesus' life and teaching and links it with today's world by using contemporary photographs. It adopts a liberal approach. It has been written for exam classes and contains suitable activities.

Basic Issues: A Christian View

by RICHARDS, Clare
Nelson Blackie 1990
ISBN:0 216 92893 1
AGE: Upper Secondary Pupils
This book concentrates on fifteen key issues which concern young people and deals in a simplified way, with the Christian attitude to them. These issues include; family and friends, prejudice, feeding and educating the world, addiction and evil, crime and the law. The material is presented attractively and is full of activities and exercises.

Be A Church Detective–A Young Person's Guide To Old Churches

by FEWINS, Clive
The National Society and Church House Publishing 1992
ISBN: 0 7151 4790 0
AGE: Lower Secondary Pupils
Through enthusiasm and cartoons this book aims to bring to life the story of mediaeval churches. It provides facts and details on many aspects of church buildings from their position in the landscape down to (wooden) church mice. Whilst it gives ideas of what to look for in exploring old churches, this book does not provide classroom activities and is definitely an information book for pupils.

Beggars, Beasts and Easter Fire: A Book of Saints and Heroes

by GREENE, Carol
Lion Publishing plc 1993
ISBN: 0 7459 2221

AGE: Secondary Pupils

Twenty stories about heroes and heroines of the Christian faith are recounted in this book. These include Nicholas, Patrick, Teresa and Francis. The historical context of each story is explained and colour illustrations make it attractive.

The Christian Faith In Today's World

by KEENE, Michael
Basil Blackwell Ltd 1990
ISBN: 0 631 90447 6
AGE: Upper Secondary Pupils
As the title suggests this examines the Christian response to controversial issues. Using a variety of source material drawn from real contemporary incidents, this book also aims to encourage students to consider their own response to these problems. These issues include divorce, abortion, AIDS, nuclear weapons and conservation.

Christian Issues In The Gospels

by BROMLEY, Eileen
Stanley Thornes (Publishers) Ltd 1991
ISBN: 0 7487 0582 1
AGE: Upper Secondary Pupils
The contents covered in this book can be divided into the four themes—beliefs, responses, celebrations and concerns. The diversity of Christian practice today is represented in the source material which comes from a broad spectrum of Christian traditions. The wide range of activities that accompany the chapters have been designed to stimulate and encourage discussion and research.

Christianity

by BENTLEY, James and Audrey
Longman Group UK Ltd 1988
ISBN: 0 582 22342 3
AGE: Upper Secondary Pupils
This book explores the origins and teachings of the Christian faith. It covers Church history, forms of worship, the Bible and Christian views on moral issues. Designed for exam classes, it contains questions and ideas for coursework.

Christianity

by CLOSE, Brian E & SMITH, Marion
Hodder & Stoughton 1992
ISBN: 0 340 54692 1
Age: Sixth Form
Designed for sixth form exam students and undergraduates, this book assumes a basic knowledge of Christianity. It concentrates on topics such as the schism between Orthodoxy and Roman Catholicism, the Reformation and events in the twentieth century as well as Jesus and the break with Judaism.

Christianity

by OWEN COLE, W
(World Religions Series), Stanley Thornes 1989
ISBN: 1 871402 08 5
AGE: Upper Secondary Pupils
This book covers Jesus, the spread of Christianity, festivals and forms of worship. It explains Christian beliefs and ethics and relates them to moral and social issues. It is well laid out and provides questions and discussion starters.

Christianity

by JENKINS, Joe
(Examining Religions Series), Heinemann Educational 1989
ISBN: 0 435 30312 0
AGE: Upper Secondary Pupils
This book covers Jesus and the birth of the Church, Christian beliefs, the different Christian denominations, worship, Christian views on modern world problems. Designed for exam groups it provides activities, quotes and illustrations and is attractively laid-out.

Christianity: A Way Of Life

by RICHARDS, Clare and Hubert
Nelson Blackie 1991
ISBN: 0 216 93063 4
AGE: Upper Secondary Pupils
This book has been written to cover material for the Christianity paper of GCSE examinations. It reflects the many facets of the religion through contributions from twenty different people describing what Christian beliefs and values mean to them. The topics covered include

creeds and beliefs, festivals and feast days and Church leaders. Each chapter ends with questions and assignments.

Christianity – An Approach For GCSE

by O'DONNELL, Kevin
Edward Arnold 1988
ISBN: 0 7131 7730 6
AGE: Upper Secondary Pupils
This book contains a considerable amount of factual information on Christianity. It examines beliefs and practices, and their meaning for Christians. A variety of pictures illustrate the text, and questions and suggestions for activity-based learning are provided.

Christianity For GCSE

by MINNEY, Robin
Basil Blackwell 1989
ISBN: 0 630 90149 3
AGE: Upper Secondary Pupils
Christian festivals, forms of worship and rites of passages are explored in this textbook. It explains Christian beliefs and their meaning for Christians, as well as Christians' active role in today's world. Designed for exam classes it gives ideas for group and project work.

Christianity in Today's World

by JENKINS, Simon & SMITH, Linda
BBC Educational Publishing 1992
ISBN: 0 563 34984 0
Age: Secondary
There is also a video which complements this book but they can be used autonomously. The book focuses on Christianity in a worldwide context and particular attention is given to England, Brazil, Italy, South Africa and southern USA. Christian beliefs, spirituality and personal values are just some of the areas explored through a range of activities. The book is colourful and attractive.

The Christian Story

by TAYLOR, James P.
Edward Arnold 1988
ISBN:0 7131 7667 9
AGE: Upper Secondary Pupils

This book examines the history of the Christian Church through describing some of the people and events that have contributed to its development. It begins with looking at the past and present impact of Pentecost and continues by looking at Christianity during the Roman period, through the dark ages to the Reformation. It concludes by looking at recent efforts to 'heal the breach' between different denominations. Each chapter contains black and white photographs and drawings, activities and questions based around the text. Imaginary dialogues between people at various events add an interesting dimension to the book.

Christianity: An Activity and Resource Pack

by BROMLEY, Eileen
Stanley Thornes (Publishers) Ltd 1992
ISBN: 0 7487 1396 4
AGE: Upper Secondary Pupils
The activity sheets, worksheets and resource sheets in this spiral bound pack are photocopiable. All the sheets have been designed to stimulate and interest pupils. The material has been written specifically for examination classes but could also be used for non-exam groups. The subjects covered include: beliefs, the Bible, the history of Christianity, the nature and worship of the Church, festivals and rites of passage.

Christianity Explored

by COURTIE, Brenda & JOHNSON, Margaret
Lion Publishing plc 1990
ISBN: 0 7459 1800 X
Age: Upper Secondary Pupils
Christianity Explored is a textbook specially designed to help teach the requirements of the GCSE exam. Parts of it are also relevant for the Scottish Standard Grade Religious Studies Course. It covers a range of topics including: The Christian Documents, Jesus the Messiah, Pentecost and after, Christian Teaching, and Creeds and Councils. The book is illustrated with black and white photographs and line drawings.

Christianity Is Born–A Creative Approach To The Acts Of The Apostles

by TAYLOR, James P
St Paul Publications 1988

ISBN: 0 85439 275 0
AGE: Secondary Pupils
This book explores the foundation of Christianity as described by the evangelist Luke. Imaginary documents, stories, dialogues, dramatic readings and plays are included in the chapters as well as questions on the Biblical passages concerned.

Christianity: A Living Faith

by WINTERSGILL, Barbara
Macmillan Education Ltd 1989
ISBN: 0 333 37644 7
AGE: Upper Secondary Pupils
This book aims to inform exam candidates as well as encourage activity-based learning. It achieves this through exercises on the text, photograph analysis and 'learning by thinking'. It contains suggestions for original and creative coursework. The subjects covered include the Christian family–then and now, sacraments and ceremonies of commitment, the Christian year, worship, pilgrimage and living a Christian life. Christian response to the world of work, war and peace and health and wholeness is also examined.

Christianity–A Pictorial Guide

by East Sussex RE Advisory Service
Christian Education Movement 1988
ISBN: 1 85100 045 3
AGE: Secondary Pupils
This pictorial guide includes illustrations of church buildings, sacraments, vestments, Christian symbols, the Church Year, some Christian denominations, the stations of the cross and some places of pilgrimage.

Clues and Choices–New Testament

by Copley, Terence
Religious and Moral Education Press 1993
ISBN: 0 900274 57 3
AGE: Upper Secondary Pupils
In providing an introduction to Biblical interpretation, this examines the following five Bible stories: The Virgin Birth, The Feeding of The Five Thousand, The Man Called Legion, The Riddle of the Coins, and The Resurrection of Jesus. In each case the Bible story is told and then historic background information is provided in an interesting way

bringing the story alive for the reader. These notes and ideas are interspersed with questions and topics for discussion in the classroom.

Considering Meaning

by GREEN, Janet
Bible Society 1989
ISBN: 0 564 05315 5
AGE: Secondary Pupils
This book examines the nature of the Bible, taking the Gospels as a major example. It looks at what the writers were trying to achieve and includes lots of investigation tasks and activities. It is an attractive resource, well laid out with plenty of illustrations.

Considering Origins

by GREEN, Janet
Bible Society 1989
ISBN: 0 564 05315 5
AGE: Secondary Pupils
Looking at how the Bible came into being, how it has reached us, and what we can deduce about its contents. This book studies questions of truth, bias, evidence and honest reporting. It includes lots of investigation tasks and activities and is attractively designed.

SERIES: Exploring Christianity

by WINDSOR, Gwyneth & HUGHES, John
Heinemann Educational 1990
AGE: Lower Secondary Pupils
The design, colour and illustrations make the books in this series an attractive resource for the classroom. They have been written for lower secondary age providing a foundation for examination work. The books provide information and accompanying activities for a wide spectrum of themes and encourage an active learning approach with ideas on group work, drama, role play and using information technology.

Exploring Christianity: Worship & Festivals

ISBN: 0 435 30273 6
This book looks at the family of God, rites of passage, the Christian year and ways of worshipping.

Exploring Christianity: The Bible and Christian Belief

ISBN: 0 435 30271 X

This book explains how the Bible came about, what it says, basic Christian beliefs and presents some of the Christian churches.

Exploring Christianity: Jesus and the Birth of the Church

ISBN: 0 435 30270 1

The life of Christ, the beginning of Christianity and how it spread throughout the world are the topics covered in this book.

Exploring Christianity: Christian Life, Personal & Social Issues

ISBN: 0 435 30272 8

This book explores how Christians face life and how they respond to contemporary personal and social issues.

Faith in History

by COOLING, Margaret
Eagle 1994
ISBN: 086 347 106 4
AGE: Lower Secondary Pupils

Offering ideas for RE, history and assemblies, this book explores the way Christianity and history have been entwined in Great Britain. It has been divided into the following topics; Romans, Saxons and Vikings, Tudors and Stuarts, Victorian Britain, Britain since 1930 and Churches Through the Ages. The book contains background information, source material, practical activity suggestions and photocopiable elements.

Faith and Struggle in Central America

- Resource pack for teachers and pupils
Christian Aid & Cafod 1989
ISBN: Not applicable
AGE: Upper Secondary Pupils

This pack contains several posters reflecting life in South America. It also contains three worksheets, one addressing the problems of land and justice in El Salvador and the Christian response. Another looks at the attempt to build a new society in Nicaragua and the third looks at Christian base communities. The sheets help pupils to relate the problems of these countries through different activities such as role play, as well as supplying a lot of basic facts and information.

Feasting for Festivals

by WILSON, Jan
Lion Publishing plc 1990
ISBN: 0 7324 0191 9
AGE: Teacher Reference Book
This book looks at different recipes, activities and crafts that are associated with the different festivals in the Christian year. The recipes, collected from many different parts of the world are explained clearly and presented colourfully and attractively.

The Final Journey

by MILNE, Charmian
Religious and Moral Education Press
ISBN: 0 900274 98 0
AGE: Lower Secondary Pupils
This Easter play, designed to be performed in the classroom, recounts the events leading up to and following the death and resurrection of Jesus. As well as the script, the book includes notes for teachers describing in more detail how it might be used and suggesting a range of classroom activities.

The Gospels–A GCSE Activity Pack

by BROMLEY, Eileen
Stanley Thornes (publishers) Ltd 1988
ISBN: 1 871402 01 8
AGE: Upper Secondary Pupils
The activity sheets, worksheets and resource sheets come in a spiral bound book and are photocopiable. The Biblical passages set for the exams are arranged thematically. All the material has been designed to stimulate and interest pupils. Although it has been written specifically for exam classes, it could also be used with non-exam groups.

Growing Up In Christianity

by HOLM, Jean & RIDLEY, Ronnie
Longman Group UK Ltd 1990
ISBN: 0 582 00283 4
AGE: Upper Secondary Pupils or Teacher Resource Book

This book provides comments and quotes from Christians about their experience of growing up in their faith, including reflections on baptism, celebrating Christmas in different parts of the world and going on pilgrimages. There is some explanation about the different aspects of the faith and basic review questions at the end of each chapter.

High Days and Holidays

–Celebrating The Christian Year
by SELF, David
Lion Publishing plc 1993
ISBN: 0 7459 2335 6
AGE: Lower Secondary Pupils and Teacher Reference Book.
This book introduces many different Christian festivals–some familiar, some less well known. In a colourful and simple way it explains how they are celebrated around the world.

Instant Art: Teaching Christianity

by THACKER, Helen
Palm Tree Press 1991
ISBN: 0 86209 142 4
Age: Lower Secondary Pupils
The simple, photocopiable drawings in this book are designed to help teachers present different aspects of Christianity. Each section of illustrations is accompanied by explanatory notes.

Jesus In The Dock

KIRKWOOD, Robert & CLAYDON, Graham
Longman Group UK Limited 1990
ISBN: 0 582 04581 9
AGE: Lower Secondary Pupils
Despite the lack of colour, the use of black and white cartoons and pictures in this book make it visually appealing. The readers of the book are invited to be the jury for the trial of Jesus. Information on Jesus, his background and claims are presented through a defence and prosecution council, encouraging the 'jury' to think about the evidence and investigate it.

Luke–A Gospel for Today

by SMITH, Linda & RAEPER, William
Lion Publishing plc 1989

ISBN: 0 7459 1503 5
AGE: Upper Secondary Pupils
This book is divided into fifty-nine units each looking at one aspect of
Luke and designed to take one lesson. The units contain background
information, Biblical references, questions and follow up work for
exam classes.

The Many Paths Of Christianity

by THOMPSON, Jan and Mel
Edward Arnold 1988
ISBN: 0 7131 7767 5
AGE: Secondary Pupils
This book describes the history, beliefs and practices of the Orthodox,
Roman Catholic and Protestant churches as well as giving a brief
survey of ecumenism. The book is illustrated and uses questions and
tasks to encourage understanding.

Mark–A Gospel for Today

by DANES, Simon & Christopher
Lion Publishing plc 1989
ISBN: 0 7459 1504 3
Age: Upper Secondary Pupils
This book is divided into fifty-five units each looking at one aspect of
Mark and designed to take one lesson. The units contain background
information, Biblical references, questions and follow up work for
exam classes.

Our First Gospel

- A Thematic Approach To Mark's Gospel Through Worksheets
by LACEY, Anne
Kevin Mayhew Publishers 1989
ISBN: 0 86209 120 9
AGE: Upper Secondary Pupils
Containing twenty-five worksheets on Mark's Gospel this pack
includes material on the purpose and structure of the Gospel, people
from Jewish background as well as the main issues and events in the
Gospel. This has been designed to meet GCSE objectives.

Revise Mark's Gospel For GCSE

by DANES, Christopher & DANES, Simon
Lion Publishing plc 1993
ISBN: 0 7459 2506 5
AGE: Upper Secondary Pupils
This provides practical help on how to revise Mark's Gospel. It looks at use of time and planning, making revision notes and provides memory test questions and answers as well as practice.

St Mark's Gospel – A Study Guide

by KEENE, Michael
Basil Blackwell Ltd 1989
ISBN: 0 631 16762 5
AGE: Upper Secondary Pupils
This guide has been designed for students studying St Mark's Gospel at examination level. It has been divided into nine sections, each concluding with a set of questions. These sections examine John the Baptist, Jesus and His Disciples, Times of Conflict, Jesus the Story-Teller, Signs and Wonders, What Did Jesus Have to say About..? Jesus Enters Jerusalem, Towards The End, The End, and A New Beginning.

SERIES: Seeking Religion

Hodder & Stoughton 1990
AGE: Lower Secondary Pupils
Lively, easy to read text combined with colour illustrations on every page make the books in this series attractive and appealing.

Seeking Religion: The Christian Experience

by AYLETT, J F
ISBN: 0 340 49373 9
The themes covered in this book include Christian origin and belief, various forms of worship, the lifestyle of its followers and examples of the way their faith has led them to help others. The questions are designed to encourage pupils to think about these things for themselves.

Seeking Religion: Jesus

by AYLETT, J.F. & HOLDEN-STOREY, R.D.
ISBN: 0 340 49050 0

Beginning with evidence of Jesus' existence, this book leaves pupils to develop their own conclusions. It continues to examine the life and teaching of Jesus relating it to present day situations where possible.

Sudden Death at the Vicarage

by COPLEY, Terence
Religious and Moral Education Press 1993
ISBN: 0 900274 99 9
Age: Lower Secondary Pupils
Assuming the role of the detective, the reader is challenged to discover why the vicar suddenly died. Whilst capturing the pupils attention, this book also ensures that pupils read about church buildings and their symbolism.

SERIES: Teaching RE

Christian Education Movement 1992/93
Age: As indicated in the title of each book.
The aim of this series is to equip and encourage teachers in their planning, delivery and development of different religious issues. The material contained in the books includes background information for the teacher as well as ideas for activities in the classroom.

Teaching RE–Christmas 5-14

ISBN: 1 85100 0534

Teaching RE–Christmas 11-16

ISBN: 1 85100 0542

Teaching RE–Easter 5-14

ISBN: 1 85100 0577

Teaching RE–Easter 11-16

ISBN: 1 85100 0585

Two Thousand Years On

KNOX, Graham & MAYBURY, Mark
Two Thousand Years On Trust 1993
ISBN: Not applicable
Age: Lower Secondary Pupils

This resource investigates the story about Jesus Christ as recounted in Luke's gospel. It is designed as a glossy magazine and contains features, interviews, role play and even a photo story. Some questions and class activitities are included.

Understanding Christianity At GCSE

by BROWN, Janet
Edward Arnold 1989
ISBN: 0 340 49006 3
AGE: Upper Secondary Pupils
This book includes twenty-nine worksheets which explore the development of the different denominations, Christian beliefs, festivals, rites of passages and styles of worship. Designed to be used in conjunction with textbooks, it is well laid out and illustrated.

We Always Put a Candle In The Window

–Celebrating Christian Festivals at Home
by FREEMAN, Marjorie
The National Society & Church House Publishing 1989
ISBN: 0 7151 4769 2
AGE: Teacher Reference Book
This book has been written for Christian parents, providing them with ideas of how to celebrate Christian festivals in their own home. Although it is not therefore immediately relevant for RE teachers it does contain lots of activities that could be adapted and used in a classroom context. The book goes through the calendar year and as well as covering the well known festivals it provides information and ideas for exploring the more unusual days in the Christian calendar like 'Collop Monday' and 'Lammas Day'.

OTHER WORLD RELIGIONS

BUDDHISM

Buddhists in Britain

by CUSH, Denise
Hodder & Stoughton 1990
ISBN: 0 340 519487
Age: Upper Secondary Pupils

This book explores Buddhism through interviews with representatives from ten different traditions in Britain.

Discovering Religions: Buddhism

by PENNY, Sue
Heinemann Educational 1988
ISBN: 0 435 30303 1
AGE: Lower Secondary Pupils
This book gives a simple introduction to Buddhism, its central beliefs and practices. Each double page looks at a different topic through text, black and white photographs and questions, ranging from very straightforward to slightly more challenging. Buddhist teachings, holy books, Buddhist history and festivals are amongst the subjects included.

Religions Through Festivals: Buddhism

by CONNOLLY, Peter & Holly
Longman Group UK Ltd 1989
ISBN: 0 582 31789 4
AGE: Lower Secondary Pupils
Twenty-two different aspects of Buddhist festivals and religious practices are explored in this book. Each subject covers a double page and the material is presented in an interesting, colourful way. Some of the sections contain follow up questions and exercises. The range of the subjects covered include The Buddha, the Elders Path and Sangha Day.

HINDUISM

Discovering Religions: Hinduism

by PENNY, Sue
Heinenmann Educational 1988
ISBN: 0 435 30304 X
AGE: Lower Secondary Pupils
This book gives a simple introduction to the central beliefs and practices of Hinduism. Each double page looks at a different topic. These include pilgrimage, worship, the caste system, rites of passage, holy books and Mahatma Gandhi.

Hindu Festivals: Teachers Book

by MAYLED, Jon
Religious and Moral Education Press 1988
ISBN: 0 08 035095 X
AGE: Upper Secondary Pupils and Teacher Reference Book
This book accompanies the *Living Festivals Series*. It is a photo-copiable resource book containing different types of worksheets. These vary from texts on Hindu festivals to recipes and wordsearch games.

Hinduism in Words and Pictures

by THORLEY, Sarah
Religious and Moral Education Press 1993
ISBN: 0 900274 55 7
AGE: Lower Secondary Pupils
This book provides a simple and visual introduction to Hinduism describing the faith in a British and worldwide context. It covers thirteen different aspects which all form self contained chapters. These include gods and goddesses, worship, pilgrimage and holy men.

Listening To Hindus

by JACKSON, Robert & NESBITT, Eleanor
Unwin Hyman 1990
ISBN: 0 0444 8121 7
AGE: Upper Secondary Pupils
Listening To Hinduism is part of a series which explores and explains different religions through quoting members of that particular faith community. Whenever possible comments and observations from young members of the community are used. Background information, illustrations and questions make this a useful classroom resource.

Seeking Religion: The Hindu Experience

by AYLETT, Liz
Hodder & Stoughton 1992
ISBN: 0 340 49372 0
Age: Lower Secondary Pupils
This is part of the colourful *Seeking Religion* series. Through stories, rituals and personal accounts, the book offers insights into the society and culture of India, and into the lives of millions of Hindus through-out the world. Pupils activities and questions are included.

Teaching RE – Hinduism 11-16

Christian Education Movement 1993
ISBN: 1 85100 064X
Age: Secondary Pupils
The aim of this book is to equip and encourage teachers in their planning, delivery and development of aspects of Hinduism. The material therefore includes background information for the teacher as well as ideas for activities in the classroom.

ISLAM

Examining Religions: Islam

by KENDRICK, Rosalyn
Heinenmann Educational 1989
ISBN: 0 435 30314 7
AGE: Upper Secondary Pupils
This is part of a series which has been designed to support Religious Studies exam syllabuses. It can be used with thematic syllabuses or for an in-depth study of Islam. It contains black and white illustrations, as well as discussion questions and ideas for coursework. The life of Muhammad, beliefs, worship, festivals, special days, Shari'ah, the mosque, Islamic history and modern issues are all addressed in the book.

Growing Up In Islam

by ARDAVAN, Janet
Longman Group UK Ltd 1990
ISBN: 0 582 00287 7
AGE: Upper Secondary Pupils
Growing Up In Islam is one of a series of books which aim to present a child's-eye view of what it means to be a member of a religion. In this book on Islam particular attention is given to describing worship, festivals, food and relationships. Quotes from young members of the faith community are accompanied by text, pictures and extension activities.

Islam: An Approach for GCSE

by THOMPSON, Jan
Hodder & Stoughton 1990

ISBN: 0 340 52108 2
Age: Upper Secondary Pupils
Designed for an exam class, this book covers eight different aspects of Islam. These are the Mosque, Prayer, Muhammad, Scriptures and Beliefs, Ramadan, Pilgrimage, the Growth of Islam and Growing Up in Islam. Questions accompany each section.

Islam: A Pictorial Guide

by LYNCH, Maurice
Christian Education Movement 1990
ISBN: 1 85100 016 X
AGE: Upper Secondary Pupils
Through black and white line drawings and text this book attempts to illustrate many of the main areas of Muslim belief and practice.

Seeking Religion: The Muslim Experience

by AYLETT, J F
Hodder & Stoughton 1990
ISBN: 0 340 49375 5
Tracing the development of Islam from Muhammad to the present day, the book provides an insight into some aspects of Muslim experience such as forms of prayer, rites of passage and beliefs.

The Westhill Project R.E. 5-16: Islam

Stanley Thornes (Publishers) Ltd 1988
This is a series of four books that have been designed to help pupils develop an understanding of Islam as a world religion.

Muslims 3

by READ, Garth & RUDGE, John
ISBN: 1 85234 075 4
AGE: Lower Secondary Pupils
The particular aim of this book is to explore the way Muslims apply their beliefs to their personal lives.

Muslims 4

by HUNT, Dilwyn
Stanley Thornes Publishers 1989
ISBN: 1 871402 17 4

AGE: Upper Secondary Pupils
This is the fourth and final part of the Westhill Project on Islam.
Divided into five parts, it looks at the ways that Muslims involve
themselves in public life, Muslim practices to do with family life, the
Muslim community worldwide, some aspects of Muslim spirituality and
the six principal Muslim beliefs.

JUDAISM

Examining Religions: Judaism

by FORTA, Arye
Heinenmann Educational 1989
ISBN: 0 435 30313 9
AGE: Upper Secondary Pupils
This is part of a series which has been designed to support Religious
Studies exam syllabuses. It can be used with thematic syllabuses or for
an in-depth study of Judaism. It contains black and white illustrations,
as well as discussion questions and ideas for coursework. Basic Jewish
beliefs and traditions, the Jewish year, Judaism in the home, family
events, communal life, attitudes, opinions and movements and Jewish
teachings on contemporary Jewish issues are examined in this book.

Jewish Festival Omnibus

by GENT, Frank & SCHOLEFIELD, Lynne
Religious and Moral Education Press 1993
ISBN: 1 85175 003 7
AGE: Upper Secondary Pupils
This is an omnibus of Jewish festivals that were originally published
individually in the *Living Festivals Series*. The festivals included in this
descriptive volume include Rosh Hashanah, Yom Kippur, Succot,
Simchat Torah, Chanukah and Passover.

Jewish Festivals: Teacher's Book

by MAYLED, Jon
Religious and Moral Education Press 1988
ISBN: 0 08 035101 8
AGE: Upper Secondary Pupils and Teacher Reference Book
This teacher book accompanies the *Living Festivals Series* (for details
of the omnibus collection of this series see above). It is a photocopiable
resource book consisting of different types of worksheets. These vary

from texts on a particular Jewish festival to recipes and wordsearch games.

Judaism

by CLOSE, Brian E
Hodder & Stoughton 1992
ISBN: 0 340 54693 X
Age: Sixth Form
A basic knowledge of Judaism is assumed in this book. It examines the development of Mishnah, Hasidism, the Enlightenment, Anti-Semitism and Judaism after Auschwitz.

Judaism: An Approach For GCSE

by PILKINGTON, C M
Hodder & Stoughton 1991
ISBN: 0 340 51951 7
AGE: Upper Secondary Pupils
The three main areas explored in this book are the foundation and development of Judaism, Jewish life today and the importance of the ritual year in Judaism. The text is illustrated with black and white photographs. The book is supplemented by a pack of worksheets by the same author entitled 'Understanding Judaism at GCSE'.

Judaism: A GCSE Activities Pack

by BROMLEY, Eileen
Stanley Thornes (publishers) Ltd 1988
ISBN: 1 871402 02 6
AGE: Upper Secondary Pupils
This pack covers the following areas of Judaism–beliefs, scriptures, synagogues, Judaism in the home, festivals, fasts, rites of passage, history and pilgrimage. The activity sheets, worksheets and resource sheets come in a spiral bound book and are photocopiable. They have all been designed to stimulate and interest pupils. Although the material has been written specifically for exam classes, it could also be used with non-exam groups.

Living the Faith: Jewish Lives

by COUTTS, John
Oliver & Boyd 1989
ISBN: 0 05 004319 6

AGE: Secondary

The *Living the Faith* series is a collection of lively, readable stories about people and communities who have lived their faith in different ways, times and places. The stories offer insight into what it can mean to be a member of a faith community. This book tells the stories of Sir Moses Montefiore, a British Jew who lived in the eighteenth century and Lady Amelie Jakobovits who lived through the horror of Nazi-occupied France during the Second World War. It also tells the story behind the Lubavitch Community Centre in London.

The Passover Meal

by RICHARDS, Hubert J.
McCrimmon Publishing Co. Ltd 1990
ISBN: 0 85597 432 X
AGE: Teacher Reference Book

This is a simple, but detailed description of the Jewish Passover meal. It includes ideas for songs that could be sung at appropriate places, words of the blessings, questions and prayers that are used. Any comments or explanations of the festival are contained in the foot-notes, so that there can be no confusion with what is and is not included in the ritual.

Religions and Issues: Jewish Belief & Practice

by ROSE, Jenny
Oliver & Boyd 1989
ISBN: 0 05 004311 0
AGE: Upper Secondary Pupils

Designed as core material for Religious Education examinations, *Jewish Belief & Practice* looks at the response of Jews to contemporary issues of concern. These beliefs are introduced through the festivals of Shabbat, Rosh Hashanah and Yom Kippur. Contemporary issues are then studied from the perspectives of these beliefs including personal relationships, work and wealth, environmental concerns, relationships with other faiths and crime and punishment. The book includes black and white illustrations, material from a variety of different sources and ideas for activities.

Seeking Religion: The Jewish Experience

by AYLETT, Liz
Hodder & Stoughton 1990

ISBN: 0 340 49371 2
AGE: Lower Secondary Pupils
Examining the origin and history of the Jewish religion and its beliefs, this book helps pupils to understand some aspects of this faith. It is well illustrated and attractive and includes a range of questions and activities.

Religions Through Festivals

by LAWTON, Clive
Longman Group UK Ltd 1989
ISBN: 0 582 31790 8
AGE: Lower Secondary Pupils
Twenty-two different aspects of Jewish festivals and religious practices are examined in this book. Each aspect presented in a colourful, interesting way covers a double page. Some of the sections contain follow-up questions and exercises. Subjects covered include Jewish history, Shabbat, Purim, Israel–the land and the Jewish year.

Short Stories From The Jewish Bible Series No 2:
Moses And Other Stories

by PHILLIPS, Sue
Longman Group UK Ltd 1988
ISBN: 0 582 31116 0
AGE: Lower Secondary Pupils
This book contains short plays and stories which explore some of the most famous stories from the Hebrew Bible: from Abraham, Moses to King Solomon and the exile in Babylon. These are accompanied by lots of activities and cartoons.

Short Stories From The Jewish Bible Series No 3:
Trip To Israel And Other Stories

by PHILLIPS, Sue
Longman Group UK Ltd 1988
ISBN: 0 582 31117 9
AGE: Lower Secondary Pupils
The short plays and stories in this book explore Jewish life–today and after the return from Babylon. It is attractively laid out and includes lots of imaginative activities and cartoons.

The Westhill Project RE 5-16: Judaism

by MONTAGU, Sarah & BREINER, Margaret
Stanley Thornes (Publishers) Ltd 1991
This is a series of four books that have been designed to help pupils
develop an understanding of Judaism as a world religion.

Jews 3

ISBN: 1 871402 20 4
Age: Lower Secondary Pupils
This book looks into Jewish community life, the synagogue, caring for
others, holy times, life within a Jewish family and what Judaism means
to the individual.

Jews 4

ISBN: 1 871402 21 2
AGE: Upper Secondary Pupils
Book four, the final book in the series, concentrates on the worldwide
Jewish community, antisemitism, diversity within Judaism and
spirituality and beliefs.

SIKHISM

Sikhism in Words and Pictures

by THORLEY, Sarah
Religious and Moral Education Press 1989
ISBN: 0 08 035102 6
AGE: Lower Secondary Pupils
This is a simple, visual introduction to the basic elements of Sikhism.
The book is divided into short sections, each containing black and
white photographs and questions on the text. The topics covered in the
book include The Guru Granth Sahib, Gurdwaras, the Khalsa and
family life.

Religions Through Festivals: Sikhism

by BABRAA, Davinder Kaur
Longman Group UK Ltd 1989
ISBN: 0 582 31787 8
AGE: Lower Secondary Pupils
Twenty-two different aspects of Sikh festivals and religious practices

are introduced in this book. The subjects covered include the Sikh turban, Karah Parshand, Guru Nanak and Vaisakhi.

Each of these are presented in an interesting and colourful way. Some of the sections contain follow up questions and exercises.

ISSUE OR THEME-BASED BOOKS

A Beginner's Guide to Ideas

by RAEPER, William & SMITH, Linda
Lion Publishing plc 1991
ISBN: 0 7459 2136 1
AGE: Sixth Form
This book is a guide to over forty of the philosophies in the history of human thought, including a study of great thinkers like Plato, Aristotle, Augustine, Descartes, Kant, Locke, Marx, Nietzsche and Freud. This would be a useful resource for A' level students covering the Philosophy of Religions course.

Believers In One God

by KEENE, Michael
Cambridge University Press 1993
ISBN: 0 521 38627 6
AGE: Upper Secondary Pupils
This book has been written for students studying the six major religions of the world. This is the first of two volumes and looks in depth at Judaism, Christianity and Islam. Each faith is examined separately, focusing on their history, beliefs, festivals, worship and sacred texts. The text is broken up with photographs, diagrams and exercises. For details of the companion volume see *Seekers After Truth*.

A Book Of Feasts And Seasons

by BOGLE, Joanna
Fowler Wright Books/Gracewing 1988
ISBN: 0 85244 153 3
AGE: Lower Secondary Pupils
This book provides a wealth of information on all the feasts and seasons of the year and helps families and schools to have fun whilst keeping traditions alive. It contains a wealth of recipes for everything from Bara Brith to Australian Ginger Log, ideas for games, activities, songs, prayers and stories.

Coursework – A Teachers Guide for GCSE Religious Studies

by HAYEN, Dianna
Religious and Moral Education Press 1988
ISBN: 0 08 035100 X
AGE: Teacher Reference Book
This is a guide for teachers of Religious Studies GCSE on how to approach, set and mark coursework. It explains the rationale of testing in this way and offers practical examples and ideas for coursework.

Ethics and Religions

by RANKIN, J. BROWN, A. & GATESHILL, P.
Longman Group UK Ltd 1991
ISBN 0 582 03307 1
AGE: Upper Secondary Pupils
The five important ethical issues covered in this book include: marriage and family, the natural world, peace and conflict, and capital punishment. Each chapter begins by considering the main questions and ethical dilemmas. It then looks at what the six world religions have to say on these issues. This book could be used with exam students as at the end of each chapter there are assignments and ideas for coursework.

SERIES: Folens RE

by CURTIS, Peter & SMITH, Carol
Folens Limited 1990
AGE: Lower Secondary Pupils
Folens RE is a three-book course. Each of the books in the series is accompanied by a volume of photocopiable resource materials to complement each unit of the course. The books are colourful and compact, with each sections having core and extension activities.

Thinking About Living

ISBN: 1 85276 093 1
This book concentrates on 'implicit' RE. The themes it covers include; suffering, special places, authority, feelings, tradition and signs and symbols.

Thinking About Religion

ISBN: 1 85276 095 8

Thinking About Religion continues from *Thinking about Living*. Becoming more religiously explicit, it considers themes such as Worship, Holy Books, Commitment and Belonging.

Thinking Things Through

ISBN: 1 85276 097 8

This combines both explicit and implicit RE. It encourages deeper reflection than the previous two books in the series and asks questions like, 'What happens when I die?', 'What is the "best way"?'and 'How important am I?'

GCSE Questions in Religious Studies

by SIMMONDS, David
Nelson Blackie 1989
ISBN: 0 216 92666 1
AGE: Upper Secondary Pupils

This is a collection of questions and assignments on six major world religions. The style of exercises range from assignments through to short factual questions.

SERIES: Beliefs and Values

Christian Education Movement 1990/1991
AGE: Upper Secondary Pupils

Green Beliefs–Valued World

by WILLIAMS, Veronica
ISBN: 1 85100 013 5

This book attempts to reflect the beliefs and values held by different faiths about the world, nature and the environment. It contains stories and poems from different traditions, questions for thought and discussion, ideas for classroom activities and material to stimulate reflection and provide experience.

Consumer Beliefs–Valued World

ISBN: 1 85100 0275

This explores the areas of wealth, work, leisure and the spiritual, bringing the insights of the major world faiths to bear on the values promoted by the consumer society.

Human Beliefs–Personal Values

ISBN: 1 85100 0313
This books examines beliefs and values concerning the self, addiction, prejudice and disablement.

Caring Beliefs–Valued People

ISBN: 1 85100 0313
This looks at values expressed in relationships; within the family, among friends, with a partner and in the community.

How Do I Teach RE?

by READ, G et al
Stanley Thornes 1992
ISBN: 0 7487 1470 7
AGE: Teacher Reference Book
This book, a companion to the Westhill Project series of textbooks, addresses some of the central issues constantly faced by teachers of Religious Education. These include planning, some content and principles of assessment. Although the book has been based on considered theory, it is not written in a difficult academic style.

The Human Difference

by ALLAN, John
Lion Publishing plc 1989
ISBN: 0 74591284 2
AGE: Teacher Reference Book or selectively with Upper Secondary Pupils.
This book has been written around the question, 'What does it mean to be human?' It has been divided into four sections, the first is entitled 'Introducing Human Life' and it looks at birth, life and death and what makes each individual unique. The second part examines the 'Potential of Human Beings', this includes the similarities and differences with animals and how the brain works. The third section is concerned with 'People Together', asking why people do what they do. The final part questions the meaning of a person, asking what the world faiths have to say and looking at the heart of it all. The material is attractively

presented, including colour photographs, quotes from various sources and cartoon drawings.

SERIES: Learn About Religion

by O'DONNELL, Kevin
Hodder & Stoughton 1992
AGE: Lower Secondary Pupils

I Wonder...

ISBN: 0 340 55926 8
This is the first book in the series *Learn about Religion*, which aims to explore and develop the spiritual dimension of human development. This is done by encouraging an experiential approach to the themes chosen, through guided fantasy for example. In *I Wonder*, worship, life after death and wonder are amongst the subjects covered. These topics are related to different religions as well as to the students' everyday experiences.

You're Dreaming

ISBN: 0 340 57147 0
In *You're Dreaming*, light, darkness, trees, water and food are amongst the themes addressed. These topics are related to different religions as well as to the students' everyday experiences.

Life Foundations

Ed. WHITFIELD, Richard
NES Arnold 1992
ISBN: 0 946647 22 4 (Volume 2)
AGE: Secondary Pupils
This series consists of six teacher/leader resource books with three support books for students. It covers twelve inter-disciplinary topics including, feelings and emotions, time and task management, family groups and parenthood, moral dilemmas in relationships, and public policy and private life. The teacher books contain background notes and photocopiable material for pupils. The student books are also photocopiable and take the form of personal journals. The whole pack creates a complete scheme for the affective side of PSE.

Living Questions

by HASTED, Sue & TEECE, Geoff
Stanley Thornes 1993
ISBN: 0 7487 1625 4
Age: Lower Secondary Pupils
Living Questions as the title suggests is structured around a large range of questions which explore different aspects of shared human experiences. These are arranged under the following general themes; The Natural World, Celebrations, Relationships, Stages of Life, Lifestyles, Rules and Suffering. The book provides responses to the questions from a wide spectrum of religions and sources. There is a teacher's book to accompany this series with ideas for class activities and photocopiable worksheets.

SERIES: Matters of Life and Death

by HAINES, Sue & WRIGHT, Chris
Lion Publishing plc 1991
AGE: Sixth Form
The four books in this series ask searching questions about life-and-death issues. Each gives voice to a variety of views through quotations and extracts. Questions focus discussion on how beliefs impact on lifestyles.

Suffering: Why, Silent God, Why?

ISBN: 0 7459 2056 X

Living and Dying: The Ultimate Horizon?

ISBN: 0 7459 2078 0

Sexuality and Religion: The Great Celebration

ISBN: 0 7459 2079 9

Success and Fulfilment: A Search for Meaning

ISBN: 0 7459 2080 2

SERIES: Looking For . . .

by KIRKWOOD, Robert
Longman Group UK Ltd 1988/1990
AGE: Lower Secondary Pupils

Looking For Proof of God

ISBN: 0 582 20309 0

This book uses a lively and questioning approach to focus attention on the issue of God's existence. Philosophical theories such as Aquinas' first cause and the teleological argument are presented in an interesting and accessible way, making the book useful and motivating for all students, even in mixed ability classes.

Looking for Happiness

ISBN: 0 582 20311 2

Looking for Happiness explores in a simple and direct way the theme of looking for happiness through two religions; Buddhism and Christianity. The lively illustrations and tone of the book have been designed to motivate pupils of varying ages and abilities.

Moral Issues in Six Religions

Ed by COLE, Owen W
Heinemann Educational 1991
ISBN: 0435 30299 X
AGE: Upper Secondary Pupils

Useful for exam and non-exam groups, this book provides material on the moral agendas of religions. The text is divided according to the religions and although many of the issues discussed are similar the different approaches which each faith adopts are emphasised.

New Methods In RE Teaching – An Experiential Approach

by HAMMOND, John et al
Oliver & Boyd 1990
ISBN: 0 05 004303 X
AGE: Teacher Reference Book

This book is packed full of ideas on how to challenge students' inner prejudices in the RE classroom and encourages them to really think, experience and become involved in the subject for themselves. This is a controversial book – loved by some and hated by others!

Religions

by BROWN, Alan/RANKIN, John/WOOD, Angela
Longman Group UK Ltd 1988
ISBN: 0 582 22341 5

AGE: Upper Secondary Pupils

This book examines the six major world religions and can be used by pupils studying one religion or using a multi- faith approach by themes. The fifty pages about Christianity summarise its beginnings, beliefs and practices today. Designed for exam courses it contains ideas for coursework.

SERIES: Religion For A Change

by PALMER, M. O'BRIEN, J & BREUILLY, E.

Stanley Thornes (Publishers) Ltd 1991

AGE: Lower Secondary Pupils

There are three books in this integrated course in religious and personal education. It aims to present issues in a lively, appealing way relating them to the modern day. A variety of religions are represented. Ideas for classroom activities and exercises are included.

Book 1

ISBN: 0 7487 0473 6

The three main topics included in *Book 1* include creation, beliefs and journeys.

Book 2

ISBN: 0 7487 0474 4

Communities, good and evil, and death are the three main areas dealt with in this book.

Book 3

ISBN: 0 7487 0475 2

The topics in Book 3 include the environment, the unknown, the sacred, drugs and alcohol, relationships, money, religious violence and racism.

Religious Artefacts in the Classroom

by Gateshill, Paul & Thompson, Jan

Hodder & Stoughton

ISBN: 0 340 57002 4

AGE: Teacher Reference Book

The purpose of this book is to encourage RE teachers to use the objects of religion in their lessons. It provides information on the main artefacts of the six major world religions, describing their use and significance. These are accompanied with suggestions for pupil activities. Most importantly the book provides teachers with hints on what to do and what not to do when handling sacred religious objects in the classroom.

Religious Beliefs And Moral Codes

by BAILEY, John R
(Religion In Life Series), Schofield & Sims 1988
ISBN: 0 7217 3037 X
AGE: Secondary Pupils
This book looks at the main doctrines of the six world religions. For example, included in the section on Christianity, thirty pages study what Christians believe about God, Jesus, the Church, eternal life, and how Christians apply these to modern problems. It contains discussion questions, activities and photos.

SERIES: Responses...

by WINTERSGILL, Barbara with DYSON, Janet
Longman Group UK Ltd 1990/1991
AGE: Upper Secondary Pupils
The three books in this series have been written specifically for use in Religious Education but they could also prove useful for teachers of integrated humanities, PSE and sixth form general studies. They have not been designed simply to convey facts but rather to be activity books encouraging the student to learn through thinking. These books can be used with exam classes, GCSE notes for teachers are included.

Responses–Life, The Universe and You

ISBN: 0 582 02669 5
Life, The Universe and You looks at a variety of issues and some of the religious responses that they have prompted. Through questions and discussion triggers, students are encouraged to reflect on these issues themselves. The issues include; 'What's the point?', 'Who am I?' and 'Times of Trouble'.

Responses–Ways of Saying

ISBN: 0 582 02670 9
Religious expression is examined through the medium of dance, artwork, painting, manuscripts, icons, architecture and garden design.

The text and illustrations explain clearly how these different techniques have been important to various worshipping communities. Questions, activities and discussion triggers accompany the text.

Responses–What Do You Think?

ISBN: 0 582 02668 7

This book aims to make pupils think about some difficult but important issues. Information on an issue or belief is presented and followed by questions and activities designed to stimulate personal consideration. The subjects contained in the book include 'peace and suffering', 'contrasting lifestyles', 'the place of women in some religions today' and 'homelessness'.

SERIES: Seeking Religion

Hodder & Stoughton 1990
AGE: Lower Secondary Pupils
The lively, easy to read text combined with colour illustrations on every page make this series attractive and appealing.

What's Special?

by HOLDEN-STOREY, R.D.
ISBN: 0 340 49374 7

In *What's Special*, students are introduced to the idea of what's special in a religious sense. Groups of special things are examined in separate chapters including special foods, rituals, buildings, languages and discussed in relation to more than one religion.

Signs, Symbols and Stories

by AYLETT, J F
ISBN: 0 340 49051

J F Aylett introduces pupils to the idea of signs and symbols, their role in our daily life, how they function as part of myth and religion and how they can have special meaning for believers. The book provides an introduction to the variety of ways in which dress, actions, objects and names can be given significance both in the world and in religion.

Seekers After Truth

by KEENE, Michael
Cambridge University Press 1993

ISBN: 0 521 38626 8
AGE: Upper Secondary Pupils
This book has been written for GCSE students studying the six major religions of the world and is the second of two volumes. It looks in depth at Hinduism, Buddhism and Sikhism. Each faith is examined separately and information is given on its history, beliefs, festivals, worship and sacred texts. The text is broken up with photographs, diagrams and exercises. For details of the companion volume see *Believers In One God.*

Shadows of the Supernatural

by CHAPMAN, Colin
Lion Publishing plc 1990
ISBN: 0 7459 1274 5
AGE: Teacher Reference Book or selectively with Upper Secondary Pupils.
Arguing that 'time and time again the mysterious side of life touches the everyday with its shadow', this book provides a background and explanation of the origin and reasons of many of todays supersitions. These include the origin of Hallowe'en, why you 'touch wood', and begins to answer questions like 'Why do we get the baby christened?' and 'Do horoscopes work?' In many ways it is a guide to popular religion. The text is broken up with black and white photographs and questions.

Skills Challenge

–Game-based activities for Religious Education.
by COPLEY, Terence & BROWN, Adrian
Religious and Moral Education Press 1992
ISBN: 0 900274 56 5
AGE: Secondary Pupils
This is a novel resource for the RE classroom. It contains ten original games which teachers can integrate into their RE programme in order to develop and assess skills. Some of the games concentrate on just one religion, such as 'The Hindu Game of Life', whilst others incorporate more than one of the major world religions. These include the 'Holy Land Tour' and 'To Be A Pilgrim'. Some of the games aim to stimulate discussion and could be used in a wide variety of subjects such as 'Interconnect' and 'You the Jury'. With the exception of dice and

counters the photocopiable book contains everything needed to play the games.

SERIES: Strathclyde Religious Studies

Hodder & Stoughton Ltd 1992
AGE: Upper Secondary Pupils

Issues of Belief

by BARR, M. BROWN, J. & SCOBIE, E.
ISBN: 0 340 55777 X
This pack explores fundamental questions about the nature of belief, arguments for the existence of God, religion and science, suffering and death. It contains over one hundred photocopiable worksheets based around these themes designed for use with Standard Grade and GCSE students. The views of some of the major world religions are included.

Issues of Morality

by COWIE, A. JACK, D. & McLACHLAN, D
ISBN: 0 340 55776 1
A range of issues set out in situations where a moral choice has to be made are presented in this book. Empathy and reflection are encouraged through the 106 photocopiable worksheets. It has been designed for exam groups and some reference to Christian view points are included.

Teaching World Religions

–SHAP Working Party on World Religions
Ed. ERRICKER, Clive
Heinemann Educational 1993
ISBN: 0 435 30330 9
AGE: Teacher Reference Book
This has been designed to help teach world religions in the classroom in an interesting and challenging way. In section one an overview of the place of world religions in the curriculum is provided, suggesting links between RE and other curriculum areas and collective worship.

Section two looks at perspectives from the six faith traditions most commonly taught in schools and suggests how these perspectives can be used in the classroom. Section three examines some of the world views not usually included in the curriculum. Finally section four provides teachers with bibliographies and information on non-book resources.

Things That Matter

by SIMMONDS, David
Nelson Blackie 1991
ISBN: 0 216 93100 2
AGE: Upper Secondary Pupils
Things That Matter has been written for students aged 14–16 years who are taking RE as a non-exam subject. The book investigates issues of concern in a multi faith context, divided into the three main sections; things that matter to you (eg self identity, health and relationships), things that matter to different people (ie the beliefs held by the six major world religions) and things that matter to the community (eg crime and punishment, prejudice and money).

SERIES: Understanding Religions

Wayland 1992
AGE: Lower Secondary Pupils
The *Understanding Religions* series consists of six hard back colourful books looking at the way important life events are dealt with in the religions of the world.

Death Customs

by RUSHTON, Lucy
ISBN: 0 7502 0419 2

Food and Fasting

by BURKE, Deidre
ISBN: 0 7502 04214

Initiation Customs

by PRIOR, Katherine
ISBN: 0 7502 04230

Marriage Customs

by COMPTON, Anita
ISBN: 0 7502 04206

Pilgrimages & Journeys

by PRIOR, Katherine
ISBN: 0 7502 04222

Teaching RE: Harvest 11-16

Christian Education Movement 1993
ISBN: 1 85100 062 3
AGE: Secondary Pupils
The aim of this book is to equip and encourage teachers in their planning, delivery and development of religious issues relating to harvest and harvest festivals. The material therefore includes background information for the teacher as well as ideas for activities in the classroom. Material has been drawn primarily from Christianity (including perspectives from Sierra Leone), Judaism (Shavuot and Sukkot) and Buddhism. Reference has also been made to other traditions including Islam, Hinduism and primal religions.

SERIES: Weaving The Web

by LOHAN, Richard/McCLURE, Mary
Collins Liturgical Publications 1988/1989
AGE: Lower Secondary Pupils
This series develops key aspects of shared human experience and relates them to Christian and other religions' beliefs and practices. An awareness of our plural society and global community are present throughout. The books contain ideas for active tasks, remedial and extension learning.

Weaving the Web: Teacher's Book

ISBN: 0 00 599156 0

Level 1: Community–Story–People

ISBN: 0 00 599149 8

Level 1: Communication–Celebration–Values

ISBN: 0 00 599152 8

Level 2: Community–Story–People

ISBN: 0 00 599150 1

Level 2: Communication – Celebration – Values
ISBN: 0 00 599153 6

Level 3: Community – Story – People
ISBN: 0 00 599154 4

Level 3: Communication – Celebration – Values
ISBN: 0 00 599154 4

STORIES & ANTHOLOGIES

SERIES: Bible Stories for Classroom & Assemblies

by PRIESTLEY, Jack G
RMEP 1992
AGE: Lower Secondary Pupils
Fifty short dramatic episodes are presented in each book in the series. Modern idiom rather than Biblical paraphrasing is used. Each Bible story is accompanied by background information and ideas for exploring further. Although they have been written with primary age children in mind they could easily be adapted for use in lower school assemblies or in the RE classroom.

The New Testament
ISBN: 0 900274 54 9

The Old Testament
ISBN: 0 900274 53 0

SERIES: REsource Banks

by Margaret Cooling & Diane Walker
Bible Society 1993
AGE: Lower Secondary Pupils
Although these books have been designed for use in the primary school, the Bible stories in their simple, modern language could be used with lower secondary pupils in acts of worship or the RE classroom. Each book includes a comprehensive guide to using the Biblical

material, explaining points of interest and clarifying what the passages mean to Christians.

REsource Bank–Book One

ISBN: 0 564 08555 3
The topics covered in Book One include 'friends', 'family', 'people' and 'sharing'.

REsource Bank–Book Two

ISBN: 0 564 08565 0
This volume covers the topics 'promises', 'change', 'fire', and 'gift'.

REsource Bank–Book Three

ISBN: 0 564 08575 8 12.95
Book Three includes the topics 'messages from God', 'special stories of Jesus', 'prayer' and 'standing up for what you believe'.

Stories for Sharing

by ARCODIA, Charles
E J Dwyer Pty Ltd Australia 1991
ISBN: 0 85574 348 4
AGE: Secondary
This is a collection of fifty-five unusual stories gathered from the past and present, east and west, legend and history. The stories illustrating themes such as acceptance, commitment, loyalty and grief, provide a useful complement to other RE material.

Words For Easter: An Anthology

compiled by Pamela Egan
The National Society/Church House Publishing 1990
ISBN:0 7151 4791 9
AGE: Lower Secondary Pupils
Many of the words ordinarily chosen to tell the story of Holy Week and Easter are difficult but familiar, such as 'sacrifice', 'denial' and 'resurrection'. This anthology tries to illustrate these through readings and poems. They are not the usual readings offered for Easter: many have been taken from well-known children's books.

BIOGRAPHIES

Something Of A Saint

by OWEN, David M
Triangle SPCK 1990
ISBN: 0 281 04481 3 2.95
AGE: Upper Secondary Pupils
Owen provides a glimpse into the lives of fifty-two great, but very different Christians who have left their mark on society over the last two thousand years. The saints included range from St Clement through to Martin Luther King. The passages briefly describe their lives and explain the background behind some famous prayers.

SERIES: Faith In Action

Religious & Moral Education Press
AGE: Secondary Pupils
There are over thirty titles in this series all dealing with Christian lives that have been noteworthy or unusual in some way. The books follow the same format, containing quite detailed information, black and white photographs and pictures, but they do not take long to read. The most recent titles in this series include the following:

A Living Memorial: Sue Ryder

by CONSTANT, Audrey
ISBN: 0 08 036349

The Way Of Peace: The Corrymeela Community

by CONSTANT, Audrey
ISBN: 0 900274 86 7

SERIES: Heroes of the Cross

Marshall & Pickering
AGE: Secondary Pupils
Each book in this series traces the life and achievement of individual Christians. The small paperback books are easy to read and full of detail. Examples of the series include:

George Müller

by STEER, Roger
ISBN: 0 551 01138 6

Christina Rossetti

by CLIFFORD, Joan
ISBN: 0 551 02013 X

SERIES: Leading the Way

Mel Thompson
Hodder & Stoughton 1992: Secondary
AGE: Secondary Pupils
This series seeks to present social issues and religious movements
through descriptions of particular people who are 'leading the way' in
them. Of the ten people featured in these books some are well-known,
such as Desmond Tutu and Bob Geldof whilst others are less so. A
majority of them are Christian, but some belong to other world religions or to none. All speak personally about their commitments and
encourage pupils to reflect on their own.

Leading the Way: Book 1

ISBN: 0 340 51955 X

Leading the Way: Book 2

ISBN: 0 340 52347 6

SOURCES OF HELP FOR RELIGIOUS EDUCATION TEACHERS

ASSOCIATION OF CHRISTIAN TEACHERS (ACT)

This Association aims to advance and apply the Christian faith in schools and colleges by supporting, uniting, equipping and representing Christians employed in education.

ACT:
- provides support in various ways for Christian teachers as individuals and as professionals.
- represents Christian views on education to the media, local and national government, and Parliamentary committees.

Its publications include:
- *ACT Now* a general magazine for all members.
- *Digest* a review of Religious Education resources.
- *Spectrum* an academic journal developing Christian perspectives on education.

For further details contact:

ACT
94A London Road
St Albans
Herts
AL1 1NX
Tel: 0727 840298

ACT (SCOTLAND)
2 Oxgangs Path
Edinburgh
EH13 9LX
Tel: 031 445 4125

ACT (WALES)
17 Brymawr Place
Masteg
Mid Glamorgan
CF34 9PB
Tel: 0656 734118

ACT (NORTHERN IRELAND)
182 Meadowvale Park
Limavady
County Londonderry
BT49 0SL
Tel: 05047 63503

PROFESSIONAL COUNCIL FOR RELIGIOUS EDUCATION (PCfRE)

PCfRE is the professional association for all those who teach RE.
PCfRE:
- runs courses, day conferences and consultation meetings.
- monitors official pronouncements from the government or governmental bodies on RE and responds appropriately.

- sends all members regular mailings.
- members can subscribe to all or selected termly journals.

These are:

- *RE Today* a magazine giving practical help to the classroom teacher. It is aimed mainly, but not exclusively, at teachers working with the 8-14 age range.
- *British Journal for Religious Education* is an internationally respected academic and professional journal.
- *Look Hear!* reviews RE materials, both audio-visual and printed.

For further details contact:

PCfRE
Royal Buildings
Victoria Street
DERBY
DE1 1GW
Tel: 0332 296655

STAPLEFORD HOUSE EDUCATION CENTRE

Stapleford House is the national training and conference centre of the Association of Christian Teachers. It runs day and weekend courses for teachers from all over the country covering a wide range of subjects.
For further details contact:
Stapleford House Education Centre
Wesley Place
Stapleford
Nottingham
NG9 8DP
Tel: (0602) 396270

DIPLOMA IN RELIGIOUS EDUCATION

This course has been designed for Christian teachers who wish to obtain a professional qualification in Religious Education.
The Diploma:

- is run jointly by St John's College and Stapleford House Education Centre.
- is validated by the University of Nottingham.
- is a two year part-time correspondence course.
- is taught by extension: the bulk of the course work is covered

through extensive distance learning study materials, coupled with tutors who relate to students by post or telephone.
- includes two summer schools which form an important part of the course and are held in Nottingham.

For further details contact Stapleford House, see address above.

THE STAPLEFORD PROJECT

The Stapleford Project is a curriculum development initiative based at Stapleford House Education Centre. It will produce a range of classroom resources for teaching Christianity in secondary schools.

For further details contact Stapleford House, see address above.

LIST OF CONTRIBUTORS

PAUL BEE is currently Head of Religious Education at Chipping Campden School in Gloucestershire.

ADRIAN BROWN is an ex-natural scientist who now teaches RE, Philosophy and General Studies at Ecclesbourne School in Derbyshire.

MARGARET COOLING has taught in both the primary and secondary sectors. She is at present a writer and trainer attached to the Association of Christian Teachers.

TREVOR COOLING, former head of RE at Aylesbury Grammar and Director of Stapleford House Education Centre is currently Projects Officer for the Association of Christian Teachers.

CAROL DUNBAR is a Lecturer in Education and Religious Studies at Stranmillis College, Belfast. A former special needs co-ordinator, Carol was a member of the Northern Ireland RE Core Syllabus Drafting Group. She has also contributed to the writing of the related Guidance Materials.

JOAN FURLONG has wide experience of teaching and advisory work which has included establishing a model for spiritual development in the primary school. Joan is currently Schools Adviser for the Lichfield Diocesan Board of Education.

DON HAWTHORN is presently a Lecturer in Religious and Moral Education in the Department of Social Studies, Northern College, Aberdeen and the former Chair of Grampian Racial Equality Council. Don served for four years on the Review and Development Group 5 which produced the consultative stages of the Religious and Moral Education 5–14 as well as the Personal and Social Development.

GUY HORDERN was a member of Birmingham City Council for ten years. He has been a member of Birmingham SACRE since 1976 and was Chairman for two years. He is Vice-Chairman of the Birmingham Agreed Syllabus Statutory Conference.

FRED HUGHES was formerly the Director of Stapleford House Education Centre. He is presently a Senior Lecturer at the Cheltenham and Gloucester College of Higher Education. He has researched developments in assessment methods in RE in secondary schools.

STEPHEN AND WENDY KENYON Wendy is Head of Religious Education at Sheffield High School (GPDST), having also taught in the state sector. Stephen is Head of Religious Education at Birkdale School, Sheffield and taught at Highfields School, Matlock prior to this.

JANET KING taught for twenty years before joining the Association of Christian Teachers as Religious Education and Worship Development Officer. She has had several books published. After four years in this post, she returned to the classroom as Head of Religious Education at Stewards Comprehensive School in Harlow.

JEAN MEAD is a Senior Lecturer in Religious Education at the University of Hertfordshire. She has taught RE in ILEA and Essex, then worked for some years abroad. Until recently she taught in Waltham Forest in East London in multifaith schools with many Muslim pupils, and has worked in a Multicultural Development Service.

GEORGE OLIVER was Head of Religious Education at South End High School for boys from 1957 to 1970. He became RE Adviser for the London Borough of Redbridge in 1970 and was an RE Inspector for ILEA from 1979 to 1986.

PETRA OWEN is an RE, drama and dance specialist who teaches at Ecclesbourne School in Derbyshire.

JOANNE PIMLOTT leads 'Hands and Feet' with her husband, Nigel. This group works in schools, prisons and churches using music, drama and other creative means to encourage young people to think about themselves, the world and God. Joanne has taught drama in secondary schools in Nottingham.

GEORGE SKINNER trained as an RE specialist and taught RE and maths. He then worked as a travelling secretary for the Interschool Christian Fellowship and was Field Officer for the Association of Christian Teachers. He is currently Lecturer of Education in the University of Manchester, working mainly in the field of inter-ethnic relations and equal opportunities in education. He also runs PGCE courses in RE.

J CLIVE TOUGHER is presently Head of Religious Education at Queen Elizabeth's Grammar School, Ashbourne, Derbyshire. He is also a member of the Religious Studies Subject Committee for the Northern Examination and Assessment Board.

TOM VANCE is a Senior Lecturer in Religious Studies at Stranmillis College, Belfast. He is also Chairman of the RE Advisory Group for non statutory guidelines in RE (NICC) and member of the drafting group of the core syllabus.

BRIAN WAKEMAN is an RE teacher and Deputy Head at South Luton High School. He is interested in teacher education and relating Christian ideas to schools in a secular setting.

ALISON WILKINSON worked at Beauchamp College, Oadby, Leicester where she was assistant Head of RE until 1992. It was a large successful department with some 350 GCSE students and 50 'A' level students. Presently she is studying for an MEd in Human Relations at Nottingham University, while working part time in Elm Hall Drive Methodist Church and Liverpool University Chaplaincy.

CHRIS WRIGHT teaches at Peers School, Oxford. He is Coordinator of Community. In this role he is responsible for coordinating the Humanities Department (History, Geography, RE and Social Studies), Modern Languages, and Physical Education. He is also a part-time Lecturer at King's College, London.

We are also grateful for the contributions we have received from Maureen Collins and Mike Phillips, Heads of RE at Bramcote Park School, Nottingham; Sue Hookway, Head of RE at Gillotts School, Henley; Nick Pollard, a Scripture Union associate worker and evangelist working specifically with sixth formers; and Christine Martin, Head of RE at Streetly Comprehensive School, Sutton Coldfield.

286 304 3453